Thomas Watters

A guide to the Tablets in a Temple of Confucius

Thomas Watters

A guide to the Tablets in a Temple of Confucius

ISBN/EAN: 9783743340985

Manufactured in Europe, USA, Canada, Australia, Japa

Cover: Foto ©ninafisch / pixelio.de

Manufactured and distributed by brebook publishing software (www.brebook.com)

-

Thomas Watters

A guide to the Tablets in a Temple of Confucius

A

GUIDE TO THE TABLETS

IN A

TEMPLE OF CONFUCIUS,

BY

T. WATTERS,

H.M'S. CONSUL FOR WUHU.

SHANGHAI, CHINA:—

AT THE AMERICAN PRESBYTERIAN MISSION PRESS.

MDCCCLXXIX.

PREFACE.

The aim of the following pages is to give the names of the men who have been canonized as followers of Confucius, with a few notices of the circumstances in which these men, were born, and lived, and of the work which they severally accomplished. A slight general sketch of each individual is all that has in most cases been attempted, but the authorities given in the foot notes will supply more complete information to those who wish to pursue the study, and will also enable the reader to correct errors and mistranslations in the present work. The differences of opinion to be found in these authorities are often considerable and they occasionally do not agree as to matters of fact. Sometimes the difference arises from a misprint, sometimes from carelessness in transcribing, and sometimes from imperfect information. The reader has consequently often to exercise his judgment in the selection and rejection of conflicting statements.

Much valuable assistance in compiling the Guide has been derived from the writings of several western authors whose names are generally given. The kindness of one or two native scholars deserves mention also, and one of these, the Principal of a College, supplied some books not easily obtained. But the Compiler's thanks are specially due to the Rev. W. S. Holt, of the American Presbyterian Mission Press, who has performed the arduous and wearisome task of revising the pages in going through the press.

ICHANG, *April*, 1879.

NOTE.

The principal authorities used in the compilation of this book and not generally mentioned in the foot-notes are the

Shêng-yü-shu-wên (聖域述聞), edition of 1824.

Wên-miao-ssŭ-wei (文廟祀位), reprint of 1872.

Much use has also been made of the five volumes of Legge's Chinese Classics, and references are not always given. They are most frequently quoted simply as L. Ch. Cl. Other sources of information not in every case specially acknowledged are Mayers' Chinese Reader's Manual, the Chia-yü, Shi-chi, Wên-hsien-t'ung-k'ao of Ma Tuan-lin, and the Mirror of History. The full title of this last treatise is Tzŭ-chĭ-t'ung-chien-kang-mu (資治通鑑綱目), with its various supplements. It is found generally quoted as the T'ung-chien, and Ma Tuan-lin's work is usually referred to merely by his name.

INTRODUCTION.

ACCORDING to the laws of China there must be a Wên-miao (文廟) or Temple of Confucius attached to every Prefecture, Sub-Prefecture, District, and in every market-town throughout the empire. Consequently not only has each town its temple but all Prefectural cities contain two and some three.

A Wên-miao may be built on any convenient site within the walls of a town but it must in all cases face the South. There are differences of detail from place to place but the essentials of the temple are much the same everywhere, and vary only in size and completeness. It must consist of three Courts which generally follow in a line from South to North. The outermost of these is called the P'an-kung, (泮宮) from the name given to the state College of a feudal principality during the period of the Chou dynasty. It is bounded on the South by a wall called the Hang-ch'iang (礐墻), a name which recalls that of the Government Colleges during the Han period. The colour of this wall, as of the temple generally, is red, that having been adopted by the Chou rulers as their official colour. It is not provided with a gate until a student of the district to which the temple is attached succeeds in obtaining the title Chuang-yuan, that is, first among the Chin-shi of his year. When this occurs the middle portion of the wall is taken away and a gate substituted, through which, however, only a Chuang-yuan and an Emperor or Prince may pass. A little to the north of this wall is an ornamental arch of wood or stone called the Ling-hsing-mên (欞星門) and beyond this is a pond called the P'an-chi (泮池). This pond is of semicircular shape properly, and extends from East by South to West according to the rule established for state colleges during the Chou period. These had "half-ponds" while the Emperor's College had a complete circular pond. Hence came the name of the former, the character *p'an* being composed of two elements one meaning *water* and the other a *half*, though the name is also given as (半頁) and said to denote diffusion, that is of political knowledge. The pond is spanned by the Yuan-ch'iao (圓橋) or Arched Bridge, also reserved for the use of a Chuang-yüan or Emperor, and often called the Wang-ch'iao, or Royal Bridge. The chief entrances to the Court are by two gates, one in the east wall and one in the west. At the upper end on the west side is the Tsai-shêng-t'ing (宰牲亭), a room in which the animals for sacrifice are kept, and at the opposite corner is a chamber for the private use of the chief worshipper. In this he rests for a short time, on coming to the temple and it is hence called the Kuan-t'ing (官廳) or Official Pavilion. It is known also as the Kêng-yi-so (更衣所) because the mandarin here changes his ordinary robes for Court uniform.

The north side of this Court, which is usually planted with trees, is occupied by a large hall in the middle of which is the Ta-ch'êng-mên, opened only for a Chuang-yüan or Emperor. This is also known as the Chi-mên (戟門) or Spear door, because for some time it was adorned by two stands of antique spears. On each side of this is a small door leading into the next or principal Court, on entering which two long narrow buildings are seen extending along the east and west walls. These are called respectively the Tung-wu (東廡) and Hsi-wu (西廡), and they contain the tablets of the Former Worthies and Scholars arranged in chronological order. Between these buildings is an open space called Tan-ch'ǔ (丹墀) or Vermilion Porch, that having been the name of a corresponding open square in front of a palace during the Chou dynasty. This part of the Court is usually planted with cypresses or in their absence with oleas and other handsome trees. Here all ordinary worshippers kneel and prostrate themselves when celebrating the worship of Confucius.   Above the Tan-chŭ is a stone platform called the Yue-t'ai (月臺) or Moon Terrace, also a survival from the Chou times.   This adjoins the Ta-ch'êng-tien (大成殿) or Hall of Great Perfection, the Temple proper.   In many places this is an imposing structure with massive pillars of wood or stone and embellished with quaint devices in painting.   In the middle of the north wall, "superior and alone," sometimes in a large niche and sometimes merely resting on a table, is the Sage's tablet.   Before it stands an altar on which are usually a few sacrificial vessels, and overhead are short eulogistic inscriptions.   Next below the Sage are the Four Associates, two on his left hand and two on his right.   Their tablets are in niches or frames and have altars before them.   Lower in the Hall and arranged along the walls are the tablets of the Twelve " Wise ones," six on each side, also furnished with altars.

The next Court, which is behind the principal one, or, if space requires, at its east side, contains the Ch'ung-shêng-tzŭ (崇聖祠) Ancestral Hall of exalted Sages.   In it are the tablets of five ancestors of Confucius, of his half-brother, of the fathers of the Associates and of certain other worthies.   With a few exceptions the men worshipped here have been canonized on account of the merits of their posterity and not from any great virtue in themselves.

The official residence of the Director of Studies is in close proximity to the Confucian temple which is under the care of that mandarin. Certain buildings for the use of government students and chambers for the worship of deceased local celebrities, or deserving officials, are also sometimes found either within the temple precincts or immediately outside.   The Wên-chang-kung, moreover, or Hall of the God of Literature is now often found close beside the Temple of Confucius.*

---

* Legge, Chinese Classics, Vol. IV. p. 616. Li-chi-chi-shuo (禮記集說) Ch. 3.

HISTORICAL SKETCH.

One of the last recorded utterances of Confucius is a lament over the failure of his teachings. The rulers of the time did not appreciate him and would not adopt his theories or follow his counsels. Among the people also, the Sage had not much influence and his death was not followed by any popular manifestation of sorrow. The Chief of Lu, Duke Ai, professed to be greatly distressed at the event, but his grief, if genuine was selfish. It is said, however, that he "caused a temple to be erected, and ordered that sacrifice should be offered to the Sage, at the four seasons of the year." The worship was continued, according to tradition, for many years, but was interrupted in the troubled times about the reign of Ch'in Shi Huang Ti.

But the origin of the magnificent honours now paid to Confucius is to be found in the history of the Han dynasty. The founder of that dynasty, when returning in B.C. 195, from a campaign against a rebel prince in the country about the present Fêng-yang (in Anhui) and Hsü-chow (in Kiangsu), passed through Lu. On his way he visited the Sage's grave and presented the T'ai-lao (太牢) sacrifice, a *Suovetaurilia*, or offering of a pig, a sheep, and an ox. About fifty years afterwards Prince Kung, a son of Ching Ti, built a temple at Confucius' native place, and called it the Ling-kuang-tien (靈光殿). Here worship was offered for some time to the Sage alone, but in A.D. 72, Ming Ti visited Ch'ui-li and sacrificed to the Master together with his Seventy-two Disciples. Several other Emperors of this dynasty made pilgrimages to Confucius' home, and Ming Ti's successor introduced the use of music at the worship. For a long time the rites were performed without the help of any visible symbol, but in A.D. 178, a likeness of the Sage was substituted for the simple tablet.

In the course of time the Ling-kuang-tien fell into ruin, and Wei Wên Ti, in A.D. 221, ordered the Chief of Lu to have it rebuilt, but the work was not finished for a long period. The first Emperor of the next dynasty in the year 267 decreed that at the Imperial Academy and at his native place, sacrifices should be offered to Confucius at each of the four seasons with the three animals named above. A new temple was built at Ch'ui-li by Wên Ti, of the Liu'Sung dynasty, who reigned from 424 to 450, and its Courts were planted with pines and cypresses. This Emperor also drew up regulations for the Confucian service and decreed that the rites observed in it should be the same as those used to a Chow chief or noble. The common people had long ago come to invest the Sage with divine powers and his help was sought in times of trouble. Hence it was found necessary in 472 to issue an Edict forbidding women to frequent his temple for the purpose of praying for children. The Emperor who gave this order, Hsiao Wên of the Wei kingdom, afterwards erected a temple to Confucius at his seat of government. In the South, his contemporary Ch'i Wu Ti also showed great reverence for the Sage, and revived the code of ceremonies which had been instituted by Wen Ti, of the previous dynasty.

At the beginning of the North Ch'i dynasty about A.D. 555, an Imperial Decree was issued that a temple should be erected in every prefectural town to Confucius and Yen Hui, in which worship should be offered to these Sages every month. The founder of the T'ang dynasty adopted the principle of ancient times and, in 624, made Confucius the Associate of Chou Kung whom he styled the Hsien-Shêng or Former Sage. But his successor a few years afterwards restored this title to Confucius to whom he joined Yen Hui as Associate. This emperor also ordered temples to be built to the Sage in each Prefecture and District, and canonized twenty-two worthies. In 712 Tsêng-tsŭ was made a second Associate, and the titles Senior Guardian and Senior Preceptor were given to him and Yen Hui respectively. In the reign of Hsüan Tsung (Ming Huang) a new honour was added to Confucius by placing his tablet or image on the north side of the Hall, it having been up to that time on the east side. About the same time the class of the "Ten wise ones" was instituted, sitting images of whom were introduced into the principal Hall, while Tsêng-tsŭ's image was placed in an elevated position apart. The protraits of the other worthies were painted on the walls of the temple.

The images were all, for sometime, made of wood, but in the year 960, Sung T'ai Tsu ordered clay figures to be substituted. Two years afterwards he ornamented the great entrance to the temple at the capital by a stand of spears. Yen Hui was restored to his place as an Associate, and in 1084, Shên Tsung introduced Mencius as another Associate, the only good thing that Sovereign did, according to the historian. In 1103 the name Ta-ch'êng-tien, was given to the Principal Hall in the temple of Confucius at K'ai-fêng-fu, its name up to that time having been Wên-hsüan-wang-tien (文 宣 王 殿) from a title of the Sage, and six years afterwards the change was ordered to be made over all the empire. The Four Associates as they are now, were first appointed by the Emperor Tu Tsung in 1267, and Tuan-sun Shi was then promoted to Yen Hui's place among the Ten.

The Mongol Emperors, more from policy than conviction, bestowed honours on the Chinese Sage and his canonized followers. Several were also added to the assembly, new titles were conferred, and in 1306 a Confucian temple was built at Peking. In 1368 Ming T'ai Tsu appointed the first *ting* days of the second months of Spring and Autumn for the Confucian sacrifices. He also caused the Ling-hsing-mên to be erected and made the Tung-wu and Hsi-wu for the tablets of the Disciples and Scholars. One of T'ai-tsu's successors decreed that the ceremonies should be changed to those used at imperial worship, increasing the numbers of the musicians and minuet-movers. In 1530 all the arrangements and regulations of the temples and worship were revised and several changes made. The clay images were removed and wooden tablets substituted, all official titles were abolished, the words Former Worthy and Former Scholar, were inscribed above the names on the tablets according to their temple rank and the term *tsŭ*, Philosopher, was added to all. The sacrificial honours were reduced to their former proportions to appease the vexed shade of the punctilious Sage, for is it not written, "Confucius said of the head of the Ke family, who had eight rows of pantomimes in his area, "If he can bear to do this, what may he not bear to do?"

The Emperors of the present dynasty have out-done all others in the services they have rendered to the honour and worship of the Sage and his saints. Under them has been enforced, for the first time, the rule that every city and town should have its temple, and Shun-chï ordered that the chief civil official at each place should conduct the worship. The next Emperor, Kanghsi, rebuilt the temple at Ch'ui-li, and performed sacrifice in it to the Sage. He also revised the regulations and ordered that the military officials should be present at the services. He promoted Chu Hsi to the Principal Hall, making him the Eleventh Wise one, and added honours to several others. Yung-chêng, who ascended the throne in 1723, was also a magnificent benefactor of Confucian worship. In the second year of his reign, the temple at Ch'ui-li was burnt and he caused a new one to be built, so grand and beautiful that there is nothing like it in all the land. A new image, or statue of the Sage was made for it, which was draped in robes sent from the Imperial wardrobe. This ruler conferred the title of king on each of the five canonized ancestors of Confucius, and changed the name of their temple from Ch'i-shêng-tzŭ (啓聖祠) to Ch'ung-shêng-tzŭ. He also caused an examination to be made into the constitution of the temple, the arrangement of the tablets, and the solemnities of worship. Chia-ching had discanonized a large number of scholars and several of these were now restored by Yung-chêng, who also added several others. He ordered a new arrangement of the tablets, framed a new code of ceremony, and abolished certain superstitious customs. The next Emperor again revised the arrangement of the tablets and adopted a purely chronological order. Yu Tzŭ-yo was now moved into the Principal Hall and made the Twelfth Wise one. Chien-lung also made several alterations and restorations in the rites of worship and other matters connected with the temple.

It is the custom for each Emperor, on his accession, to prepare an inscription which is copied on tablets and hung up in the Confucian Temples, the manuscript being generally sent to Ch'ui-li. The last inscription thus presented was that drawn up for the present Emperor in 1875, the words of which are *Ssŭ-wên-tsai-tzŭ* (斯文在茲), meaning, "the manifestation of truth is with me." The expression is derived from a memorable passage in the Lun-yü which Legge thus translates, "The Master was put in fear in, K'wang. He said, "After the death of King Wăn, was not the cause of truth lodged here *in me?* If Heaven had wished to let this cause of truth perish, then I, a future mortal, should not have got such a relation to that cause. While Heaven does not let the cause of truth perish, what can the people of K'wang do to me?" *

THE WORSHIP OFFERED IN THE TEMPLE.

Dr Edkins and Mr. Doolittle have described at some length the ceremonies which take place at the biannual worship of Confucius, and consequently it is not necessary to enter into details respecting these at present. It may be of use, however, to add a few explanations and additional remarks, while stating briefly in what the service consists.

The first *Ting* day in the second month of Spring, and the same day in the second month of Autumn, are fixed as the times for the worship. The Ting (丁), which comes under the element of Fire, is the fourth of the Ten Stems or Cyclical signs and so the first *ting* occurs within the first third of the month. These two were the days on which, during the Chou period, the Spring and Autumn Sessions of the State Colleges were opened by the Minister of Music.

Throughout the Provinces the person who performs the worship to Confucius, is the chief civil authority of the town in which the temple is situated. He is accompanied by the subordinate civil and military officials, the former of whom assist at the services to the Associates and other Worthies. A band of musicians and a company of boys, who make certain minuet-like movements following the music, also take part in the proceedings. The appointed number of the former is fifty and of the latter thirty six, both having leaders or conductors.

On the morning of worship the tables and altars in the Principal Hall are covered with offerings which have been prepared the day before. In front of the Sage's tablet is an altar on which are an

---

* Yuan-chien-lei-han (淵鑑類函) Ch. 161: Ma Tuan-lin's Wĕn-hsien-t'ung-k'ao (文獻通考) Ch. 43. *Peking Gazettes* for 1875, p. 27: Legge, Ch. Cl. I. p. 18

incense vase and two large candles which are lighted. A table in front of this altar is spread with bowls of grain, cups and goblets of wine, and certain other articles, while on the east and west sides are tables furnished with vessels containing various articles of food. In the centre of the Hall a roll of white silk is laid out conspicuously, and before it are the three victims, a bullock in the middle, with a sheep on one side, and a pig on the other. Offerings of a like description, but fewer in number, and in all cases without the bullock, are set out in front of the other tablets.

The Mandarin who is to officiate as chief worshipper is supposed to have fasted and purified himself during the three preceding days. He arrives at the temple before daylight and assumes his Court dress in the Kuan-t'ing. Under the guidance of the Master of Ceremonies, he then takes his station at the head of the Civil officials on the east side of the Court below the Principal Hall, while the military officials are arranged on the west side. The service begins by the playing of some shrill music after which the chief mandarin ascends to the Hall entering by the east door. He then kneels, prostrates himself, and offers up incense on the altar before Confucius' tablet. This being finished he descends to his station, and at the order of the Master of Ceremonies re-ascends and continues the sacrifice. This is done for three times and in the intervals music is performed to which the boys go through certain figures with gestures, all done according to rule and in a grave and solemn manner. Certain hymns of praise are also sung or chanted in a loud shrill voice, all the music, vocal and instrumental, being of the most disagreeable kind. The roll of silk is reverently presented before the Sage's tablet and then burnt in the Court, and the flesh of the victims is, or may be, distributed among the inferior ministrants.

All the ceremonies of this service recall the golden age of Chinese antiquity, the days of Wu Wang, and Wên Wang and Chou Kung, and the times of simpler virtue long before. The same airs were played with the same sort of accompaniment, four thousand years ago, and the sacrifices and worship have meanings brought from a far-off period. Nearly everything in them is a type or symbol. The white silk, emblem of faithful purity, was the present by a chief to the man whom he wished to take into his service. The ox, head of domestic animals, leaves broad, lasting foot-prints; the pig, as its bristles symbolize, has a will of its own; and the sheep, plump for food, is also soft with wool to make woollen clothing. The incense typifies the fragrance of virtue, and the wine and food the abundance of a happy Kingdom. The music is supposed at one time to rouse the hearer to valiant deeds and at another to lap him in soft measures expressing peace and harmony. The boys who perform the curious moving accompaniment are dressed in the old uniform of Hsiu-ts'ai's or graduates of the first Degree. They bear a flute in the left hand and a pheasant's feather in the right, the former the symbol of the refinement produced by music and the observance of social laws, and the latter of the adornment of learning.

The performances of these boys cannot be understood without a reference to the old Chinese writings. In the Great Preface to the Shi-ching we read that when the "prolonged utterances of song are insufficient" for excited feelings, unconsciously the hands and feet begin to move. This tendency was turned to practical account and the movements were adopted and regulated to be the visible representation of what music was supposed to express. Hence in very early times we find a Kan-wu (干舞) and a Wên-wu (文舞), that is, a warlike and a peaceful accompaniment. The actors in the former held a bow in the left hand and an arrow in the right, and imitated the gestures of an archer shooting in the presence of his chief. The performers in the latter held a flute and pheasant's feather. When the Emperor Shun failed in his attempt to conquer the Miao, by arms, he resolved to win them over to submission and allegiance by gentle persuasives. So he had an exhibition of "war and peace posture-makers" in the Court before his palace and within two months the savage chief tendered his submission. During the Chow dynasty, exhibitions of these performers were held at the sacrifices to deceased Kings and Emperors, and on all grand festive occasions of state. Their numbers were also settled by law, sixty-four being allowed to an Emperor and thirty-six to a Prince or Chief. These *wu* were originally, perhaps, athletic and military exercises performed at the end of a war or at a military review before the ruler. When a Chow Emperor held a durbar, the feudal chiefs showed their skill in archery in the Court before the Palace. There was an established etiquette for them in taking up the bow, advancing from their position, bowing, and retiring, and the boys at the Confucian worship still, to some extent, imitate these actions. But only the civil performance of posture-making takes place in the temples of the Sage, the idea of war being inconsistent with the solemnity of the place and the nature of the service.

The worship described above cannot properly be called religious, for the Chinese have not made a god of Confucius. Prayer is not offered to him, nor is his help or intervention besought on any occasion. The ceremonies used at his service are the same as those used in the Temple of Kings and Emperors. It has been the custom in China, from a very remote age, to pay posthumous worship to the great benefactors of the country and especially to the promoters of learning and culture. Hence Yao, and Shun, and Yü, were all worshipped after death, and similar honour was paid to Chow Kung not only in his own country but also in Lu. These, however, were all summed up in Confucius who was the actual founder of learning, the teacher not for one age or country but for all time and all the Empire. So the titles and honours of Former Sage and Former Teacher were transferred to him, and scholars and officials were required to do him homage. In process of time the rank of Prince or King, was conferred on him, and the worship offered to him then took the character of that offered to a feudal chief of the time at which the Sage lived. It is not as a king, however, but as their great teacher and pattern, that the Chinese worship their Sage. The idea involved in the ceremonies is to forget for the time that he is dead and to treat him as though he were present in the flesh. Even to the schoolmaster now, the scholar kneels and prostrates himself and at stated times reverently presents certain articles of food. Much more is reverence due to him who first made learning accessible, taught the way of virtue, and settled the laws of social and political order. No day, say the Chinese, can pass without an experience of the benefits derived from Confucius, and his influence among men is like that of Heaven and Earth in the world. Hence comes their deep respect for him and all about him, and hence the worship they pay him, which is a perpetually renewed service of gateful remembrance. Offerings are presented to him at other seasons besides those mentioned above, and his birth-day is observed as a solemn fast in all the public departments. But he must be worshipped in his own temple and it is forbidden to set up any image or likeness of him in a Buddhist or Taoist temple. The school-boy may do him obeisance in the school, and the student in the College, for these are institutions which are eminently the result of Confucius, teaching and influence.*

GENERAL REMARKS.

A Temple of Confucius is supposed to present a visible outline of the course of old truth and right principle from the days of the Sage, down to modern times. But even a cursory glance will shew that the outline is deficient, and that the names on the tablets very imperfectly represent the history of orthodox learning in China. Moreover in the selection and rejection of men it will be seen that bigotry and caprice have exercised no little influence.

The persons who have been chosen for the honour of worship with Confucius are his immediate disciples, the developers of his teachings, the preservers, transmitters and expositors of the ancient classics, the popularizers of their philosophy, and the men who have in life eminently fulfilled the requirements of their practical maxims. By a recent Edict it has been decided that hereafter only those are to be admitted who shall have elucidated the learning of the sages and transmitted the body of truth.

It is admitted by all, that of the disciples worshipped, many have no other title to the honour than that they were privileged to hear the

---

* See Edkin's in Journal N.C. Branch R. A. Soc. N.S. No. VIII. p, 79.; Doolittle, Social Life of the Chinese Vol. 1. p. 359.; Ta-ch'ing-hui-tien, Ch. 45; Li-chi-chi-shuo, Ch. 3 et al.; Chou-li, Ch. 14; Ma Tuan-lin, Ch. 43.; Legge, Ch. Cl. Vol. III. p. 66; Vol. I. Proleg. p. 90.

Master's discourses. It is supposed, indeed, that when they returned to their homes they taught the doctrines of the Sage in their native places. This, however, is only a supposition, and one which is refuted rather than supported by history. But among the disciples were ten who, in a well-known passage of the Lun-yü, are represented as having ceased to enter the Master's door, and who are there enumerated grouped in four classes. These ten were afterwards formed into a superior order, and their tablets or images were fixed in the Principal Hall—Yen Hui being replaced by another disciple. For this distinction there was not the slightest justification, and it has been severely censured by several Confucianists, notably by Ssŭ-ma Kuang. It is very evident, as Ssŭ-ma points out, that the Master did not regard all these ten as eminent above their fellow-disciples. On the contrary, as will be seen, he speaks of some of them occasionally in slighting or condemning language, as Tsai Yü for example. Moreover among the other disciples were several whom he singled out for special praise, and on account of their possessing merits of a superior kind. So it was plainly not the Master's intention to create a hierarchy among those whom he was wont to style collectively his " children ; " and to make a superior order of ten, calling them the " wise ones " was a capricious and improper proceeding. Among the general body of the worthies also are some who have been admitted into the Temple merely to satisfy a personal liking. Thus Luh Chiu-yuan, was introduced to please Wang Shou-jen, and Ou-yang Hsiu to please the Chia-ching Emperor of the Ming dynasty. But the number of those who have thus entered the Temple is very small, and in general conspicuous merit has been required.

There were, moreover, several men of fame who once received worship with Confucius and who enjoy that honour no longer. The enumeration of the principal among these will help to illustrate the rule which is supposed to be followed in making additions to the occupants of the Temple, and at the same time to show how caprice can interfere. The earliest was Hsün K'uang (荀况) who lived shortly after Mencius in the bad times of the warring states. He was a follower of Confucius, but not of Mencius, whose theory of man's nature he combated vigorously.   Hsün-tzŭ was a bold, clear thinker, a skillful reasoner, and an accomplished writer, and on many points he was far in advance of his age.   Holding that man is born into the world with a disposition which is evil, he yet taught that man is raised above all other creatures by the possession of a faculty for discerning and judging between right and wrong.   For a long time his name was always joined with that of Mencius, and Han Wên-kung who so refers to Hsün-tzŭ gives him qualified praise.   In latter times, however, he has been regarded as not strictly orthodox or at least as holding some erroneous opinions.   His tablet was admitted to the Temple together with those of Yang Hsiung and Han Yü (wên-kung) by Sung Shên Tsung, in 1084.   Of the Han scholars there were Tai Shêng (戴聖) renowned for his labours on the Li-chi; Liu Hsiang (劉向), a high official and learned in all the classics, who also did good service to the orthodox learning; Chêng Chung (鄭衆), a faithful official and good scholar; Chia K'uei (賈逵), the Universal Scholar who wrote on the Tso-chuan; Ma Yung (馬融) of varied accomplishments, and vast learning, who taught Confucian philosophy to more than a thousand disciples; Lu Chĭ (盧植) an illustrious scholar of the last and a loyal official; Fu Ch'ien (服虔) a learned expositor of the Ch'ün-ch'iu; Ho Hsiu (何休) well versed in all the classics and author of a celebrated treatise on Kung-yang's Commentary; Yang Hsiung (楊雄) better known as Tzŭ-yun (子雲), a follower of Confucius but halting between the opinions of Mencius and Hsün-tzŭ.   His best known work is the Fa-yen (法言) a small philosophical treatise on which much learning has been spent and to an edition of which Ssŭ-ma Kuang contributed a Preface.   In subsequent times were Wang Suh (王肅), of the Wei dynasty in the period of the Three Kingdoms, who wrote the Chia-yü and other treatises; Wang Pi (王弼), of the Chin dynasty, who wrote a Commentary on the Yih and another on the Tao-tê-ching, and who had acquired a fame for learning and genius when he died at the age of twenty four in A.D. 249; Tu Yü (杜預), a contemporary of the last, famous as a statesman, a warrior, and a scholar, and author of a highly esteemed treatise on the Ch'un-ch'iu and Tso-chuan.   Of the Sung period were Wang An-shi (王安石), the learned, astute statesman, execrated as an innovator; Wang Yü (王雱) his base, worthless son; Sun Fuh (孫復), a profound scholar and famous teacher, who wrote a Commentary on the Ch'un-ch'iu. Su Shi (蘇軾), better known as Su Tung-p'o, a celebrated poet, commentator and official, but of doubtful orthodoxy and of imperfect character.

Of the above Wang An-shi was canonized in 1104 and expelled in 1241, and his son, who was canonized in 1109, was ejected in 1177. These two ought never to have been in the Temple and every good Confucianist regards their removal as reparation for the offence of having allowed them to enter. Yang Hsiung was uncanonized in 1395, and the strictly orthodox think that he had no claim to Confucian worship, for he did not hold the whole truth and he never wrote a commentary on one of the sacred books. Su Tung-p'o and Sun Fuh were admitted together in 1235 and removed together in 1845. All the others, together with a few who have since been restored, were uncanonized by Ming Shi Tsung in the year 1530. This proceeding has been severely condemned by Ku Yen-woo and others, who believe that the scholars thus dismissed will be restored in better times. There was no right principle involved in the conduct of the Emperor who merely wished posterity to forget the profligate debauchee in the regulator of Confucian worship.

Among the scholars and officials, moreover, who have deserved well of the orthodox learning, are many whose names have never been enrolled in the Wên-miao. A false step taken turned the fate of some, and timid doubt in others made good resolve to miss the name of action. Not a few have passed into utter oblivion or are remembered only in the petty homage of a village shrine. Chance has had much to do with the posthumous destinies of Confucian scholars, and there is often no explanation to give for one being taken and another left. The Han dynasty affords several examples, and none more conspicuous than the case of Prince Hsien of Ho-chien (Ho-kien) in Chihli. He gave a great stimulus to learning by his exertions in the recovery and preservation of the ancient classics and his labours on the Li-chi. Yet while Kao T'ang-shêng, Mao Chang, and Fuh Shêng have been admitted to the Temple for similar, though inferior merits, Prince

Hsien—perhaps because he was a Prince—has not been so honoured.
So late as 1876 a Petition for his canonization was presented to the
Throne but it does not seem to have received a favourable answer.
Several Petitions of a like nature for the admission of other scholars
into the Temple were made at an earlier period of this dynasty and
were refused.   It is probable, however, that a new revision will sometime be made which will lead to numerous and important changes with
reference to the persons who will hereafter be worshipped with
Confucius.*

* Wên-kung-wên chi (溫公文集) ch. 13; Jï-chï-lu (日知錄) ch. 14; Translation
  Peking Gazettes for 1876, p. 86.

THE TABLETS.

At the north end of the Temple and facing the South, the only one so placed, is the tablet of Confucius. It bears the following inscription (至聖先師孔子) Chĭ-shêng-hsien-shĭ-K'ung-tzŭ, that is, The Perfect Sage, the Former Teacher, the Philosopher K'ung.

The life of Confucius has been told so often that it is needless to give an account of it here. Legge and Plath, in particular, have put together all that can be learned of his history and teachings, and his fortunes after death, and the details collected by these two Sinologues have been widely made known. For the present purpose it is enough to recall a few of the important facts relating to the Sage.

K'ung Ch'iu (孔丘) or K'ung Chung-ni (仲尼) was born B.C. 551 or 550, at Ch'ui-li (闕里), a village near Ch'ang-p'ing (昌平) which was a small town in the district of Tsou (陬) a city of La—"somewhere within the limits of the present department of Yen-chow, in Shantung." His father was named Shu-liang-ho (叔梁紇), and his mother was Yen Chêng-tsai (顏徵在), according to some a daughter of a relative of Yen Hui's father. Shu-liang-ho had nine daughters by a previous wife and a son by a concubine before Confucius was born. This last was "the Benjamin of his father's old age," and the only son of his mother.

Neither in private nor public life was Confucius happy. He

divorced his wife and was not content with his son who, moreover, died before him. The chiefs and Princes of the time did not adopt his counsels, his teachings could not prevail, and he had to mourn over the deaths of several of his best disciples.

He himself died in the year B.C. 478, and all the good he had done at once began to live. But many years'had to pass before the fullness of time came for the spread of his teachings and their perfect influence on all the ways of individual, social, and public life in China.

The title now found on his tablet was first given in 1530. The Emperor Shun-chĭ, of the present dynasty, changed it in 1645 for a more flowery one, but the former one was restored in 1657. It is the last of a long series of titles conferred on the Sage by the Emperors of the various dynasties from Han P'ing Ti down.*

THE SSŬ P'EI (四配) OR FOUR ASSOCIATES.

1. Fuh-shêng-Yen-tzŭ (復聖顏子), the Philosopher Yen, the Sage who returned. Yen Hui (顏回) S. Tzŭ-yuan (子淵) or simply Yuan.

Yen Hui was descended from an old family long settled in Lu. The surname was originally Ts'ao (曹) and Yen was adopted by one of his ancestors whose father had gained distinction under that name in the service of the chief of Lu. The descendants of this first Yen continued to hold high offices in their native state down to Wu-yab (無繇) the father of Hui. This latter was born, according to one account, in B.C. 519 but according to another in 514. His father Wu-yao was a disciple of Confucius and he sent his son, while still a boy, to be educated by the Sage. Hui soon became the most distinguished of all the disciples, and his love and admiration for his master, whom he regarded as a father, were unbounded. None equalled him in love of learning. He studied with unwearied diligence, and always tried to put in practice the rules of life which he learned. When only 29 years of age his hair turned gray, and three years later he died, in 488 (or according to the other account 483), "perished in his summer day."

---

* Legge, Chinese Classics, Vol. 1. Proleg. p. 56: Plath, Leben des Confucius (Transactions of the Bavarian Academy, 1870): Shĭ-chi Ch. 6.: Mayers, Chinese Reader's Manual p. 100.

He was buried near Chü-fou (kio-fu 曲阜), and his grave remains to this day, with the temple erected at the place for his worship.

As a disciple Hui was silent and attentive. He seldom asked questions and he never offered criticisms. To him the Master's doctrines were sublime and exhaustless in application. He was content with the pursuit of virtue and wisdom, though living in deep poverty. A bamboo joint for a cup, a gourd for a bowl, his elbow for a pillow, rice and water for his food, and a hovel in a lane for a house—such was his lot, and yet not only did he not repine but he never lost his cheerfulness. This traditional picture of his poverty, however, is most likely overdrawn. One day Confucius hinted to him that he should go into office. Hui replied that his small patrimony gave him food and clothing, music afforded him enjoyment, and his Master's teachings all the pleasure he wanted. Confucius said of Hui that he nearly reached perfection and that for three months he could be free from any violation of virtue. He never allowed his anger, on account of one matter, to influence him in another, and he never repeated a fault. If he erred it was only for an instant, and his return was easy, for he had chosen that good way which lies between too much and too little. The free-thinking scoffer says—why teach that virtue brings long life when Yen Hui died only 32 years of age? But the believing Confucianist replies—To him there came instead of a prolonged mortal life an immortality of fame, and endless glory is better than added years.

Hui was distinguished for a virtuous life, and he had more faith than Confucius, as the latter owned. He was a simple-minded, tender-hearted man. The hopeless wailing of the woman who had to sell her son to bury her husband fell on his ear as distinct from ordinary weeping. He won the life-long affection of Confucius, whose gloomy and desponding moods could always be charmed away by Yen Hui's harp and song. The Sage looked to him for the future propagation of his doctrines, and when "the finger of God touched" the disciple the old Master wept bitterly, giving way to despair and crying out that Heaven had ruined him.

From the time of the Han dynasty, Yen Hui has been associated with Confucius in the worship offered in the temples of the latter, and he has received various titles and designations. Thus his tablet bore for a long time the title Hsien-shī (先師) which was afterwards given to Confucius. Under the T'ang dynasty he was made Yen Kung, or Duke of Yen, a district in the south of Shantung. In 1330 the reigning Mongol emperor changed this for the longer inscription Yen-tzŭ-yen-kuo-Fuh-shêng-kung (顏子兖國復聖公). The title Duke was taken away by the Chia-ching emperor of the Ming period in 1530, and the inscription which still remains was then substituted. Legge translates Fuh-shêng in one place as "Continuator of the Sage," and in another place as "The second Sage." But Hui did not live to continue the Sage, and Mencius is generally known as the second Sage, though the term is applied to Yen Hui also, the expression used being Ya-sheng (亞聖). By some the word *Fuh* is supposed to refer to the exposition of the diagram so named, the 24th in the Yih-ching. Others derive it from a passage in the Lun-yü in which Confucius explains to Yen Hui, the way of attaining perfect virtue. "By self-conquest to return to the moral law of man's being is perfect virtue," is the saying of Confucius, and the phrase "K'o-chi-fuh-li (克巳復禮) is very often used as describing Yen Hui. The character 禮 in this expression has not its ordinary signification but that of the character 理. *Fuh-shêng* may mean, however, the Sage who repeated, or reported, the lessons taught by the Master, but it is better to understand it in the sense of *returning* as explained above.*

Facing Yen Hui's tablet and next to it in order of succession is that inscribed :—

2. Tsung-sheng-Tsêng-tzŭ (宗聖曾子) that is, the Philosopher Tsêng, the Founder-Sage, or as Legge translates the words *Tsung-shêng* "Exhibiter of the Fundamental Principles of the Sage."

Tsêng Shên (曾參) S. Tzŭ-yü (子輿) or (子與).

Tsêng-tzŭ was born in the year B.C. 506, at South Wu-ch'êng (武城), a town of Lu, whence he is sometimes distinguished as Lu-shên.

---

* For Yen Hui see Legge's Ch.Cl. 1. Proleg. 113 ; p. 18, 114 et al : 2.p. 211 : Plath, Die Schüler des Confucius p. 14 : Chia-yü. Ch. 4. etal.; Lie-tzŭ Ch. 4.; Kao-shī-chuan (高士傳) Ch. 上 ; Mayers' Chinese Reader's Manual p. 275 : Shêng-yü-shu-wên (聖域述聞) Ch. 3. Tao-t'ung-lu (道統錄) Ch. 上.

His father was Tsêng Hsi (曾晳), a cruel, selfish man and apparently a hypocrite. Shên was only 15 years of age when he was sent to study under Confucius, at that time living in the State of Ch'u, corresponding nearly to the modern Hu-kwang. Dull and slow of speech, he had no showy abilities, but he soon rose to distinction among the disciples as a man of great learning, and it was to him that the Sage entrusted the education of his grandson Tzŭ-ssŭ.

It is, however, rather for his great filial piety and his general high moral character that Tsêng-tzŭ is celebrated. There are several well known ancedotes illustrative of his devotion to his parents. On one occasion while weeding a garden of cucumbers he accidentally broke one of the plants. Hereupon his father took a stick and beat him nearly to death. As soon as Shên was able to move he went to his father and expressed his anxiety lest the old man might have hurt himself in administering the lesson, and then sat down and played the guitar to put his father's mind at ease. For his conduct on this occasion Confucius rebuked Tsêng-tzŭ as going to excess.

To his mother he was still more devoted, and between these two there was a real electric cord of sympathy. To recall her son from the hills where he was gathering firewood the mother bit her own arm. The pain was at once communicated to the heart of the son, who hastened home with his bundle of firewood. We need not wonder to read that in after life he divorced his wife for serving up an ill-cooked pear to his mother.

On the death of his father first, and afterwards on that of his mother, Tsêng-tzŭ observed the funeral rites with great care and precision, and ever afterwards he burst into tears when reading that part of the Li-chi which treats of the ceremonies for the dead. His loving remembrance of his parents continued also through all the rest of his life. The elder Tsêng had not been a man of a kind or noble character, but after his death the son could not even bear to eat any "Sheep-dates" because his father had been fond of that fruit. Up to old age and in his last illness he showed his honouring remembrance of his parents by his anxiety to keep whole and unharmed that body which was their gift.

Tsêng-tzŭ said he examined himself every day on three points—had he been self-interested in what he did for others, had he been unfaithful in his intercourse with friends, and had he failed to embody in life the Master's teachings. He was very poor, dressed meanly, and had to support himself by tilling the land. But riches and greatness in others did not affect his contentment with benevolence and righteousness. His favourite topic of conversation was filial piety, which he described as serving one's parents while they live, burying them when dead, and worshipping them afterwards, all according to the due forms and laws.

After the death of Confucius, Tsêng retired to his native place where he became the chief of a school and had many disciples some of whom afterwards rose to eminence. Tzŭ-ssŭ is reported to have received from him the materials out of which he made the Ta-hsiao, and Tsêng is recorded to have written several treatises. The small work on Filial Piety known as the Hsiao-ching (孝經) is ascribed to him, though it was inspired at least by his Master, and tradition represents Tsêng as the only one of the disciples who handed down Confucius. teachings in their original purity. The Sage speaks very warmly of him, and Mencius seems to have known much about him and to have esteemed him highly.

Tsêng was always very careful of his life and limbs. His moral courage may have been great, but he showed a discretionary valour when the rebels invaded Wu-ch'êng. He was one of the first to run away and he did not return until his house was put in order. His regard for the proprieties of ceremony remained to the last, and he died while his sons and attendants were adjusting his mat in B.C. 437.

"His name was heard over all the world," says a biographer of Tsêng-tzŭ, but a long time passed before his merits were openly recognized. His tablet was first admitted to the Temple of Confucius in A.D. 720, in the reign of T'ang Hsüan Tsung, and in 1267, it was placed among the Associates. The epithet Tsung-shêng was given in 1330 by Yuan Wên Ti, and the title which now remains was adopted in 1530.*-

---

* For Tsêng-tzŭ, see Legge, Ch. Cl. 1. Proleg. p. 118 and the Four Books; Plath, Die Schüler &c. p. 65; Tao-T'ung-lu (道統錄) Ch. 上; Shêng-yü &c as above.

3. Shu-shêng-Tzŭ-ssŭ-tzŭ (述聖子思子), The Philosopher Tzŭ-ssŭ the Transmitting Sage, or as Legge translates, "The Philosopher Tsze-sze, Transmitter of the Sage."

K'ung Chi (孔 伋). S. Tzŭ-ssŭ (子 思).

Tzŭ-ssŭ was the son of Poh-yü and grandson of Confucius. The dates of his birth and death cannot be ascertained with accuracy, but he is supposed to have been born about the year B.C. 490 (or 500 according to some), and to have lived 100 years, though one account makes him to have died when only 62 years old. He was left an orphan at an early age and consigned to the care of his grandfather who seems to have done his best for the boy. The latter was clever but apparently · rather precocious. One day when Confucius was sitting absorbed in gloomy thought the child divined his thoughts, that they were about the doubtful fate of his doctrines. He then told his grandfather that he was anxious to become able to bear the bundle made by his father—to transmit to posterity the Sage's teachings. The sad old man smiled and felt no more despondent.

Tzŭ-ssŭ afterwards became a disciple of Tsêng-tzŭ, but he outstript his master, at least in knowledge of the Code of Ceremonies. From Tsêng-tzŭ and others, as also from the Sage himself, he received the substance of Confucius' teachings, and embodied much of it in the Ta-hsiao and Chung-yung. There is some doubt, however, as to his having written the former of these books, but all are agreed that he is the author of the latter—perhaps the best of the early Confucian writings.

Tzŭ-ssŭ held various offices under several of the small princes who then divided the country. When Minister of State to the Chief of Wei, he remained at his post during the invasion of a party of rebels, though advised to fly. This, Mencius says, was the proper thing for him to do as a Minister, just as to run away at once on the same occasion was the proper thing for Tsêng-tzŭ to do as a teacher. Hsion Kung of Lu, otherwise known as Duke Muh, had to give Tzŭ-ssŭ an attendant, otherwise he would not have continued in his service. Duke Muh also wanted to treat Tzŭ-ssŭ as a friend, but the latter would not agree. The ancients had not mentioned such a thing, and the prince was, as to official position, his superior, and as to virtue, he should be the prince's teacher. But Duke Muh did not treat him as a teacher nor appreciate his merits properly.

In old age Tzŭ-ssŭ retired to his native town and devoted himself to study, writing, and teaching, soon collecting a large number of disciples. He was very poor, at times not having even the simple necessaries of life. When in such straits he accepted a gift of food but he refused wine and other luxuries, especially when given with a bad grace. Misery came with poverty. His mother committed the social crime of marrying again after the death of her husband, and this must have caused him pain for the rest of his life. Then his wife did not please him and he divorced her. When she died his son Tzŭ-shang refused to observe the usual mourning. Tzŭ-ssŭ defended his son's conduct, and from this arose the custom in the K'ung family of not going into mourning for a mother who died divorced.

Tzŭ-ssŭ seems to have been a man of strong will and great self-confidence. He was bold and faithful in counsel but could not bear to be slighted or thwarted. While inheriting something of his grand-fathers' genius he seems to have inherited his temper also.

The tablet of Tzŭ-ssŭ was first admitted to the sacrifices in the Confucian temples by Sung Hui Tsung in 1108. In 1236 it was placed among the "Wise Ones," and 1267 promoted to its present position. The title Shu-shêng-kung was inscribed on the tablet in 1330, and this was changed for the present title in 1530. Sung Hui Tsung had ennobled Tzŭ-ssŭ posthumously as Yi-shui-hou (沂水疾), and Tu Tsung of the same dynasty made him Yi-kuo-kung (沂國公), Yi being the name of a district in the South of Shantung.*

---

* For Tzŭ-ssŭ see Legge, Ch. Cl. 1. Proleg. p. 36; 2. p. 105 et al. (Legge's account of the life and sayings of Tzŭ-ssŭ is very detailed and gives all the information about him that can be obtained). Shêng-yü &c. as above! Shi-chi, Ch. 6 at end.

4. Ya-shêng-Mêng-tzŭ (亞聖孟子), the Philosopher Mêng, the Sage who is Second (*i.e.* to Confucius).

Mêng K'o (孟柯) S. Tzŭ-ch'ê (子車) or Tzŭ-chü (子居) or Tzŭ-yü (子與).

Mencius was a native of Tsou (鄒 otherwise written 騶), a small State in the South of the present Shantung, and he was related to the local family of Lu named Mêng or Mêng-sun. He was born in B.C. 371 or, according to one account, in 372. The mother of Mencius is a lady of noble fame in Chinese history, but little or nothing is known of his father except that his name was Chi (激), and that he died when his son was only three years old. His mother took very great care of the fatherless boy, changing her place of residence twice on his account, or as the Chinese express it " thrice changed her abode." She moved first from the neighbourhood of a cemetery because the child was learning to make fun of funeral ceremonies. Then she took a house in the market place, but her child began to learn the bad ways of tradesmen and she had to move a second time. Her next house was near a public school where the mimicking boy could use his natural faculties to advantage in imitating the solemn gestures of salutation which passed between scholar and master. In course of time Mencius was sent to school, but he does not seem to have been very diligent at first. A well known story tells how his mother roused him to earnestness by cutting asunder a web she was weaving, and the words Tuan-chi-ch'üan-hsiao (斷機勸學) "She cut through her web to exhort to learning," are household words in China to this day.

Mencius took the lesson to heart and applied himself diligently to study. From disciples of Tzŭ-ssŭ he is said to have learned the doctrines of Confucius—the truth thus getting free course. He became a follower and, to some extent, an imitator of the Sage. For some time he was employed as State adviser by the king of Ts'i, and was otherwise engaged in public life for a number of years. He was a stern and faithful adviser though at times impracticable. Sometimes his counsels

have a haughty tone, and he was not wanting in self-appreciation.
In old age he retired into private life and gave himself up to learning.
Many disciples followed him and with these he discoursed on morals
and politics not without a slight mixture of metaphysics. Assisted by
some of these disciples he edited the Shi and Shu, handed down the
meaning of Confucius, and compiled the book which bears his own
name. He died in B.C. 288.

Mencius' admiration for Confucius was unlimited, and his esteem
for some of the disciples, especially Yen Hui and Tsêng-tsŭ, was great
and apparently sincere. His own recorded sayings and teachings
are often interesting and instructive, and his thoughts and language
are more definite and precise than those of Confucius. His greatest
merit with the orthodox is that he was an uncompromising enemy to
heterodoxy. He "blew out" Yang and Mêh and held aloft the
brightly-burning torch of truth first lit in the world's prime and handed
down from sage to sage, a light to the feet of all who dwell in the land.
He taught plainly and distinctly that man is born good, but that his
physical, no less than his spiritual nature, requires careful fostering.
He too first dwelt on Jen (仁) and Yi (義) as complementary
elements of man's moral being. The former is the fullness of virtue
in the man as a separate individual, the attainment of which ends in
the perfection of the moral nature. The latter is the due observance
of all man owes to his fellow creatures. But the two cannot be parted
in actual life, and are mutually dependent.

Mencius was admitted into the Temple of Confucius as an Associate
in 1088 by Sung Chê Tsung, who at the same time conferred titles on
the Sage's father and mother. The previous Emperor had made
Mencius Tsou-kuo-kung (鄒國公) or Duke of the State Tsou in 1083.
The inscription on his tablet was changed in 1330 to Ya-shêng-kung.
The first Emperor of the Ming dynasty removed the tablet from its
place in the Temple but restored it a short time afterwards. In 1530
the inscription which still continues was settled by Ming Shĭ Tsung.
A title and sacrificial honours have also been awarded to Mencius'
mother at her home in Shantung.*

---

* For Mencius see Legge, Ch. Cl. 2. Proleg. Ch. 2; Morrison's Ch. Dict. Vol. 1. art.
孟 ! Tao-t'ung-lu, as above. Remusat. Nouveaux Mélanges Asiatiques.T . 2. p. 115.

The Shǐ-êrh-Chê (十二哲), The Twelve Men of Genius, or, as Legge translates "The Twelve Wise Ones."

The tablet of each of these bears the title Hsien-hsien (先賢), Ancient or former Eminent One (or Worthy).

(1.) Hsien-hsien-Min-tzǔ (先賢閔子), The Philosopher Min. Min Sun(閔損). S. Tzǔ-ch'ien (子騫).

Min Tzǔ-ch'ien was a native of Lu, and 15, or, according to one account 50, years younger than Confucius. His family was poor and he was afflicted in childhood with a cruel stepmother who treated him very badly notwithstanding the sacrifices he made in order to please her and make her comfortable. Her husband wanted to put her away on account of her treatment of Tzǔ-ch'ien, but the latter pleaded for his stepmother and she was at length won over to kindness.

Min became a disciple of Confucius, and rose to considerable eminence. When he first joined the Sage he had a poor appearance, but the food of philosophy gradually made him well-looking and contented. His filial piety was acknowledged by all, and he was distinguished among the disciples rather for virtue than for genius. His manner was precise and bland as he stood beside the Master, who said of him on one occasion—"This man seldom speaks; but when he does, he is sure to hit the point."

When the Chief of the Chi (季) family wished to make Min Governor of P'i (費), the latter politely declined, and threatened to go out of the country if the offer were repeated. Yet we find him afterwards in that capacity consulting Confucius about the theory of government.

He seems to have been of an economical and conservative nature, and he is praised for purity and uprightness. He would not serve a usurping chief, nor take the pay of a disreputable prince. Confucius held him in high esteem, and pronounced him to be a model man, Chün-tzǔ (君子). Later writers have also admired him very much, and by one of these he is placed next to Yen Hui and equal to Tsêng-tzǔ. He died before Confucius, and it is not recorded that he ever committed anything to writing.

Min was admitted to the Confucian Temple as one of the Ten "Wise Ones" in A.D. 720 by T'ang Hsüan Tsung. By the same Emperor he was afterwards ennobled as P'i-Hou (費疾), Marquis of P'i. Under the Sung dynasty he received still further posthumous titles, having been made Lang-ya-kung (琅邪公) in 1009, and P'i-kung in 1267. The present designation was settled in 1530.*

(2.) Hsien-hsien-Jan-tzŭ (先賢冉子), The Philosopher Jan. This is the first on the west side and faces Min Sun.

Jan-kêng (冉耕). S. Poh-niu (伯牛)

Poh-niu was a native of Lu and was only seven years younger than Confucius. Little is known about him. He was noted among the disciples for his high moral qualities, and he won the esteem of the Master, who gave him an official appointment.

When confined to his room by the loathsome disease which ended in death he was visited by Confucius. The latter did not go into the house, however, but shook hands with the patient through the open window, and said—"It is killing him. It is the appointment *of Heaven*. Alas that such a man should have such a sickness! That such a man should have such a sickness!" But there is a difference of opinion as to the reason why Confucius did not go into the room, the older commentators supposing it was on account of the nature of the disease, and Chu Hsi thinking it was because the patient's bed had been placed on the south side of the room. Poh-niu died and the Master sighed for him along with those other good disciples who came no more to his door.

Jan Poh-niu was "daring in word and upright in conduct." Under the T'ang dynasty he was ennobled as Yun-Hou (鄆侯), Marquis of Yun, and under the Sung dynasty he was made Tung-p'ing-kung (東平公) and afterwards Yun-kung, Duke of Yun. Tung-

---

* For Min Sun and all the other disciples of Confucius see Legge, Ch. Cl. 1. Proleg. Ch. V. Sec.; Plath, Die Schüler des Confucius; The Chia-yü; Shêng-yü-shu-wên, ch. 4, &c.

p'ing, sometimes used for Yun, was a town of the latter which was a district in the South-east of the present Shantung. He was canonized in A.D. 720, along with the others who made up the Ten, though, like them, he had long before been sacrificed to along with Confucius as one of the Disciples. When it is said of any of these Ten that he was admitted to the Temple in that year, the statement is to be understood as referring to *the formation of them into the superior group called the Ten Wise Ones.**

----

3. Hsien-hsien-Jan-tzŭ (先 賢 冉 子), The Philosopher Jan. Jan Yung (冉 雍). S. Chung-kung (仲 弓).

Chung-kung was of the family from which Jan Kêng came, but he was born 21 years after the latter, and was consequently 29 years younger than Confucius. His father was a notoriously mean, bad man, but the calf of the brindled cow was red and horned—the son was good and worthy though sprung from a base father.

Chung-kung became a disciple of Confucius, and took a high place for solidity of character and a virtuous life. The Master said he would do for a prince, and defended him against the objection that he was not a ready talker. He became a high officer in the employment of the chief of the Chi (季) family, and he must have made a good Minister if he carried out his own principle that the ruler should be reverently circumspect in character though indulgent to others. When Confucius explained to him in what *jen* (仁) or perfect virtue consisted he said—"though I am not clever I beg to make these words my business." He talked, says Tzŭ-kung, and thought of filial piety until his thoughts became his principles. In attendance on his chief and in all the affairs of office he was strict and careful. He did not change his anger, nor keep resentment, nor record old offences. Confucius spoke very highly of him and said he was one of the few who could persevere in virtue up to death—quoting with reference to him the words of the Shĭ-ching,—"All are good at first, few can keep so to the end."

----

* Legge, Ch. Cl. 1. p. 52, and 101.

The date of Chung-kung's death is not known, but it occurred some years before that of Confucius.   Under the T'ang dynasty he was ennobled as Hsie-Hou (醉書) Marquis of Hsie, and under the Sung dynasty he was promoted to be Hsie-Kung.   The title was taken from the name of a small state of the kingdom of Lu, and corresponding to part of the present Yen-chow in the South of Shantung.*

---

4. Hsien-hsien-Tsai-tzŭ (先賢宰子).   The Philosopher Tsai. Tsai-yü (宰子). S. Tzŭ-wo (Go) (子我).

Tsai yü was a native of the state of Lu, but it is not known in what year he was born.   For some time he was a disciple of Confucius, and exposed himself on several occasions to severe rebuke from the Master.   Thus he was found once sleeping during the day and Confucius thereupon observed, "rotten wood cannot be carved nor a wall of dirty earth be plastered," that is, reproof would be useless.   Again when Yü told Duke Ai (Gae Kung) that the founder of the Chou dynasty planted the chestnut at the altars of the Gods in order thereby to symbolise the sharp, severe rule he was about to initiate, Confucius heard the remark with regret, but the words having been uttered it was of no avail to find fault.   On another occasion his question as to whether "a benevolent man on" hearing "There is a man in the well" would "go in after him" elicited from the Sage the famous reply—"Why should he do so? A superior man may be made to go *to the well*, but he cannot be made to go down into it.   He may be imposed upon, but he cannot be befooled."   Again Tsai wished to shorten the period of mourning for a deceased parent from three years to one year, and gave fairly good reasons for the proposal. But Confucius put him down with the crushing reply that "a superior man" would act differently.   He afterwards remarked to his disciples that Yü showed in this he was not a man of perfect human feeling—a child had to be carried in the arms of its parents for the first three years of its life, and all the world observed the term of three years' mourning,

---

* Legge, Ch. Cl. 1. pp. 48, 50, 101, 115, 127; Chia-yü Ch. 8. Sec. 12; Legge, Ch. Cl. 4. p. 505.

adding "Had Yü three years' affection from his father and mother?" These were convincing arguments though Legge calls them "puerile."

Tsai was a man of a sharp and ready tongue, and he was always asking puzzling questions which Confucius did not like. When he enquired whether Huang Ti (黃帝) was a man seeing he had lived 300 years, the Master gave a characteristic reply that as the histories of Yü, T'ang and the founders of the Chou dynasty could not be thoroughly investigated, the disciple was asking about Huang Ti who lived long before these, merely for the sake of asking a difficult question. Tsai explained, however, and the Master then told him of Huang Ti and the four other Ti's in succession. But at the end he added the ungracious remark that the disciple was not able to comprehend what he had said. In general Confucius seems to have had a low opinion of Tsai. It was through him, he said, he had learned not to take men by their speeches but "to hear their words and look at their conduct." Yet he sent him on a mission to the Prince of Ch'u (楚) and approved of the answer which Tsai gave to the Prince when refusing on behalf of Confucius an "easy carriage adorned with ivory" which the former wanted to send as a present. His reply to the Prince is really excellent, and when Tzŭ-Kung showed how he might have embellished it, Confucius said that his flowery praise was not so good as Yü's plain truth.

Tsai entered the service of the Chief of Ch'i (齊), and was appointed a high officer at Lin-k'uei (臨箵) or, according to another version, Lin-tzŭ (臨淄). In B.C. 480, the powerful and popular minister of Ch'i known variously as Ch'ên Hêng (陳恒) or Ch'ên Ch'êng (成) and T'ien Ch'ang (田常) revolted against his chief Chien Kung and murdered him. Confucius, on hearing of this, at once took a solemn bath and went to the court of Duke Ai to ask that a force might be sent to punish the murderer. Unfortunately Tsai was mixed up in the revolt, and he was put to death with three generations of his family. After this Confucius said he was ashamed of him.

During the T'ang period Tsai was ennobled as Ch'i-Hou (齊侯) and under the Sung dynasty he was made first Lin-tzŭ-Kung (臨子公) and afterwards Ch'i-Kung. Lin-tzŭ was a town of Ch'i and was situated in what is now called Ch'ing-chow-foo (青州府) in the north part of Shantung.*

---

5. Hsien-hsien-Tuan-mu-tzŭ (先賢端木子), The Philosopher Tuan-mu.

Tuan-mu Tzŭ (端木賜) Tzŭ-kung (子貢).

Tzŭ-kung was born in B.C. 520 of parents apparently not rich who resided in the kingdom of Wei. In early life he became a disciple of Confucius, and it is said that at the end of his first year of education he thought himself beyond the Master, at the end of the second he thought himself equal to him, and at the end of the third he found he did not come up to him. Afterwards he took office, his first appointment being Chief Magistrate of Sin-yang (斜陽). He subsequently rose to high position not only in Lu but also in his native state.

信

As a disciple he had an unbounded admiration for Confucius of whom he is represented as speaking in the most rapturous and enthusiastic language. Ching, Duke of Ch'i, asked him whether the Master was a man of excellence. He is a Sage, said Tzŭ-kung, and then went on to illustrate the immensity of his resources, the endless store of learning he possessed, thus showing that he himself had wisdom to know a Sage, to use the words of Mencius. He had a straightforward look, was a man of great abilities and strong feeling, and was specially clever as a talker. In this last quality he excelled the Master himself. On one occasion Confucius said of him— "With one like Tzŭ I can begin to talk about the Odes. I told him one point and he knew its proper sequence." Another time the Sage compared him to a Sacrificial vessel made of precious stone. He wished to have the ceremony of sacrificing a sheep on the first day of the moon abolished, but Confucius dissented, saying that Tzŭ-kung grudged the sheep and he the rite. Tzŭ-kung disliked the prying, the impudent, and the babbling, and he said that he wished not to do to others what he would not have others do to him. This, Confucius said he had not attained

---

* For Tsai Yü see Legge, Ch. Cl. 1. p. 26, 40, 56, 101, 191, et al.; Chia-yü. Sec. 23 ;Shi-chi Ch, 6; Ch, Cl. 5 p. 838 &c.

to, and assented to his statement that he was not equal to Yen Hui. Yet he had a high opinion of Tzŭ-kung and there was a mutual affection between master and disciple. It was he whom the Sage recommended to be sent into Ch'i to expostulate with the rebellious T'ien Ch'ang. He was rebuked, indeed, for his habit of making comparisons and his fondness for talking, and the Sage once said to Tsĕng-tzŭ—"after my death Tz'ŭ will wane," because he would not make friends of the proper persons.

When Confucius died the disciples all mourned for him the full period of three years, but Tzŭ-kung built himself a hut near the grave and remained there for three years more. He himself died in Ch'i, but in what year is not known. It was through him, says a biographer, that Confucius' name was spread abroad over all the empire. He liked to publish men's virtues and could not conceal their vices. He spoke with a generous enthusiasm of several of the other disciples, and he seems to have held a high place among them. Ch'ên Tzŭ-chin once said to him, "You are too modest. How can Chung-ne be said to be superior to you?" The character he bore among men was very good, for he had not been servile when poor and riches did not make him proud. Still he was fond of making and owning money, and of living in a style of comparative splendour.

Under the T'ang and Sung dynasties he was ennobled, first as Li-Hou (黎侯), then as Li-yang-Hou (黎陽侯) and afterwards as Li-Kung. Li or Li-yang was a place in the kingdom of Wei situated in the north of the present Honan.*

---

* For Tzŭ-kung see L. Ch. Cl. 1. p. 6, 8, 25 et al.; 2 p. 130 et al.; Lie-tzŭ Ch. 1 & 4.; Shang-yu-lu (尚友錄) s.v.

6. Hsien-hsien-Jan-Tzŭ (先賢冉子), The Philosopher Jan. Jan Ch'iu (冉求) S. Tzŭ-yu (子有).

Jan Ch'iu, a native of Lu, was born in B.C. 520, and was a kinsman of Jan Kêng and Jan Yung. He was noted among the other disciples of Confucius for his great abilities and specially for his administrative talents. He was frank and honest, of a modest, cautious disposition, and needed to be urged and encouraged. Once he said to Confucius that he had not strength to follow his teachings. but the Master said—" Those whose strength is insufficient give over in the middle of the way, but now you limit yourself." The desire which he expressed for himself was, that he might be appointed to a small state into which he would bring plenty within three years, waiting for a " superior man " to teach the people " the principles of propriety and music." When Confucius left Lu in disgust and disappointment, among the disciples who went with him was Ch'iu who acted as carriage-driver for the Master when going to Wei.

He took office under the ambitious chief of the Chi family and rose to be one of his ministers. Though unable to reform his chief he yet helped him to enrich himself by the levy of a grain-tax double that which had been formerly collected. This conduct brought down on him Confucius' displeasure. " He is no disciple of mine," said the Master, " You may proclaim him, children, with beat of drum." It was wrong for Ch'iu to take service with this chief, and it was doubly wrong to help him in his unprincipled measures for adding to his wealth, already very great. On another occasion the master rebukes him for continuing in the service of Chi while the latter was pursuing a policy of wicked aggrandisement.

With his chief, however, Ch'iu seems to have had considerable influence, which he was able to use in favour of Confucius. Not only did he speak of him in terms of high praise, but he succeeded also in obtaining the restoration of the Sage to his native land. Confucius was then in his old age, but the disciple, in the flower of manhood, died before the Master. His loss was greatly lamented by the people of Wu-ch'êng, where he had been living for some time and where he had collected about him 300 disciples.*

In the period of the T'ang dynasty Jan Ch'iu was ennobled as Hsü-Hou (徐 侯). In the Sung period he was promoted to be Peng-ch'êng-Kung (彭 城 公) and afterwards Hsü-Kung, Peng-ch'êng and Hsü being different names for the same place, a district corresponding nearly to the present Hsü-chow-foo in the North of Kiangsu.

----

7. Hsien-hsien-Chung-tzŭ (先 賢 仲 子), The Philosopher Chung. Chung Yu (仲 由) S. Tzŭ-lu (子 路) al. Chi-lu (季 路),

Tzŭ-lu, who was born in B.C. 543, was a native of Pien (卞), a town of Lu, situated in what is now the Prefecture of Yen-chow in the South of Shantung. He became a disciple of Confucius but left the study of philosophy for public life. While studying with the Master and indeed through all his life he had a warm and thorough affection for him. The latter seems to have had a high opinion of the purity, fidelity, and courage of his disciple, and to have regarded him with no little fondness. "Since I have had Chung Yu," he says on one occasion, "no bad words are heard in my ear." Yet he had several times to rebuke the fierce eagerness, and dashing rashness of the disciple, and his desire to give unbecoming state and dignity to his master. Tzu-lu was one of the few who ventured to dictate to the Sage, and his remonstrances were heeded. When Confucius wanted to obey the summons of the rebel Kung-shan Fuh-jao (公 山 弗 擾) Tzu-lu was displeased and said—"Indeed you cannot go! Why must you think of going to see *Kung-shan*." It is not to be wondered at that the Sage called him rude. So also when Confucius was inclined to accept the invitation of Pi Hsi (佛 肸), another rebel, Tzu-lu expostulated with him, reminding him of his own sentiments.

Of his filial piety the Master spoke in terms of high commendation, saying that he served his parents while they were alive with all his

* For Jan Ch'iu See L. Ch. Cl. 1. Proleg. p. 84. p. 52, 107, 111, et al.; 2. p. 180; The Lnn-yü &c. (論 語 集 註 本 義 匯 叅) Chuan 11.

energy and when they were dead with all his thoughts. In the days of his prosperity he sighed for the early years in which his own food was wild herbs while he carried rice on his back for his parents.

Tzŭ-lu had a bold, dashing manner and a stubborn will which would not conform to circumstances. Generous and fearless, he disliked all cowardice and hypocrisy in others and was always willing to hear of his own faults and shortcomings. He was a great lover of war and of every thing that was military and the Master did not like this trait in his character. Confucius could not even endure the disciple's warlike music at his door, and could not be induced to praise his daring rash spirit. Yet the Sage once said that if he resolved to float on a raft out of the world into the ocean, Tzŭ-lu would be his companion, a statement with which the latter was much delighted. Indeed this disciple seems to have taken a personal interest in the Master beyond what any of the others took. He was equally ready to argue, fight, be silent, pray for his master, and die with him. So it is very unfair in Dr. Legge to call him a "kind of Peter," meaning of course Simon Peter, a man who lacked faith, courage, and fidelity, and who moreover cursed and swore.

Tzŭ-lu held office under the house of Chi, in Lu, and under the chief of Wei. He was at one time P'u-yi-t'ai-fu (蒲邑大夫), or Chief Magistrate at P'u, a town situated in what is now the Prefecture of Chêng-ting in Chihli, and complained to Confucius of the difficulty of ruling the place. His administration, however, there and elsewhere seems to have been successful, and it obtained high praise from the Master on several occasions. He never slept over a promise and could settle a lawsuit, Confucius said, with half a word. But his ardent impetuous spirit could not be restrained, and the Master foretold that he would not die a natural death, a prediction which proved correct. A plot against the Chief of Wei was suddenly put into execution and the government was seized by a usurper. Tzŭ-lu spoke and acted with his wonted generous daring and remained loyal to the end. Tzŭ-kao met him going into the palace and said—"you are not implicated—avoid the Chief's difficulties." "I have had his pay," said Tzŭ-lu, "and I will not shun his difficulties." He spoke of setting fire to the tower and thereupon men were sent to kill him. They hacked him with spears and left him dying. In the struggle, Tzŭ-lu's official cap was knocked off, and saying, the perfect man does not die without his cap, he tied it on and died. This event occurred in the year B.C. 479, and none mourned for him more than the forlorn old Sage, who sorrowed for him as a father for a son.

The honorary title conferred on Tzŭ-lu during the T'ang dynasty was Wei-Hou (衞 侯). In the Sung period he was created Ho-nei-Kung (河 內 公) and at a somewhat later period Wei-Kung.*

---

8. Hsien-hsien-Yen-tzŭ (先 賢 言 子), The Philosopher Yen.

Yen Yen (言 偃) S. Tzŭ-yu (子 游)

Tzŭ-yu belonged, according to the Chia-yü, to Lu; but according to another and the correct account, to the Kingdom of Wu (吳). He was born near what is now the town of Ch'ang-shou (常 蕭), in the Prefecture of Soochow, and his descendants still live in that neighbourhood. The Chia-yü says he was 35—other authorities, say 45—years younger than Confucius, the former being the more probable. Inflamed with a zeal for learning he travelled to Lu, and became a disciple of the Sage, and he must have studied with great diligence and success. While in Lu, he took office and became Governor of Wu-Ch'êng (武 城), a town in what is now the sub-prefecture of Lin-ch'ing in Shantung. In this capacity he distinguished himself by the selection of good subordinates and by his efforts to reform the people of his jurisdiction by the introduction of culture, teaching them classical music and the laws of refined society. Confucius at first, though pleased, ridiculed the work as like using "an ox-knife to kill a fowl," but when he heard Tzŭ-yu's defence he retracted and said he had only been joking. Elsewhere the Master is represented as speaking very highly of this disciple. Thus on one occasion he says of him—"Wishing to have ability he learns, wishing to know he asks, wishing

---

* Legge, Ch. Cl. I. p. 15, 39, 62, 84 et al; II. p. 81; V. p. 848,; Li-chi, Ch. 2.; Lie-tzŭ Ch. 4.

to do things well he is careful, wishing to be ready he prepares."

But Tzŭ-yu does not seem to have been of a very amiable and friendly disposition. He speaks rather disparagingly of Tzŭ-hsia's disciples as amateur scholars, and says of Tzŭ-chang that though he did hard things he had not perfect virtue. Some jealousy also seems to have existed between him and Tsêng-tzŭ, but Tzŭ-Kung gives him generous praise. "To perfect his thoughts," he says "before applying them in action so that he did not err in conduct, was the moral character of Yen Yen." His learning was celebrated and he excelled in knowledge of the rites and ceremonies due on solemn occasions, his decision in such matters being generally accepted as final. Mencius says he had one member of a sage, and he is classed with Tzŭ-hsia as distinguished for "literary acquirements." In some matters he was of a very practical way of thinking, even when it led him near to heresy. "Mourning for parents," he says on one occasion, "should stop when grief has reached its height."

One utterance of his is greatly praised. Some time after Confucius died, Chi Kang-tzŭ asked Tzŭ-yu how it came to pass that, while on the death of Tzŭ-ch'an (Kung-Sun-Ch'iao 公孫僑), all the people of Chêng had gone into public mourning, on the death of Confucius the people of Lu did not show any signs of mourning. Tzŭ-yu replied, "Where overflowing water reaches, there is life, and where it does not reach there is death, and so all know of it. But the enriching rain spreads everywhere and all receive its benefits, but do not recognize whence they come. Confucius is to Tzŭ-ch'an as the enriching rain to the overflowing water."

Nothing is known of the date or manner of Tzŭ-yu's death. In the T'ang period he was created Wu-Hou (吳侯) and in the Sung period Tan-Yang-Hou (丹陽侯) and afterwards Wu-Kung. Tan-Yang was a town of Wu, and was situated in what is now the prefecture of Chin-kiang.*

---

* See L. Ch. Cl. I. p. 53 &c.; II. p 69. T'ang-tzŭ-yi-shu (楊子遺書) Ch. 3. Li-chi, Ch. 2.

9. Hsien-hsien-Pu-tzŭ (先賢卜子), The Philosopher Pu.
Pu Shang (卜商). S. Tzŭ-hsia (子夏).

Tzŭ-hsia was born about B.C. 507, and belonged to the State of Wei. After he became a disciple of Confucius he applied himself diligently to study and became distinguished for his "literary acquirements." He was apparently well read in the Books of Rites and History, but he was specially noted for his learning in the Shi-Ching, and afterwards in the Ch'un-ch'iu. The texts of these two works are said to have been delivered to him by Confucius. The latter on one occasion referring to Tzŭ-hsia's explanation of a passage in the Shi, said that he could "begin to talk about the Odes with him." It is said that he penetrated the meaning of the Shi, and that his teachings were handed down to Mao, the illustrious editor of the Classic in the Han dynasty.

Tzŭ-hsia held office for some time in Lu, as Chief magistrate of the town Ch'ü-fu (莒父). He does not seem to have been held in high esteem by his contemporaries except in his own country where he gained the reputation of a "Sage." Confucius said that he did not come up to the due mean, and that he was a miser. So when he asked "about government" the Master said; "Do not be desirous to have things done quickly; do not look at small advantages." In office he was very strict and careful, and Confucius applied to him the words of the Shi, saying that "by acting fairly he kept worthless men from becoming dangerous." He was punctilious and ceremonial, and though learned he had not wide views, but was rather fond of arguing about minutiæ. Yet Chu Hsi says that of the disciples "after Tsăng-sin there was no one of such firm sincerity as Tsze-hia." He certainly seems to have been a man of strong affection for it is said that on his son's death he wept himself blind.

Confucius said "after my death Tzŭ-hsia will wax day by day" because he knew to choose proper friends. When the Sage was no more, Tzŭ-hsia retired to a hill near Hsi-ho (西河) in the present

Province of Shansi, where he built himself a mud hut. He gave himself up to study and teaching, and as his fame was great he had many disciples. In the evenings he amused himself with lute and song, sitting outside his cottage door, and killing care and grief of heart with music brought down from the days of old world virtue and purity. His old fellow-disciple Tsêng-tzu visited him in this retreat to condole with him on the death of his son. Tsêng wept and Tzu-hsia's grief was renewed. "It was Heaven"—he exclaimed, "I was without guilt." "How are you without guilt?" Tsêng replied, and went on to show that his friend had three sins on his head. He had grown old at Hsi-ho, and made the people doubt whether he had been a disciple of Confucius; he had buried his parents without letting others know, and he had destroyed his sight by mourning for his son. Tzu-hsia, leaning on his staff, bowed and owned his faults, pleading in excuse for not having known them before that he had been long living apart from his friends. In old age he seems to have gone back to court life for a time as we find it stated that he was Preceptor to Wên (文), the Marquis of Wei, about B.C. 406. Neither place nor date of his death is recorded, but he must have lived to the age of more than 100 years.

Though Tzu-hsia was noted for his great learning yet he does not make book-knowledge the great business of life. He says that the official should devote his leisure to study, and the student his leisure to official life. Many other sayings of Tzu-hsia are recorded and some of them are very interesting. Thus we have his famous reply to Ssŭ-ma Niu, who complained sadly that while all others had brothers he alone was without any. "Death and life," answers Tzu-hsia, "have their determined appointment; riches and honours depend upon Heaven. Let the superior man never fail reverentially to order his own conduct, and let him be respectful to others and observant of propriety; then all within the four seas will be his brothers. What has the superior man to do with being distressed because he has no brothers." Again he says that he would call that man learned who had come to prize virtue instead of beauty, who did his duty to the utmost of his abilities towards parents and ruler, and whose words among friends were always faithful.

Tzŭ-hsia was first introduced into the Confucian temple along with several others by T'ang T'ai Tsung in A.D. 647, but he was made one of the Ten in 730. His first posthumous title, given in the T'ang dynasty, was Wei-Hou (魏 侯). Under the Sung dynasty this was changed for Ho-tung-Kung (河 東 公) and afterwards he was promoted to be Wei-Kung.*

---

10. Hsien-hsien-Tuan-sun-tzŭ (先 賢 顓 孫 子), The Philosopher Tuan-sun.

Tuan-sun Shi (顓 孫 師). S. Tzŭ-chang (子 張).

Tzŭ-chang was a native of Ch'ên (陳), part of the present Honan, in which State he was born B.C. 504. Of his life we know very little, and the statements given about his character are not always consistent. He was a disciple of Confucius but apparently had an independent way of thinking. The other disciples were friendly with him but did not respect him because he did not lay enough stress on "benevolence and righteousness." Confucius said he went too far, that is, he went beyond the Mean, and he characterized him as "specious," or pretending to be what he was not actually. His questions show that he was sometimes not quite satisfied with the Master's teachings, and it was said that he wanted more sublime doctrines. But he had a great respect for the Sage. He treasured in his memory the latter's answer about the duties of one in office, and wrote on his sash the exposition he gave of conduct which would be everywhere appreciated. Tzŭ-Kung, who in one place says he was not virtuous, in another gives him high praise. "Of excellent deserts," he says, "and not boasting of them, of honourable position and not taking merit for it, neither insolent nor luxurious, and not rude to the dependent; such was the character of Tuan-sun Shi." His kind, frank, and easy disposition seems to have made him too indulgent, but it led Confucius to apply to him the lines of the Shi; "The happy and courteous sovereign; the parent of his

---

* For Tzŭ-hsia see L. Ch. Cl. I. p. 4, 116, and Book xlx, p. 203 &c.; Chia-yü Ch. 2; Li-chi, Ch. 2 et al.

people." Yet in another place Confucius is represented as saying that Tzŭ-chang surpassed him in gravity of deportment. This seems scarcely possible.

Some of the sayings attributed to Tzŭ-chang are admirable. "The scholar in office," he says, "who on seeing danger risks even life, on seeing personal gain thinks of public duty, whose thoughts at sacrifice are reverential, and at a funeral sad, is all that is wanted." Of the "principles of intercourse" he says, "The superior man honours the talented and virtuous, and bears with all. He praises the good, and pities the incompetent."

On the death of Confucius, Tzŭ-chang retired to his native State, and lived there in seclusion all the rest of his life. It is reported that when he felt death approaching he said to his son Shên-hsiang (申 詳). ' Of the superior man it is said ' he ended,' of a common man ' he died,' I am to day near the former I think."

In A.D. 720 Tzŭ-chang was admitted to share in the Confucian sacrifices, and in 1267 he was promoted to be the tenth " Wise one," by Sung Tu Tsung. Under the T'ang dynasty he was made Ch'ên-Po (陳伯) or Earl of Ch'ên, in 1108 this was changed to Ying-Chuan-Hou (潁川侯), and afterwards under the same dynasty to Ch'ên-Kua-Kung (陳國公). Ying-chow, formerly called Ying-chuan is the name of a Prefecture in the north of Anhui and was formerly in the State of Ch'ên.*

---

* For Tzŭ-chang see L. Ch. Cl. I. p. 107, 203 et al., 4. p. 489; Li-chi Ch. 2.; Lie-tzŭ Ch. 4.; Chia-yŭ Ch. 3. Sec. 12, et al.

11. Hsien-hsien-Yu-tzŭ (先賢有子), The Philosopher Yu.

Yu Jo (有若) S. Tzŭ jo (子若) or according to the Chia-yü Tzŭ-yu (子有).

The date of Yu Jo's birth is given by some as B.C. 516, and by others as 539. He was a native of the State of Lu, but it is not recorded in what village or town he was born. Among the disciples of Confucius he was noted for his powers of memory and his love for the ways of antiquity. He praises a high officer of Ch'i for having worn a fox-skin coat for thirty years, and he was evidently a man fond of economy. But his name is not often mentioned and little is known of his history. It is probable that he held office under the ruler of his native State, for we find Duke Ai consulting him as to the means of raising a sufficient revenue. Yu Jo advised a light taxation and said, "If the people have plenty, their prince will not be left to want alone. If the people are in want, their prince cannot enjoy plenty alone."

On the death of Confucius the disciples observed the full period of three years' mourning for him as for a father. At the expiration of this period some among the disciples proposed to make Yu Jo the chief of the school. His way of talking and his outward manner and appearance were very like those of their late Master. There was apparently no other reason for the proposal, from which Tsêng-tzŭ specially expressed his utter dissent and which soon fell to the ground. But its rejection did not imply any slight on Yu Jo or any demerit on his part as compared with the other disciples.

Yu died in battle brought on by an invasion of his native State, Lu, by forces from the State of Wu, sometime about the year B.C. 450, and it is recorded that the Chief of Lu, caused state ceremony to be used at his funeral.

The tablet of Yu was first placed in the Temple of Confucius as a Worthy in A.D. 730, and it was promoted to its present position in 1738. In the period of the T'ang dynasty he was ennobled as Pien-poh (卞伯) or Earl of Pien, and in the Sung period he was made P'ing-yin-Hou (平陰侯), Marquis of P'ing-yin. Pien and P'ing-yin are names of towns which were formerly in the principality of Lu, and at present belong to the southern part of Shan-tung, the former being one of the names for the place near which the battle was fought in which Yu was killed.*

---

12. Hsien-hsien-Chu-tzŭ (先賢朱子), the Philosopher Chu. Chu Hsi (朱熹) S. Yuan-hui (元晦). al. Chung-hui (仲晦).

The family of which Chu Hsi came belonged to Wu-yuan (婺源), a town of Hsin-an (新安)—now Hui-chow-foo in An-hui. But Hsi's father Chu Sung (朱松), who will re-appear hereafter, had been appointed District Magistrate of Yu-K'i (尤溪), a town within the Prefecture of Yen-p'ing in the Province of Fuh-keen, and when his term of office there had expired he obtained the loan of a friend's house on the opposite side of the river from Yu-K'i, and being very poor continued to reside there for some years. The little town of Yu-K'i, or as it is also frequently called Nan-K'i (南溪), is beautifully situated amid romantic mountainous scenery on the left bank of the small river Yu, at a distance of about 140 miles from Foochow in a north-westerly direction. It was in this place, in the house borrowed by his father, that Chu Hsi was born in the year A.D. 1130, being the fourth in the Kien-yen period of the reign of Kao Tsung, the first Emperor of the Sung dynasty after the dismemberment of the empire by the Kin Tartars. The birth of Hsi was heralded by great signs and wonders in widely-separated districts. Two hills stand respectively on the east and west sides of Yu-K'i, facing each other, and named Kung (公) and Wên (文) from a fancied resemblance in their outlines to these two characters. This night a "wild fire" arose and burnt down all the trees and grass on these hills, and in the morning the characters *Wên* and *Kung* were clearly visible on them. At Wu-yuan, the home of his ancestors, an arc of vermilion light was seen to stream from a well for

---

* For Yu Jo See L. Ch. Cl. I. Ps. 2, II. 119. p. 130; Mêng-tzŭ-chi-chu &c., (孟子集註 &c.) Ch. 5. p. 52.; Li-chi-Ch. 2.

three days. Moreover the baby was found to have exactly seven black spots on one side of his face, a circumstance which every body said was strange.

The father and mother of Hsi were persons of no ordinary character, and they began early to train up their child in the way he should go. When only three years of age he surprised his father by asking what was above the sky, a question to which through all his life he could not gain a sure and complete answer. In his next year he began the Little Learning, and continued for some time to be educated by his parents. Even as a child he had quiet, grave ways, and when his comrades were playing he sat down by himself and solemnly traced Pa-kua on the mud with his finger.

The family removed to Kien-ning-foo, and here in 1144 Hsi's father died. The latter on his death-bed appointed a friend, Liu Tzŭ-yü, his executor, and enjoined on Hsi to become as son and disciple to Hu Hsien (胡憲), Liu Chĭ-chung (劉致中) and Liu Yen-ch'ung (劉彦冲), three friends of good repute for virtue and learning. After the father's death his executor, Liu Tzŭ-yü, built a house and gave it to the widow and family of his late friend. Hsi was prompt to obey his father's order, and put himself at once under the instruction of the three scholars, who treated him with great affection but did not always teach him what was quite orthodox. Liu Chĭ-chung gave him his daughter in marriage, and some years after he and the other Liu died, leaving Hsi to the sole care of Hu Hsien.

After having passed the necessary examinations, Chu Hsi was made a Chin-shi in his nineteenth year, and shortly afterwards he went to Wu-yuan to visit and worship at his ancestors graves. In 1151 he received his first official appointment as Assistant Magistrate at T'ung-an, a town not very far from Amoy. On his way to this place he went to Yen-p'ing to visit Li T'ung (李侗), better known as Li Yen-p'ing (李延平), a great scholar and philosopher, who was teaching there the doctrines derived from the brothers Ch'êng. He remained at T'ung-an for three years, and wrought much good, fostering learning among the people and reforming their bad customs. When released from duty he returned home, paying another visit by the way to Li

T'ung, who won him over from studying Buddhism and Taoism.

Being very poor he asked for a new appointment that he might be enabled to support his mother, and, according to his request, he was made superintendent of the Nan-Yo Temple in Hunan. As this was a sinecure office he had abundant leisure for study, and he now became a constant disciple of Li T'ung. In 1163 he was summoned to Court by the new Emperor Hsiao-Tsung, and at once presented an earnest Memorial on the bad state of public affairs. But he did not like the Capital, and after a short stay he went back to his home and studies. On being again appointed to the Nan-yo Temple he went to live at T'an-chow, and here he met the philosopher Chang Ch'ih. His mother died in 1169 and his wife in 1176, and he had no desire to return to active official life. But he was forced, in 1178, to accept the post of prefect of Nan-k'ang in Kiangsi. His administration at this place was very successful, and he did much for the moral and material improvement of the people. Afterwards he was appointed to special duty on the east coast of Chekiang. While on this mission he ordered the demolition of the Hall which had been built for sacrificial honours to Ch'in K'uei, the Minister of State who had counselled peace with the Kin Tartars, at Yung-chia in the Prefecture of Wênchow.

Numerous other appointments were offered to him, but he generally refused them and only went into office with great reluctance. In the meantime he continued to do what he considered his public duty, teach orthodox philosophy and bring into publicity the classical literature of his country. But in 1196 an official named Hu Hung (胡紘) as the agent for others, brought false charges against him of teaching corrupt doctrines, and he was stript of all his honours and titles. Some of these were restored to him three years afterwards when a new appointment was given to him. Now, he was old and broken down by sickness and he obtained leave to resign. For a long time he had been afflicted with something like rheumatism in one of his feet, and latterly he had suffered from acute pains in the bowels. Yet he did not "bate a jot of heart or hope," and continued to teach his disciples and correct his manuscripts, anxious to leave his work as perfect as

possible. In 1200 he became very much worse, and it was plain that
life was ebbing quickly. He regretted the long absence of his sons
and wished to see them once more. The disciples visited him often
but Ts'ai Ch'ên (蔡沈) remained with him constantly and tended him
with great care and affection. When Hsi knew his end to be near he
signed to Ts'ai to have his dress adjusted, and after much suffering he
passed gently away in the arms of his beloved disciple. Some nights
before he died a dreadful roaring noise, such as had never been heard
before, echoed through all the surrounding hills, and the people knew it
was a warning of some great calamity. On the night of his death also
a mighty wind arose which blew down houses and tore up trees, the
rivers suddenly overflowed their banks and great hills were rent
asunder, for "the fading away of a Sage is no slight event in nature."
The ceremonies of antiquity were observed at his funeral and he was laid
beside his wife.

Chu Hsi was known by many names and soubriquets, some given
by others and some adopted by himself. His baby name, given by his
father, was Ch'ên-lang (沈郎), Gentleman of Ch'ên, an old name of
Yu-k'i, and his style as an infant was Chi-yen (季延), or Young
Yen-p'ing. In boyhood he received two other names denoting his
place among his kindred. His teacher Liu Yen-ch'ung called him
Yuan-hui (元晦), Greatness latent, and Hsi modestly changed this
for Chung-hui (仲晦), Mediocrity latent. Afterwards he styled
himself *Hui-yen* (晦菴), from the name he gave to a retreat he had
made near Kien-yang, *Hui-wêng* (晦翁), old man of obscurity, and in
old age *T'un-wêng* (遯翁), the old man hidden away. Besides these
there are a few other designations which are still sometimes used.
The posthumous epithet conferred on him was Wên, accomplished, and
he is usually known as Chu-wên-kung, or Chu-foo-tzŭ. He was
admitted to the Temple of Confucius in 1241 as one of the "Scholars,"
and in 1642 he was promoted to be one of the "*Hsien,*" placed below
the Seventy disciples. In answer to a Memorial, the Emperor Kanghsi in 1712 caused him to he advanced to the Hall of Great Perfection
next below the "Ten Wise Ones." When Tzŭ-yo was promoted to a
place in this Hall for the sake of symmetry in 1738 Hsi was transferred

from the East to the West side, Yu Jo having at least the qualification
of having died before him.

The amount of literary work achieved by Chu Hsi is almost
incredible, specially when its general excellence is taken into considera-
tion. He regarded it as his fated duty to restore the geniune texts of
the ancient classics, and to set forth their true meanings. With these
ends in view he confirmed to the Ta-hsiao, and Chung-yung their
independent places, divided them into chapters and sections, and added
elaborate commentaries. He revised also and annotated the *Lun-yü*
and Mencius, and the *Ching*, giving Mencius that high place which he
has since retained. He composed five works on the Yih-ching and
short treatises on several of the other classics. Of the principal authors
whose works shed light on the canonical books he took Han Yü, Chou
Lien-ch'i, the two Ch'êng, and Chang Tsai. The writings and sayings
of these philosophers he collected and published with notes and
criticisms. In History he revised the T'ung-chien of Ssŭ-ma Kuang
and, with the help of his disciples, published it in a new form as the
T'ung-chien-kang-mu. He corrected also the Chi-ku-lu of the same
author, and wrote accounts of the eminent men in the previous part of
the Sung dynasty. Morover he composed biographical or critical
sketches of the most distinguished rulers, scholars, and statesmen of
former times, a large number of poems, and Essays on Buddhist and
Taoist subjects. In addition to all this he had many disciples to whom
he lectured or gave advice daily for several years, and he kept up a
correspondence with not a few literary and philosophical friends. The
Yü-lu, or Record of his sayings, and *Wên-chi*, or Collection of his
Letters and Miscellanies, form volumes of considerable size and great
value.

The life of Chu Hsi is beautiful for its simplicity and purity, and
its long history of self-sacrifice and devotion to noble aims. He was
wont to rise while it was still dark and perform the morning service
of remembrance to his ancestors and the ancient Sages. He began his
studies immediately after an early breakfast and continued at them
until he was interrupted by his disciples. With these he was unwearied
in teaching, and often remained with them until after midnight in

order to clear away all doubts and darkness from a youthful mind. He was a man of immense erudition, but of a liberal spirit and generous sympathies. He did not cry out in the streets against error and heresy but wrote and reasoned against them in his study. True wisdom, he thought, once made known to the people would win them away from false doctrine and evil living. Hence in his writings and conversations he taught that philosophy was for every day life—that the Ultimate Principle—the law and source of moral life—is embosomed in every man and woman, and that the sum of all doctrine was to lead a life of duty free from reproach. Philosophy was to make men wise and good, above all fitting them for the active service of their country. Chu Hsi's daily thoughts, said one who knew him, were about his country and he was always affected to tears by any new story of national trouble or disgrace. In his speculations about a Supreme Being, the future of the world, and other subjects beyond the ken of man, he had little dogmatism, and was wont to say that the matter required further reflection. But he did not shrink from discussing any problem which the Buddhist learning and religion had raised, though his solutions of such problems are often very unsatisfactory. Confucianism was enough for him, and he preferred its plain maxims for this working-day world, and human examples of wisdom and holiness to airy speculations about gods, and heavens, and the dark hereafter. "Hostile criticism" has attacked much of his work on the ancient classics, and tried to make him out a schismatic and an innovator, and the priests of western sects have called him materialist, and atheist. But none can deny the perfect purity of his life, his grandeur of soul, and the wonderful influence of his teaching and example. "Ille est optimus [Philosophus], non qui plurimum disputat, sed qui optimé vivit et optimé vivere docet," if we accept the Confucian view of philosophy, and thus judged, Chu Hsi has a high place among the philosophers of the world. For though statements may be disproved and faults discovered in his theories, yet the good results of his life and doctrines remain imperishable. He has joined "the choir invisible

Of those immortal dead who live again
In minds made better by their presence; livé
In pulses stirred to generosity,
In deeds of daring rectitude, in scorn
For miserable aims that end with self,
In thoughts sublime that pierce the night like stars,
And with their mild persistence urge men's search
To vaster issues."*

* See Chu-tzŭ-nien-p'u (朱子年譜); Nan-ch'i-chǐ (南溪鄴); Chinese
    Repository, Vol. XVIII. p. 187 &c.; Mayer's Ch. R. M. p. 25; Ch. Recorder Vol. IV.
    No. 12; Hsing-li-hui-yao (性理彙要) ch. 12.

The *Hsien Hsien* (先 賢) *or Former* "Worthies."

The tablets of these form the inner rows arranged along the sides of the main part of the temple—the "outer Court." The order is the same as in those above, the first from the North on the East side being the First, and the first on the West side being the Second and so on throughout. The epithet *Hsien-hsien* is prefixed to the surname on each tablet, but is not given here.

1. Kung-sun Ch'iao (公 孫 僑). S. Tzŭ-ch'an (子 產)

Kung-sun Ch'iao, generally known by his second name Tzŭ-ch'an, was some years senior to Confucius, but the date of his birth is not known. He first appears in history in B.C. 565, when marauders from Chêng his native state, invaded Ts'ai and captured its Duke's son, who was at the time Minister of War. On this occasion Tzŭ-ch'an was the only one in Chêng who had the morality to condemn the expedition. He said—"There can be no greater misfortune to a small State than to have success in war while there is no virtue in its civil administration." At this time he must have been very young, for his wise and politic father in rebuking him for the above language about the invasion says—"If a boy like you talk about it so, you will get into disgrace."

The State of Chêng (鄭), corresponding to nearly the northern half of the present Honan, did suffer, however, and Tzŭ-ch'an was not disgraced. On the contrary he is next found as Chief Minister of the State, and conducting the government in such a way as to make it a model to other States. He selected the best men for office using them according to their natural abilities, and he then allowed each to do his best in his own department, while he exercised over all a constant but light control. Thus the State Decrees and other official documents passed through the hands of several officers from P'i Shên (稗 諶) the counsellor, who could think well only when he was out in the open country—who drafted then, down to Tzŭ-ch'an who gave them the "proper elegance and finish." So it came to pass that during his administration this little State seldom came into collision with other States, and at the same time its chief commanded the respect due to his position.

Confucius had a very high opinion of Tzŭ-ch'an, and said that he "had four of the characteristics of a Superior man ; in his conduct of himself, he was humble ; in serving his superiors, he was respectful ; in nourishing the people he was kind ; in ordering the people, he was just." Elsewhere he says that Tzŭ-ch'an was fit to be the "foundation of a State," and on another occasion he calls him "a kind-hearted man." Mencius on the other hand thinks that the way in which he showed this kindness, for example in conveying people across a river in his own carriage, was evidence that he did "not understand the practice of government" Confucius himself says that Tzŭ-ch'an was kind to the people as a mother to her children, and that he did not instruct them. But this seems not to agree with a statement about his conduct towards public schools found in the Chia-yü and the Tso chuan. He gave the people a Penal code, and secured to them peace in a time of general Confusion. His dying advice to Tzŭ-T'ai-Shu (子太叔)—the Shi-Shu of the Lun-yü amounts to this—Be generous first, and be severe rather than indulgent. So he himself had acted while in office, being stern and severe to the bad because he loved the people. He was eminently patriotic, and always wanted the little State of Chêng to hold her own and be respected. His political sayings are often good, Such as, "It is being prepared which keeps a State from being made little of." He was also a skilful debater and an eloquent speaker. Though respectful to his superiors he did not shrink from telling them their faults and duties in plain and sometimes cutting language. He stands out in history as one of the very few men in authority during those dark times who were able and pure, true to their chief and generous to their people.

Tzŭ-ch'an died in the year B.C. 521, and all the State mourned for him with a deep and general sorrow. When Confucius heard of his death he went out and wept, for this man as he had said, "had a love bequeathed by the ancients."

The tablet of Tzŭ-ch'an was admitted to the temple in the year 1857. It took the place formerly occupied by that of Chü Yuan, which was moved across to the opposite side. This comes next.*

---

2. Chü Yuan (蘧瑗) Poh-yü (伯玉).

Chü, known best by his second name Poh-yü, was a contemporary and, as some say, a disciple of Confucius. His native place and the dates of his birth and death are not recorded, and we have only occasional notices of him from which to cull our information. We know that he belonged to Wei, and nearly, if not quite all his public life seems to have been spent in that State. He served under three of its Dukes and was for some time a Chief Minister.

The first mention of Poh-yü in history is on the occasion of the trouble in the State of Wei, which led to the flight or expulsion of its Duke Hsien, in B.C. 558. At this time he appears proclaiming the doctrine of non-resistance even as a matter of expediency. As he rose in office, his fame grew, and it was said that Wei could not be invaded while Po-yü was at the head of the administration. Then we find him in the service of the wicked Duke Ling, and still keeping his high notions of respect for the ruler. Once the Duke had been sitting up very late with his fair but infamous consort Nan-tzŭ. As morning was drawing near, the noise of a quickly-going carriage was heard approaching the palace. The noise then ceased and the carriage moved slowly until it had passed the palace. "That is Chü Poh-yü who is driving past," Nan-tzŭ said to her lord. And then she explained that she knew it was he by the ceremony observed in passing the palace—"an eminent, high officer of the State, virtuous and wise, reverential in serving his chief, he is a man who could not take advantage of the darkness to fail in etiquette."

Confucius when in Wei, made the acquaintance of Poh-yü and

---

* For Tzŭ-ch'an see L. Ch. Cl. I. p. 42, 142; 2. p 193, 223; 5. p. 434 et al.; Chia-yü. Ch. 9 et al.,

was his guest on one occasion. This acquaintance ripened into a close
friendship, and the Master was evidently highly satisfied with Poh-yü.
He calls him a "superior man," and says of him; "when good
government prevails in his State, he is to be found in office. When bad
government prevails, he can roll his principles up, and keep them in
his breast." When the Sage had returned to his native State, Poh-yü
sent a messenger to enquire about him. Confucius asked him what
his master was doing, and the messenger replied that he was wanting
to make his faults few but had not then succeeded. It is said of
him, however, that at 50 years of age he knew all the failings of his
previous life, and that at 60 he was converted (hua 化), or refined
to purity.

His death is supposed to have occurred about B.C. 500, but this is
apparently only a conjecture. His tablet was first admitted to the
Confucian honours in A.D. 739. It was removed, however, in 1530,
and was not restored until 1724, when it was put first on the East
side—the place which it continued to occupy until 1857. Poh-yü was
ennobled in 1267 as Nei-huang-Po (內黃伯), Earl of Nei-huang—a
town in the present Honan.*

---

3. Lin Fang (林放) S. Tzŭ-ch'iu (子邱).

Lin Fang is said to have been a native of Lu and a disciple of
Confucius. He is known, however, only by a question which he asked
Confucius, viz ;—What is the first thing to be attended to in ceremonies?
—which Confucius said was a great question.

He was admitted to the temple in A.D. 739. Chia-ching in 1630
removed his tablet, but it was restored in 1724. He was also honoured
by territorial titles during the T'ang and Sung dynasties.†

---

* For Chü Poh-yü see L. Ch. Cl. I. p. 149, 160.; 5. p. 461 et al.; Shi-chi, K'ung-tsŭ-
shi-chia.: Li-chi, Ch. 2.
† L. Ch. Cl. L p. 19.

4. T'an-t'ai Mie-ming (澹臺滅明). S. Tzŭ-yü (子羽).

T'an-t'ai was born in B.C. 513, or according to another account 503, in Wu-chêng (武城), a town in what is now Lin-ch'ing-chow, in Shantung. He was introduced to Confucius as a disciple, and the Sage at first formed a low opinion of his character and abilities, judging from his plain features and ungainly bearing. Afterwards, however, Confucius had to own that he had been mistaken, and that, taught by his experience in this case he had ceased to take men by their personal appearance. But this story does not agree very well with another statement which ascribes to this disciple the outward semblance of a "superior man."

T'an-t'ai took office in his native town, and we find him a subordinate of the disciple Tzŭ-yu (子游) when the latter was Governor of Wu-Ch'êng. At this time Confucius one day asked Tzŭ-yu what kind of officers he had to help him. Tzŭ-yu replied that he had T'an-t'ai Mie-ming who never took a short cut and never came to his official residence except on business. From this low position T'an-t'ai rose to be a State counsellor in Lu. His character as a public servant was very good, and it is thus given by Tzŭ-kung—"He shows no joy when honoured, and no anger when slighted. Profuse in what benefits the people and exacting in all that concerns himself, he serves his superiors by helping his subjects." Confucius, too, says that he was upright and disinterested. He was indeed endowed with many talents but too generous and self-forgetful, caring neither for an easy life nor a decent burial.

It is related of T'an-t'ai, that he was once crossing the Huang Ho, bearing his massive gold badge of office, when two dragons at the bidding of the guardian demon of the river, tried to take the piece of gold by violence. T'an-t'ai told them that while he could be prevailed on by fair entreaty he would not yield to force. So he killed the dragons with his sword and afterwards destroyed the piece of gold.

T'an-t'ai's fame grew and went abroad into every State. He came to have about 300 disciples and these followed him in his travels which he extended as far south as the Yang-tze. He survived Confucius and spent the last years of his life in the State of Ch'u (楚), among his books and disciples.

Under the T'ang and Sung dynasties successively he was ennobled, and in A.D. 739, he was admitted into the Confucian temple as one of the "Worthies." This is the date of all the other disciples in this department except when a different date is mentioned.*

---

5. Yuan Hsien (原憲) S. Tzŭ-ssŭ (子思).

Yuan Hsien, who was born in B.C. 516, was a native of Lu, according to one author, but, according to another, of Sung. He became a disciple of Confucius, and when the latter was Minister of Crime, in his native State, he made Yuan his chief administrator, or as some interpret the expression, Governor of a town. In this office the salary wa "900 measures of grain" which Yuan wished to refuse, but Confucius said " Do not—suppose you give them away in the neighbourhoods, hamlets, and villages." Afterwards he asks Confucius as to what was shameful. The latter replied that it was shameful to draw salary alike in times of good and bad government. Yuan would serve without pay himself and he thought it was a shame for a public servant to take remuneration. But Confucius held that if the country was in a state of order, and an officer was able to do his duty according to his principles he should take salary. It was shameful to enjoy the emoluments of an office only while its duties could not be properly performed. The passage in question, however, is translated by Legge, following Chu Hsi, thus—" When good government prevails in a State, *to be thinking only of his* salary ; and, when bad government prevails, *to be thinking, in the same way, only of his* salary ; this is shameful." Thus translated, the answer of the Sage had no special meaning for Yuan Hsien.

---

* For T'an-t'ai see L. Ch. Cl. I. p. 53; Chia-yü Ch. 5. sec. 19, et al.; Po-wu-chī (博物志) Ch. 7.

Yuan is described as a plain, modest man, of clean hands and pure heart, poor, but having his delight in truth. After the Master's death he retired to Wei, and lived there in studious seclusion. Hu An-kuo doubtingly attributes to him the compilation of the Fourteenth Book of the Lun-yü, but there is no record apparently of his literary occupations. He lived in a hut made of branches of trees and dried grass, caring only to have a dry floor and a stanch roof. He wore a leathern cap, straw sandals, and raiment from the woodland. Content with his books and happy in the study of truth, he recked little of the outside world, and could enjoy his lonely lute in the hours of evening leisure. There is a well-known story—told with many differences of detail—about Tzŭ-kung visiting Yuan in his hermitage. The old fellow-. disciple came in all the grandeur of a State Minister, with carriages, and horsemen, and grand display. The recluse went out to receive him clothed in the tattered weeds of every-day wear. "Are you ill, Hsien-shêng (Sir)?" said Tzŭ-kung with a sigh. "I have heard," replied the other, "that to be without riches is to be poor—that to learn truth and be unable to carry it into practice is to be ill. I am poor, not ill." Tzŭ-kung at once took his leave, ashamed through all his being, to have uttered such ill-advised words.

It is not known when Yuan Hsien died nor is anything related about him after the above event. Like the other disciples he received titles of nobility from Emperors of the T'ang and Sung dynasties in succession.*

---

* For Yuan Hsien consult L. Ch. Cl. I p. 50, 139; Lun-yu-chi-chu, &c. Ch. 6 p. 10, Ch. 14 p. 1: Kao-shi-chuan ch I. at end.

6. Fuh Pu-ch'i (宓不齊) S. Tzŭ-chien (子賤).

The surname is also written 伏 and 虙 both pronounced Fuh.

Tzŭ-chien was a native of Lu, and was born in B.C. 513, or according to another account in 503. In his youth he became a disciple of Confucius, and he must have applied himself to learning with great zeal and devotion. He was distinguished among the Sage's disciples as a man wise and clever, and at the same time kind and affectionate. After he left Confucius he took office in his native State, and became Governor of Tan-fu (單父), a town in what is now the Prefecture of Tsao-chow in Shantung. In his administration of this place he won golden opinions of all. Confucius on learning about his success said of him—"He is a superior man indeed ! If Lu had not excellent men, could he have acquired this merit ? ." On another occasion Confucius asked him how he acted in government so as to please all the people. Tzŭ-chien thereupon explained his system to the Sage. He said that he sympathised with the people in their various relations and duties, that he had three men who were fathers, five who were elder brothers, and eleven who were friends, to teach the people the laws of domestic and social morality, and lastly that he had five men of the place wiser than himself to consult with and to teach him the art of governing. "It is in this last that there is greatness," said Confucius warmly, or, according to another author—"Is there anything greater than this ? " Yao and Shun in old times, he added, in like manner sought out men of ability and virtue to help them in governing the Empire. It is a pity that Pu-ch'i has only the administration of a small place.

Tzŭ-chien was a humane and large-minded ruler. He took care to choose his subordinates well, employing only such as were like-minded with himself. He then left to them the practical working out of his rules and theories. So he is said to have merely sat still and played his harp, and thereby to have secured good government for his subjects, none of whom could bear to impose on him. He was also an author, and the names are given of some of his writings, but none have been preserved. In the period of the T'ang dynasty Tzŭ-chien was ennobled as Tan-poh (單 伯) and under the Sung as Tan-fu-Hou (單 父 侯), Marquis of Tan-fu, the place in which he ruled so well. In later authors he is sometimes referred to under this latter title.*

---

7. Nan-Kung Kuo (南 宮 适) S. Tzŭ-jung (子 容).

This man appears under many different names, and there are several reasons for thinking that two individuals have been mixed up in the old histories. We find Nan Jung (南 容), Nan-Kung Kuo (括), and the *name* is also given as T'ao (綯) and as *Ching-shu* (敬 叔), but this last is said to be a posthumous appellation. According to the Han history there were Nan Jung, known as Nan-Kung T'ao, and Nan-Kung Ching-shu also called Nan-Kung Kuo, and Chung-sun-yue (仲 孫 閱). In the Sung dynasty, however, these two were said to be one, and this judgment has been adhered to in the temple arrangements.

The family surname was Mêng (孟), and Tzŭ-jung was the son of Mêng Hsi-tzŭ (孟 僖 子) and brother of Mêng Yi-tzŭ (孟 懿 子). He thus belonged to one of the three powerful families of Lu, which in the 6th century B.C., kept that State in trouble and confusion. But he himself is represented as a man of great abilities and genuine goodness. His father sent him to be a disciple of Confucius, with whom he soon found favour. The master said of Nan Jung "that if the country were well governed, he would not be out of office, and if it were ill governed, he would escape punishment and disgrace." He was accustomed to repeat three times a day certain lines in the *Shi-ching* to the effect that "a flaw in a white sceptre-stone may be ground away; but for a flaw in speech nothing can be done." Confucius was pleased with him and gave him his crippled brother's daughter to wife.

---

* For Tzŭ-chien see L. Ch. Cl 1. p. 37.; Lun-yü-chi-chu, &c.; Ch. 5 p. 2.; Chia-yü Ch. 3 p. 11.

While attached to the Court of the Duke of Lu, Tzŭ Jung lived in the Nan-Kung or South Palace, and the name by which he has come to be known arose from this accident. He went with Confucius to the Royal Court at the capital of Chou. But he fell into disgrace with Duke Ting and went to live in the State of Wei. He took his badge of office with him and used it in his efforts to obtain employment under the chief of that country. On hearing of Confucius' strongly expressed disapproval of this conduct, he desisted, and soon after he was allowed to return to his native State and was restored to office. We read that when a great fire broke out in the palace of Duke 'Ai, in B.C. 491, Nan-Kung Ching-shu saved from destruction the official archives, and the copy of the Chow-Li which was in the palace library. So he has the "great merit" of having preserved that valuable canonical treatise.

The dates of Nan-Kung Kuo's birth and death are apparently not known, and very few incidents of his life are recorded beyond those stated above. He seems to have reciprocated the affection and esteem which the Master had for him, and to have been in public life a man of tender conscience and upright conduct. "A superior man indeed is this!", exclaims Confucius, "An esteemer of virtue indeed is this!" And Tzŭ-kung in his usual style sums up his character in these words —"when alone, his thoughts were on perfect virtue, and when in company, his conversation was on righteousness." *

* See L. Ch. Cl. I. p. 37, 102, 141, 11 ; Lun-yü. Chi &c. Ch. 5, & Ch. 14. ; Shang-yu-lu
(尚友錄) Ch. 22 p. 30. ; Chia-yü, Ch. 3 sec. 12. The Story about the badge of office is told in different ways.

8. Kung-ye-Ch'ang (公冶長) S. Tzŭ-oh'ang (子長).

It is doubtful whether Kung-ye's name and second name were as above, or one Ch'ang and the other Chĭ (芝). *Ch'ang* is also written 萇 and *Chĭ* is also written (之). But nothing is known about the man beyond what is told of him in the Lun-yü. We read there—"The Master said of Kung-ye Ch'ang ' he is fit to have a wife—though he was in bonds it was not for any crime he had committed.' He gave him his own daughter to wife." This is said to indicate the Sage's appreciation of Kung-ye Ch'ang's high moral character.

One account makes Kung-ye to have been a native of Ch'i (齊) and another says he belonged to Lu. It was in the latter State that he was buried, and his grave was a few miles from an old town situated in what is at present the Prefecture of Tsao-chow, in Shantung.*

----◆----

9. Shang Chü (商瞿). S. Tzŭ-mu (子木).

The surname of this disciple is usually given as Shang, but in the Han-shu it is given as Shang-chü. He was a native of Lu, and was born in B.C. 523 or 513 for the accounts vary. He became a disciple of Confucius in the old age of the latter. But he studied diligently and attained to a good knowledge of the old classical literature.

Shang Chü seemed destined to be childless, and one day the disciple Yu-Jo lamented this failure of progeny to Confucius. The Master, however, prophesied that Shang would become the father of five sons after he had attained the age of forty years ; and so it befell.

The great merit of Shang Chü, is that Confucius delivered to him a perfect Copy of the Yih-ching (易經) with his own commentary. Shang kept this text carefully, and at length delivered it over to a disciple. From him it was transmitted without interruption or danger down through a succession of hands until the time of the Han dynasty. This text was used by all the Scholars of that illustrious period who studied the Yih-ching.†

* L. Ch. Cl. 1. p. 36; Shang-yu-lu Ch. 21 p. 34.
† For Shang Chü, see Han-shu, Ch. 88 ; Shang-yu-lu Ch. 11 p. 20.

10. Kung-si Ai (公皙哀). S. Chi-tz'ŭ (季次).

The name of Kung-si is also given as K'o (克), and his second name as Chi-ch'ên (季沈). He was a native of Ch'i, or of Lu, according to one account, but the dates of his birth and death are not known. It appears that he was for some time a disciple of Confucius, and little more is known about his life. He became disgusted at the number of scholars who took office about this time under the chiefs of powerful but usurping families, and he persistently refused to bend to the acceptance of such office. For this conduct he won the high esteem of Confucius. Legge says—"Confucius commended him for refusing to take office with any of the families which were encroaching on the authority of the Princes of the States, and for choosing to endure the severest poverty rather than sacrifice a little of his principles."*

11. Ch'i-tiao K'ai (漆雕開). S. Tzŭ-K'ai. (子開).

The name of Ch'i-tiao was at first Ch'i (啓) and it was chan ge to K'ai on the accession of Han Hsiao-ching in B.C. 156 in order to avoid the use of that Emperor's name. Instead of Tzŭ-k'ai for the second name we find Tzŭ-jo (子若) and Tzŭ-hsiu (子脩), but there were several men of the surname Ch'i-tiao with whom Confucius had intercourse—three disciples bearing that surname—and it is possible that they have been mixed up by later writers.

Ch'i-tiao K'ai was born in B.C. 541, and belonged to the State of Ts'ai, corresponding partly to Ju-ning-foo in Honan, though one account makes him to have been born in Lu. He seems to have been plain-looking and deformed, but his moral character was excellent and his mental powers above the average. Confucius once said that it wad time for Ch'i-tiao to take office, but the latter replied that he was not yet able to believe intelligently all the Shu-ching—an answer which

* For Kung-si Ai, see Shang-yu-lu Ch. 21 p. 88.

pleased the Master. This story is told differently in the Lun-yü, where he is represented as replying that he could not fully understand Confucius' teachings. He did not care for official life, however, and he was very fond of reading, and specially of the Shu-ching.

The date of Ch'i-tiao's death is not recorded. His tomb was a few miles from Shang-ts'ai in Ju-ning-foo.*

---

12. Kao Ch'ai (高 柴). S. Tzŭ-kao (子 羔).

The *Kao* of the second name of Kao Ch'ai is also found written as (臯) and he is called Chi-kao (季 羔). One says he was born in Ch'i (齊), and one in Ts'ai (蔡), while another says in Wei (衛), and the date of his birth is variously given as B.C. 522 and 512. He was for some time a disciple of Confucius, but afterwards went into public life and held several offices. When Tzŭ-lu appointed him Governor of Pi, Confucius said "you are injuring a man's son," that is, you are doing a wrong to Tzŭ-kao in appointing him to a difficult office for which he has neither abilities nor training.

The Master evidently did not think much of Tzŭ-kao's intellectual powers, and in another place he describes him as simple, that is, having a good heart but no head.

Yet Tzŭ-kao was very successful as an official. While Criminal Judge in Wei, he had to order the feet of a criminal to be cut off, that being the statutory punishment for the crime which the man had committed. Afterwards the judge, during the time of a tumult in the city in which he was living, had to run for his life. The gate through which he wanted to pass was kept by the man whom he had made footless. He offered to help the judge over the city wall, but the judge said a "superior man" does not climb over the wall. Then the man offered to hide him in a hole, but no "superior man" would hide in a hole, and at last the shelter of the man's house was offered and this the judge accepted. He then talked about the sentence which he had formely passed on the man who was now his preserver, and the latter admitted

---

* See L. Ch. Cl. I. p. 38 ; Lun-yü-chi &c. Ch. 5 p. 5 ; Shang-yu-lu Ch. 22. p. 51 Mê-tzŭ (墨 子) Ch. 9 at the end.

fully that the judge had only done his duty. This incident showed that Tzŭ-kao dispensed justice with strictness and impartiality, combined with great personal kindness and humanity. Confucius saw in it a rare blending of severity and goodness.

Kao Ch'ai is described as being dwarfish in stature—several feet smaller than Confucius—and of very plain features. He was eccentric in manner, and of a very gentle, harmless disposition. He was too candid and sincere for an official, and he had no genius or brilliant accomplishments. But his love and friendship were sincere and lasting. The prescribed term of three years' mourning he kept for each of his parents with the utmost faithfulness. He wept tears of blood, says one author, and he never relaxed his mouth to a smile, says another, that is, during all the period of mourning. In respect of these matters Confucius spoke of him in terms of high praise. It is not known when he died, and accounts vary as to where he lies buried. He was serving in Wei, at the time of the tumult in which Tzŭ-lu lost his life, but Tzŭ-kao does not appear to advantage in this crisis, as he evidently deserted his chief in the latter's hour of danger. *

---

13. Ssŭ-ma Kêng (司馬耕) S. Tzŭ-niu (子牛).

The second name of Ssŭ-ma Kêng is often given simply as Niu, and he is generally quoted under the designation Ssŭ-ma Niu. The family surname was Hsiang (向) or Huan (桓), an older name which was still used by his elder brother. His *name* is also given as Li (黎) or Li-kêng. Ssŭ-ma that is, Master of the horse, was an office or title hereditary in the family, and hence it came to be used as a surname.

The date of Ssŭ-ma Niu's birth is not recorded, but we read that he was a native of Sung, a State corresponding to parts of the present Honan and Anhui, and that he was for a time a disciple of Confucius. He had an elder brother known as Huan T'ui (桓魋) who caused him much trouble and anxiety, so that he spoke of himself as not having

---

* See L. Ch. Cl. I. p. 107 et al. Lun-yü-chi-chu &c. Ch. 11. p. 20 et al.; Shang-yu-lu Ch. 7 p. 6.; Chia-yü, Ch. 8, sec. p. 12.

any brother. This was partly because T'ui had raised a rebellion and was seeking to kill the Duke of Sung, and Niu feared that this conduct would lead to the destruction of himself and his brothers. For some time he fled from State to State pursued by this bad big brother.

Niu was too fond of talking, and he had a rash, violent disposition. Hence when he asked Confucius about Jen (仁) or perfect virtue, the Master replied—"The man of perfect virtue is cautious and slow of speech." So also, partly because he was in constant fear and trouble about Huan T'ui, the Master replied to his question about the "superior man," by saying that he does not distress himself or fear.

The chiefs of Chên (陳) and Chao (趙) called him to their Courts but we are not told whether he served in these States. His death took place in Lu, outside the outer gate of a city, and he was buried by a stranger. The usual honours were conferred upon him during the T'ang and Sung dynasties.*

----◄◆►----

14. Fan Hsü (樊須). S. Tzŭ-chi (子遲).

Fan Hsü, better known as Fan-ch'i, was a native of Lu, or of Ch'i, it is not certain which, and the date of his birth is variously given as B.C. 516 or 506. He was a disciple of Confucius for some time, but took office in the service of the chief of Chi (季), one of the great usurping families of Lu, and rose to some distinction as a military commander.

Once, while in office apparently, he asked to learn husbandry and gardening from the Master, who referred him to a farmer, and then remarked that Fan-ch'i was a small man. He tried on three different occasions to obtain from Confucius an explanation of Jen (仁), and he does not seem to have succeeded.

Though Fan-ch'i was what Legge calls a "minor disciple," yet he seems to have been much with the Master, for whom he acted as coachman, at least on one occasion. At another time we find the two "rambling under *the trees* about the rain-altars, when he asked what

---

* See L. Ch. Cl. I. p. 115 &c.; Lun-yü-chi-chi &c. Ch. 12; Shang-yu-lu, Ch. 21 p. 43.

the Master called "good questions." But he was evidently not a man of wide views or great intellect.

Nothing is recorded of his death and burial. *

---

15 Liang Chan (梁鱣) S. Shuh-yü (叔魚).

Liang's name is also given as Li (鯉), and as Chung (仲), and his second name is given as Tzŭ-yü (子魚) and Tzŭ-mien (子兒). He was a native of Ch'i (齊) and was born, according to one authority, in B.C. 523, and in 513 according to another authority. When thirty years of age he wanted to divorce his wife because she had not given him a son. Shang Chü, however, related how *he* had become the father of five sons, according to promise, after he was forty years old, and hinted that it was not necessarily the wife who was in fault. Liang did not divorce his wife, and two years after the above conversation took place he became the father of a son. This is the only circumstance of Liang Chan's life that we find recorded.

---

16. Shang Tsê (商澤). S. Tzŭ-chi (子季).

Shang Tzê whose second name is also given as Tzŭ-hsin (子秀), was a native of Lu, but nothing more is known about him.

---

17. Jan Ju (冉孺) S. Tzŭ-lu (子魯).

This disciple's name is sometimes written also Ju (儒), and his second name is also given as Tzŭ-tsêng (子曾) and Tzŭ-yü (子魚). He is said to have been born in the State of Lu in the year B.C. 502,

---

18. Wu-ma Shī (巫馬施) S. Tzŭ-ch'i (子旗).

Another name for Wu-ma, is Ch'i (期), but this is also said to have been his second name. He was born in B.C. 522, but it is not certain whether he was a native of Ch'ên or of Lu. He became Governor of Tan-fu (單父), and kept that lawless place in order by

---

* See L.-Ch. Cl. I. p. 11, 55 &c.; Lun-yü-chi &c. Ch. 2. p. 15.

hard work and constant attention to business. Tzŭ-chien (Fuh Pu-ch'i) was equally successful in the same place, and he had seemed to lead an easy, happy life. Tzŭ-ch'i asked Tzŭ-chien the explanation. "I employ men" replied Tzŭ-chien, "and you employ strength, the employment of strength makes toil, the employment of men brings ease."

There seems to be record of only one question addressed by Tzŭ-ch'i to the Master. One fine morning when about to start on a journey, the latter told his disciples to take umbrellas as there would certainly be rain. Wu-ma ch'i said—"the morning is cloudless and the sun has come out, yet you tell us, Sir, to take our umbrellas. How do you know that rain will come?" Confucius answered that it was from seeing the moon in the Hyades—the Shi-ching saying—"The moon also is in the Hyades which will bring still greater rain."*

---

19. Poh Ch'ien (伯虔) S. Tzŭ-ch'ie (子析).
This man's name is also given as Ch'u (虔), and his second name appears as Tzŭ-hsi (子皙). He was a native of Lu, and was born in B.C. 502, but nothing more seems to have been handed down respecting him.

---

20. Yen Hsing (顏辛) S. Tzŭ-liu (子柳).
This disciple's name is variously given also as Hsin (幸), Liu (柳), and Wei (韋). He too was a native of Lu, and was born in the year B. C. 506.

---

21. Jan Chi (冉季) S. Tzŭ-ch'an (子產).
The second name of this man is also Tzŭ-ta (子達). He was a native of Lu, and nothing more is told of him.

---

22. Ts'ao Hsü (曹卹). S. Tzŭ-hsün (子循).
He was a native of Ts'ai (蔡) and was born in B.C. 502.

---

* See L. Ch. Cl. IV. p. 422 for the quotation from the Shï-ching.

23. Ch'i-tiao T'u-fu (漆雕 徒 父). S. Tzŭ-yu (子 有).

Ch'i-tiao's name is also given as Ts'ung (從), and his second name is also given as Tzŭ-wên (子 文).   He was a native of Lu.

---

24. Kung-sun Lung (公 孫 龍). S. Tzŭ-shí (子 石).

For Lung we sometimes find Ch'ung (寵) as this man's name.   He was a native of Wei (衛), or of Ch'u (楚), according to another account, and was born in B.C. 499.   He is represented as being invited by Tzŭ-kung to join the school of Confucius, and he offered his services to the latter when he proposed to stop the force of T'ien Ch'ang (田 常) when it was about to invade Lu.   His services were refused, and we do not read anything more about Kung-sun Lung, except that he was the author of a metaphysical treatise according to some.   It is more probable that this treatise was the work of a later namesake.

---

25. Ch'i-tiao Ch'i (漆雕 哆). S. Tzŭ-lien (子 斂).

Instead of Ch'i (or ch'o) we sometimes find Ch'i (侈) given as Ch'i-tiao's name, and Tzŭ-min (子 敏) is given as his second name instead of Tzŭ-lien.   He was a native of Lu, and nothing more is known about him.

---

26. Ch'in Shang (秦 商). S. Tzŭ-p'ei (子 丕).

Ch'in's second name is given also as P'ei-tzŭ (丕 茲).   According to the Chia-yü he was a native of Lu, and was only four years younger than the Master.   But other authorities make him a native of Ch'u (楚) and forty years younger than the Master.   His father Chin (堇) and Confucius' father were contemporaries and were celebrated for their strength.

27. Kung-hsi Ch'ih (公西赤). S. Tzŭ-hua (子華).

This disciple, who is generally known as Kung-hsi Hua, belonged to the State of Lu, and was born B.C. 510. He appears to have been a modest, unassuming man, highly respected by Confucius and by his brother disciples. When the Master disclaimed the title of Sage and said he was only a man who learned without feeling satiety and taught without becoming wearied, Kung-hsi Hua is reported to have said— "This is just what we disciples cannot imitate you in."

On one occasion the Master asked four of his disciples among whom was Kung-hsi Hua, what aims or ambition they had with respect to taking public office. After Tzŭ-lu and Yen-yu had told their wishes, Kung-hsi, being asked his, said— "I do not say that my ability extends to these things, but I should wish to learn them. At the services of the ancestral temple, and at the audiences of the Princes with the Emperor, I should like, dressed in the dark square-made robe and the black linen cap, to act as a small assistant." On this Confucius observed to Tsêng Tien— "If Ch'ih were to be a small *assistant* in these *services*, who could be a great one?"

Kung-hsi Hua was uniformly decorous yet able to assert his dignity, his mind was set on truth (reading *tao* 道 and not *t'ung* 通) yet he loved the proprieties, he acted as master of ceremonies for two princes, and he had sincere courtesy coupled with self-control, such is the character given of him by Tzŭ-kung. He was specially noted for his unrivalled acquaintance with the laws of rites and ceremonies. People said he was perfect in these, but Confucius said that it was only in knowledge of ceremonies required in the entertainment of State guests that he was perfect, and he referred his other disciples to Kung-hsi Hua if they wished to learn these. Yet Kung-hsi's affectionate care of his parents, and his conduct as a friend showed that the kindness of his disposition prevailed over the requirements of ceremony.

On the death of Confucius, the disciples agreed that he was to be buried with the solemnities due to a father. The task of arranging and conducting the ceremonies was assigned to Kung-hsi Hua, who followed the rules of the ancient kings, and gave the remains of the Master a splendid funeral.[*]

---

28. Yen Kao (顏高). S. Tzŭ-chiao (子驕).

Yen's name in the Chia-yü is K'o (刻) and it is otherwise given as Ch'an (產). He was a native of Lu, and was born in B.C. 502. On the occasion of Confucius' visit to Wei when he was a guest of Duke Ling we find Yen Kao acting as coachman. The Duke's consort, Nan-tzŭ, whom Mayers describes as "a meretricious contemporary of Confucius," drove through the streets of the Capital in a carriage with the Duke and a eunuch, and she made Confucius and Yen Kao follow in another carriage. The Master was ashamed of himself and his hosts. Yen was again coachman for Confucius at the time when the latter was in trouble at K'uang from his great likeness to a dreaded leader of banditti. He was celebrated among his contemporaries for his great physical strength and for his skill in archery.

---

29. Jen Pu-ch'i (任不齊). S. Tzŭ-hsüan (子選).

This man is said to have been a native of Ch'u (楚) but there does not seen to be anything more known about him.

---

30. Jang-ssŭ Ch'ih (壤駟尺). S. Tzŭ-t'u (子走).

This man's surname is also found written Jang-ssŭ (壤駟), his name is also given as Chi ( ), and his second name also as Tzŭ-ts'ung (子從). He was a native of the State of Ch'in (秦), and was distinguished for his knowledge of the poetical and historical literature of his country.

---

[*] For Kung-hsi Hua, see L. Ch. Cl. I. p. 70 and 112; Chia-yü Ch. 3. (Sec. 12); Shang-yu-lu Ch. 21 p. 33,; Li-chi Ch. 2. From this down to no 69 the tablets, except when it is otherwise stated, represent immediate disciples of Confucius about whom little more than their names is known.

31. Kung-liang Ju (公冣孺). S. Tzŭ-chêng (子正).

Kung-liang's name is also found written as Ju (孺), and his second name is found as Tzŭ-yu (子有). He was a native of the State of Ch'ên (陳), part of the present Honan, but the date of his birth is not given. It seems that he was a man of wealth and distinction, and he joined the train of Confucius with five carriages. When the Master was in danger at K'uang, Tzŭ-chêng, was with him. Then when Confucius, *en route* to Wei, was stopt at the town of P'u (蒲) by the people of that town headed by Kung-shuh, Tzŭ-chêng and his five carriages were again in attendance. Tzŭ-chêng said it was his fate to get into trouble this way, but that rather than be caught in the net again he would die fighting for the Master. So he drew his sword and charged the crowd. The people became frightened and allowed Confucius and his suite to pass, the Master having been obliged to swear that he would not proceed to Wei. He did go to Wei, however, but nothing more is known of Kung-liang Ju, the rich, brave, and faithful disciple.

32. Shih Tso-shu (石作蜀). S. Tzŭ-ming (子明).

This disciple's name appears also as Chĭ-shu (之蜀) and Tzŭ-shu (子蜀), and his surname also is doubtful. He was a native of Ch'êng-Chi (成紀) the present Ch'in-chow-foo (秦州府) in Kansuh. In one edition of the Chia-yü we have yu (右) instead of Shih, perhaps a misprint.

33. Kung Chien-ting (公肩定). S. Tzŭ-chung (子中).

It is doubtful whether this disciple's surname was Kung or Kung-chien or Kung-yu (公有), or whether surname and name were Kung Chien-ting (公堅定). The *Chung* of his second name is also written in different ways, and the name of the State to which he belonged is matter of uncertainty.

34. Kung-hsia Shou (公夏首). S. Shêng (乘).

Kung-hsia was a native of Lu, but nothing more is known about him.

———◆◆◆———

35. Hsiao Tan (鄡單). S. Tzŭ-chia (子家).

This disciple, whose name does not appear in the Chia-yü, was a native of Lu. It is doubtful whether his surname was Hsiao or Wu (鄔), and there is no record of his history, his name appearing only in the *Shi-chi*.

———◆◆◆———

36. Hou Ch'u (后處). S. Tzŭ-li (子理).

Instead of *Hou* the Chia-yü gives Shih (石), and the second name of this disciple is given also as Li-chĭ (理之). The only fact recorded of him is that he was a native of Ch'i (齊).

———◆◆◆———

37. Han-fu Hei (罕父黑). S. Tzŭ-so (子索).

This man's surname appears in the Chia-yü as Tsai-fu (宰父). and his second name is variously given as Tsŭ-so, Tsŭ-su (子素), and Tzŭ-hei (子黑). He belonged to Lu.

———◆◆◆———

38. Hsi Jung-tien (奚容蒧). S. Tzŭ-hsi (子皙).

The Chia-yü gives this disciple's name as Chên (蒧) and his second name as Tzŭ-ch'ie (子楷). According to one account he was a native of Lu, and according to another of Wei (衛).

———◆◆◆———

39. Yung Ch'í (榮旂). S. Tzŭ-ch'í (子旗).

In the Chia-yü this disciple's name is written Ch'í (斯), and his second name Tzŭ-ch'í (子祺). He was a native of Lu.

40. Yen Tsu (顏祖). S. Tzŭ-hsiang (子襄).

In the Chia-yü the name appears as Hsiang (相), and the disciple belonged to the State of Lu.

———◆◆◆———

41. Tso Jen-ying (左人郢). S. Hing (行).

It is doubtful whether this disciple's surname was Tso or Tso-jen, and the Chia-yü gives his surname and name as Tso Ying (右郢) and his second name as Tzŭ-hing. Lu was his native State also.

———◆◆◆◆———

42. Kou (or Chü) Ching-chiang (句井疆) S. Tzŭ-chiang (子疆).

This man, whose second name appears also as Tzŭ-mêng (子孟) was a native of Wei.

———◆◆◆———

43. Ch'êng Kuo (鄭國). S. Tzŭ-t'u (子徒).

In the Chia-yü a disciple is given with the surname Hsie (薛), name Pang (邦) and second name Tzŭ-ts'ung (子從). By some this is supposed to be the same person as Ch'êng Kuo, and by others he is regarded as a different individual. The Commentator on the Shi-chi thinks that Ch'êng (鄭) is a transcriber's mistake for Hsie (薛), and that the State annalist of the Han dynasty changed Pang into Kuo in order to avoid using the name of the founder of that dynasty. Ch'êng (or Hsie) is said to have been a native of Lu.

———◆◆◆———

44. Ch'in Tsu (秦祖). S. Tzŭ-nan (子南).

This disciple belonged to Ch'in (秦).

———◆◆———

45. Yuan K'ang (原亢). S. Tzŭ-chi (子籍).

Some editions of the Chia-yü give this man's name as T'ao (桃) and others as K'ang (抗), and he is elsewhere given as Yuan K'ang with the second name Chi (籍). He was a native of Lu.

46. Hsien Ch'èng (縣 成). S. Tzŭ-hung (子 橫).

This disciple's second name is given also as Tzŭ-ch'i (子 祺).   He too was a native of Lu.

———◆———

47. Lien Chie (廉 潔). S. Tzŭ-yung (子 庸).

In the Chia-yü this disciple's second name is given as Tzŭ-ts'ao (曹).   His native State was Wei.

———◆———

48. Kung-tsu Kou-tzŭ (公 祖 句 茲). S. Tzŭ-chih (子 之).

The Chia-yü gives *Tzŭ* (茲) simply as the name of this disciple who was a native of Lu.

———◆———

49. Shuh-chung Hui (叔 仲 會) S. Tzŭ-ch'i (子 期).

One account makes this disciple a native of Lu, while another gives Chin (晉) as his native country.   In one place he is represented as having been born in B.C. 502, and in another place the date of his birth is put four years later.   He and a young relative of Confucius named K'ung Hsüan (孔 璇) were about the same age, and they took turns in attending on the Sage to write down his teachings.   Mêng Wu-Poh (孟 武 伯) asked the Master whether such boys as these could remember what they learned as well as full grown men.   The Master said yes.   "The attainments of early life when in accordance with the moral nature become habit by practice."

———◆———

50. Yen Chi (燕 伋) S. Tzŭ-ssŭ (子 思).

This disciple was a native of Ch'in (秦).

———◆———

51. Kung-hsi Yü-ju (公 西 輿 如) S. Tzŭ-shang (子 上).

This disciple, whose name is given also as simply Yü, belonged to Lu.

———◆———

52. Yo Kai (樂 欬) S. Tzŭ-shêng (子 聲).

Instead of Kai we have also Hsin (欣) for the name of this disciple, who was a native of Lu.

53. Kuei Sun(邦 巽) S. Tzǔ-lien (子 斂).

Instead of Kuei we find Pang (邦) given as the surname of this disciple, for his name Hsüan (選) instead of Sun, and for his second name Tzǔ-yin (子 飲) instead of Tzǔ-lien. He was a native of Lu.

54. Ti Hei (狄 黑). S. Hsi (晳).

Ti's name is given also as Moh (墨), and his second name appears in the Chia-yü as Chê-chih (哲 之). The latter is elsewhere given as Hsi-chih (晳 之). According to one account he was a native of Wei, and according to another of Lu.

55. Ch'ên K'ang (陳 亢). S. Tzǔ-ch'in (子 禽).

Ch'ên's second name is given also as Tzǔ-k'ang (子 亢) and as Tzǔ-yun, (子 元). He belonged to the State of Ch'ên, and was born in B.C. 512. By some he is said to have been a disciple of Tzǔ-kung, but the Lun-yü seems to show that he was one of Confucius' disciples. In this work he is represented as asking Tzǔ-kung how the Master, on arriving at a State, was certain to learn about its government, and on another occasion as asking Poh-yü, the son of Confucius, whether his father gave him different teaching from what he gave the disciples. "A good story is related of him. On the death of his brother, his wife and major-domo wished to bury some living persons with him to serve him in the regions below. The thing being referred to Tsz-k'in, he proposed that the wife and steward should themselves submit to the immolation, which made them stop the matter."*

56. K'ung Chung (孔 忠). S. Tzǔ-mie (子 蔑).

This man was a nephew of the Sage, being the son of his half-brother Mêng-p'i. [Legge says, "His sacrificial title is 'The ancient Worthy, the philosopher Mëë," but this is not always the case as his tablet is at least in some cases inscribed with his surname and name.

* L. Ch. Cl. 1. p 6, 179.

57. Chin Chang (琴 張). S. Tzŭ-k'ai (子 開).

Chin, whose name is also given as Lao (牢), was a native of Wei.

His second name is also said to have been Chang (張), and he is said by Mencius to have been one of those whom Confucius designated "ambitious," that is taking wildly and grandiloquently. He is mentioned only once, I think, in the Lun-yü, and on that occasion the name Lao is used.

58. Kung-hsi Tien (公 西 蒧) S. Tz-shang (子 上).

The Shang of this disciple's second name is also written 尚. He belonged to the State of Lu.

59. Pu Shuh-shêng (步 叔 乘). S. Tzŭ-ch'ê (子 車).

This man's surname is also given as Shao (少) which is perhaps only a transcriber's mistake.   He was a native of Ch'i (齊).

60. Yen Chĭ-pu (顏 之 僕). S. Tzŭ-shuh (子 叔).

This man, who was a native of Lu, is sometimes given as Yen Pu with the second name Shuh.

61. Ch'in Fei (秦 非). S. Tzŭ-chĭ (子 之).

A native of Lu.

62. Shĭ Chĭ-ch'ang (施 之 常). S. Tzŭ-hêng (子 恒).

This disciple, a native of Lu, has his second name also given as Tzŭ-ch'ang (子 常).

63. Yen K'uai (顏 噲). S. Tzŭ-shêng (子 聲).

Yen also belonged to Lu.

64. Shên Ch'ang (申棖).

In the Shih-chi there is a Shên Tang (申黨) with the second name Chow (周), and in the Chia-yü there is a Shên Chi (申績) with Tzŭ-chou (子周) as second name. We find also T'ang (棠) and Su (績) given as names to a man surnamed Shên, a disciple of Confucius. Ch'êng Kang-chêng and other scholars considered these as various names for one man. Up to 1530 there were tablets of Shên Tang and Shên Ch'ang in the temples, but in that year the tablet of the former was reu.oved. The celebrated scholar Chu Yi-tsun (朱彝尊), of the 17th century, again decided in favour of two Shên s, but only one, Shên Ch'ang, is now worshipped.

We know of this man only that he was a native of Lu, and that Confucius declared him to be a man subject to his passions.*

----◄►----

65. Yen Ho (顏何). S. Jan (冉).

The second name of this disciple occurs also as Ch'êng (稱) and he is stated to have been a native of Lu, or according to another account of Chin (晉). His name occurs in the old editions of the Chia-yü and Shi-chi, but not in the new editions. He was admitted to the Temple along with the other disciples, but in 1530 his tablet was removed. It was restored, however, in the second year of Yung-chêng, 1724.

----◄►----

66. Tso Ch'iu-ming (左丘明).

It has been much disputed whether this man's name was Tso or Tso-ch'iu, and it is not unlikely that two persons have been mixed up in the account given of Tso Ch'iu-ming. The first to maintain that the author of the Chuan was not named Ch'iu-ming was a scholar of the T'ang period, Cha K'uang (趙匡). He doubted the authenticity of the work and wished to show that it was not immediately derived from Confucius. This opinion has since been maintained

* See L. Ch. Cl. I. p. 41.

by Wang An-shi and many others.   But many hold that the Chuan
was the work of Tso Ch'iu-ming and that the author was a disciple
of Confucius.   These suppose the last part of the work to be the
addition of some later writer.

Tso Ch'iu-ming is known only by this historical treatise which
bears the simple name Tso Chuan or Tso's Commentary.   He is by
some supposed to have been associated with Confucius in the compilation of the Ch'ün-ch'iu, which treatise the Sage afterwards consigned
to his care, and to have derived at the same time from the State
records, the materials for his own work.   He is also said to have been
for a time Annalist or Historiographer in Lu, and in this capacity
he would have excellent opportunity for acquiring a knowledge of the
political transactions of the various States during the period embraced by
his History.   For the Chuan is far more than a commentary on the dry
annals compiled by Confucius.   It indeed clothes that skeleton chronicle
with flesh and blood and gives it life, but it is also a History in itself.

The positive information about Tso is very meagre, and even
the time at which he lived is still a question for discussion.   His
Commentary seems to have been very little known until the time of
Liu Hsin (劉歆) of the early Han dynasty, although it had been in
circulation among scholars for some period before.   It rose into favour
during the third century of our era and has since generally maintained
a place of superiority over the works of Kung-yang and Ku-liang.
The authorship of the Kuo-yü (國語) is also assigned to Tso, a Tso-
ch'iu, but it is doubtful whether that work was composed by the
author of the Commentary.

In A.D. 647 T'ang T'ai Tsung admitted Tso Ch'iu-ming to the
Temple of Confucius as an Associate, but in the next reign his tablet
was removed to a lower position.   In 1530 he was made one of the
"Scholars," but the last Emperor of the Ming dynasty in 1642
placed him among the "Former Worthies" next to the Seventy-two
Disciples.*

---

* See L. Ch. Cl. V. Proleg. Ch. I; The Tso-chuan-chu-su (左傳注疏) Vol. 1.
   (Yuan Yuan's edition of the Shi-san-ching (十三經).

67. Hsien T'an (縣亶). S. Tzŭ-hsiang (子象).

The name of this man is given also as T'an-fu (亶父) and as Fêng (豐). His name is not found in the Shih-chi, and some suppose that this is the same person as Hsiao Tan (鄡單), No 35. His tablet was not admitted to the Confucian temples until the year 1724. He was a native of Lu, but there does not seen to be any further record of him.

———◆◆◆———

68. Ch'in Jan (秦冉). S. Tzŭ-k'ai (子開).

Ch'in Jan was a native of Ts'ai. His tablet was admitted with the others but in 1530 it was removed. In 1724 it was restored. The Chia-yü does not mention this man as one of the Sage's disciples.

———◆◆◆———

69. Mu P'i (牧皮).

Of Mu P'i (or P'ei), as Legge says, "nothing is known. Neither the Shih-chi nor the Chia-yü contains his name. But he is mentioned once by Mencius who puts him among the "ambitious" ones to whom Confucius objected. His tablet was first admitted in 1724 and was placed on the west side, but it was afterwards removed to its present position.*

———◆◆◆———

70. Kung-ming Yi (公明儀).

Kung-ming is said to have been born in Nan, or Southern, Wu-ch'êng (武城), and to have been a man of worth and eminence in Lu. He was a disciple first of Tzŭ-chang (子張) and afterwards of Tsêng-tzŭ. On the death of the former, Kung-ming was charged with the arrangement of the funeral ceremonies, and he showed his respect for his teacher in the way he conducted these. Mencius introduces him,

---

* For Mu P'i see L. Ch. Cl. II. p. 375.

as quoting Chow Kung's words—"Wen Wang is my teacher," and adding, "Chow Kung does not deceive me," that is, Wen Wang may be my teacher also. Kung-ming's tablet was admitted first in 1853.*

71. Yo-chêng K'o (樂正克).

The surname of this man is sometimes given as above, but often as Yo simply. His second name is said to have been Tzŭ-ngao (子敖) and he was a native of Lu. He became a disciple of Mencius, and master and disciple seem to have had a mutual admiration for each other.

Yo-chêng-tzŭ, as he is generally styled, obtained official employment in his native State, and rose to a high position. He recommended his Chief, Duke P'ing, to make the acquaintance of Mencius, and defended the latter with great ability when accused to the Duke of impropriety in the matter of funeral ceremonies.

When Duke P'ing made Yo-chêng-tzŭ a sort of State Minister, Mencius was so rejoiced that he could not sleep. This was because he knew the minister to be a man who "loved what was good." He owned that Yo-chêng was not a man of vigour, or wise in council, or learned, but, as he says elsewhere, he was a good man, a sincere man. Yet we find Mencius on one occasion reproving his disciple in severe language for what he considered unworthy conduct.

In, 1115 Sung Hui Tsung ennobled Yo-chêng-tzŭ as Li-kuo Hou (利國疾) or Kingdom-profiting Marquis, and ordered him to be associated with Mencius in the worship offered in the latter's temple. He was admitted to his present place in the Confucian temple in 1724. It is possible that *Li-kuo* is the name of some old place in the north of China.†

72. Kung-tu-tzŭ (公都子).

The "philosopher Kung-tu" was a disciple of Mencius, but beyond this nothing is known about him. His name appears frequently in the conversations recorded in Mencius. Sometimes he merely questions the

---

* For Kung-ming Yi see L. Ch. Cl. II. p. 111; Shang-yu-lu, Ch. 21 p. 37 : Li-chi, Ch. 2.
† See L. Ch. Cl. II. Proleg. p. 80, M. p. 37, 54, et al.; Shang-yu-lu Ch. 20 p. 16.

Sage, at other times he reports the criticisms of the world, and on a few occasions he ventures to state opinions illustrative of his master's teachings.

In 1115 Kung-tu was ennobled as P'ing-yang-Poh (平 陽 伯), P'ing-yang being the name of a city in Shansi, and at the same time he was admitted to participation in the worship offered in Mencius' temple. In 1724 his tablet was placed in its present position in the temples of Confucius. Legge says, " In the temple of Mencius he was the "Baron of Tranquillity and Shadiness (平 陰 伯).*

73. Wan Chang (萬 章).

This man also was a disciple of Mencius, and nothing more of his history is known than this one fact. He appears very often in the work bearing the name of Mencius as a questioner of the latter. He is supposed to have become a teacher, and tradition says that his disciples assisted Mencius in the formation of his Book.

The Emperor Huei Tsung of the Sung dynasty ennobled Wan Chang with the title Po-hsing-Poh (博 興 伯), from Po-hsing, a town in what is now Ch'ing-chow-foo in Shantung. Legge translates the title " Baron of Extensive Arousing. " In the same year, 1115, he was made a participator in the sacrifices performed in the temple of Mencius, and in 1724 he was admitted to the Confucian Temple as a " Worthy. "

74. Kung-sun Ch'ou (公 孫 丑).

Kung-sun was another of Mencius' disciples, and a native of Ch'i (齊). He had a great admiration for his master, but displeased the latter by comparing him with small notables of his own State. In Mencius' work he appears often asking the Master questions, some of which were of a plain and practical nature.

He too was ennobled in 1115 and his title was Shou-kuang-Poh (壽 光 伯), or, Baron of Shou-kuang, a place in the modern Ch'ing-

* See L. Ch. Cl. II. Proleg. p. 80.

Chow-foo in Shantung, but Legge translates, "Baron of Longevity and Glory." In the same year he was admitted to Mencius' temple, and in 1724 his tablet was placed in its present position in the temples of Confucius.

------

75. Chou Tun-i (周 敦 頤). S. Mou-shu (茂 叔).

Chou Tun-i was born in A.D. 1017, being the 20th year of the reign of Sung Chên-Tsung. His birth-place was a small hamlet about six miles westward from Ying-tao, a District-town of Yung-chou in the South of Huuan. The hamlet was called Lien-ch'i (濂 溪) from the name of a stream which rises in the neighbouring mountains, flows past the hamlet, and joins the river Siang. The remote ancestors of the Chou family had originally lived in Honan, and had afterwards removed to Ch'ing-chow (青 州) in Shantung. But in A.D. 765 a member of the family, having been appointed to an office in the Yung-chou department, fixed his residence there, and some time after one of his descendants acquired property at Lien-ch'i and settled there.

The family had produced a number of scholars and officials, and Tun-i's father Fu-ch'êng (輔 成) was himself a man of learning and of good repute as a Magistrate. His mother, whose surname was Chêng (鄭), also belonged to a family of some distinction in the public service. Of the boyhood of Tun-i we have very little information, and he does not seem to have been conspicuous for any precocity of intellect or any premature exhibition of genius. He spent much of his time in angling from a bridge on the stream and in roaming over his native hills. In one of these was a vast cave with a crescent-shaped entrance on each side, eastward and westward, but round as the full moon inside. This was a favourite resort of the boy at all times, and tradition said that here the idea of the T'ai-chi first rose in his mind.

But his father died in 1031, and his mother thereupon removed to the Capital in Honan. Here her brother, a Chancellor of the Han-lin, took charge of the education of Tun-i, and loved him with all the fond affection of a father. In due time Tun-i passed his examination, and received a small appointment, but in his twenty-first year he lost his mother. When the period of mourning for her was over he returned to public life, and was sent to Fên-ning-Hsien (分 寧 縣) in the Nan-ch'ang Prefecture of Kiangsi, where he distinguished himself by a prompt clearing off of old cases. From Fên-ning he was transferred to Yuan-chow (袁 州) in the some Province, and here his fame as a teacher began. The next post he filled was an important one of a military character at Nan-an (南 安) in the South-west of Kiangsi. It was at this place that Chêng Hsiang (程 珦) met him, and formed a friendship with him which was destined to have important results. Hsiang entrusted the education of his two sons Ming-tao and Yi-ch'uan to Tun-i, who communicated to these youths all his learning and philosophy.

After holding several other offices in various parts of Kiangsi he was sent to Ho-chow (合 州) a town of the Ch'ungking Prefecture in Ssu-chuan. He was always a great lover of mountains and rivers, and he enjoyed the voyage up the Yangtse through the wild gorges which lead from Hupeh into Ssŭchuan. At Ho-chow also he had many disciples and the fame of his learning and virtue daily increased.

In the year 1061 when on his way to a new appointment at Ch'ien-chow (虔 州), the present Kanchow in Kiangsi, he visited the Lu Mountains near Kiukiang. Smit with the love of their grand scenery he determined to have a cottage built on their slope near a deep and dark-blue stream. The name of this stream was Ch'i-shui (溪 水), but Tun-i remembering "a secret sweetness in the stream" of his childhood called it Lien-ch'i and his cottage Lien-ch'i-shu-t'ang (濂 溪 書 堂), the Lien-c'hi study. He continued to be promoted and transferred from place to place, but he did not rise to any very high position. When fifty-five years old he retired to the Lu mountains, and at this time he had not saved enough money to maintain himself and his family. His patrimony had been signed away chiefly for the purposes of ancestral worship, and he was now poor and happy. The Emperor called him back to public life in 1073, but the Decree did not come in time, for Tun-i died in the 6th moon of that year. As his will directed he was laid beside his mother at Tan-t'u (丹 徒) a town in the Prefecture of Chinkiang.

Of Chou Tun-i's philosophical writings only two were published, the T'ai-chi-t'u-shuo (太極圖說) and the T'ung-shu (通書). These and a few miscellaneous short compositions are all the written records of him that remain. He had no thought of fame or glory, and did not care to publish. Had it not been that he consigned to his great disciples, the brothers Ch'êng, the T'ai-chi-t'u-shuo and the T'ung-shu these two would also have perished. The former, Diagrams of the Ultimate Principle with explanations, is a short pamphlet, and the T'ung-shu, or as it was originally called Yih-shu, is a small book of forty chapters. These two treatises are the source of the Sung philosophy. They give Chou's theory of the evolution of all things, and his doctrines as to the relations between the moral and physical world. He bases these on the teachings of the ancient classics, specially the Yih-ching, and endeavours to make one harmonious system. Some have traced his peculiar doctrines to previous Confucianists, some to Lao-tzŭ and the early Taoist writers, and some to a Buddhist monk. But so great a philosopher would not deign to be indebted for his wisdom to a "cropped" heretic, and there is too little resemblance between his tenets and those of any earlier writer to admit the notion of his having borrowed. It is not known who were his immediate instructors in philosophy, but his great merit is to have drawn directly from the original fountain—the texts of the sacred books as left by Confucius and Mencius. From the recorded teachings of these Sages he divined their unrecorded doctrines and so was able to supplement the memorials of them bequeathed to posterity by the first disciples.

Chou's name was at first Tun-shi (敦實), but on the accession of Ying-Tsung, Shi, being the old name of that Emperor, was changed for i. His disciples called him Lien-ch'i-Hsien-shêng, and he has continued to be known by that designation or simply as Chou Lien-ch'i. He was posthumously ennobled, and received the honorary epithet Yuan-Kung (元公), or the Chief (—according to one account Yuan-ts'ung). In 1241 his tablet was admitted to the Confucian Temple and placed among the scholars in the outer chambers. But the last of the Ming Emperors ordered that it and the tablets of the four which follow should be promoted to the places which they now occupy.

Chou Lien-ch'i was a man of great genius, and of a character singularly pure and simple. All who met him seem to have been impressed with his marvellous powers and his amiable disposition. As an official he was unequalled for the clearness, justness, and quickness of his decisions and his freedom from corruption. Tenpence and an old box were all his house at one time contained. As a philosophic scholar he stood quite alone, having an inspired, creative genius. Nor did any approach him in his thorough love of nature and appreciation of her beauty and grandeur. His favourite flower was the Lotus, which like the ideal man, grows, blooms, and dies pure in the midst of impurity. But his greatest delight was to climb up mountains and wander at pleasure among their fearful cliffs and over their lonely summits.*

---

76. Chang Tsai (張載). S. Tzǔ-hou (子厚).

Chang Tsai, who was born in the year A.D. 1020, was the son of Chang Ti (張迪), a native of Ta-liang (大梁) in the Prefecture of K'ai-fêng in Honan. His father was an official of some distinction and died while Prefect of Fou-chow (涪州), near Chungking, in Ssǔchuan. At the time of this event Tsai was very young. It is recorded of him that he was clever and studious, but shy and not fond of the company of other boys. From Fou-chou he was taken on his father's death to Hung-ch'ü (橫梁), a military station near Mei (郿) Hsien in the Prefecture of Si-an. Here he imbibed a boyish love for soldiers and fighting which culminated in an attempt to get up an expedition for the purpose of seizing some land to the west of the T'ao River in Kansuh.

About the year 1040, however, Tsai was introduced to the great Statesman and Scholar Fan Chung-yen (范仲淹), who turned his

---

* The Chou-lien-ch'i-chi (周濂溪集) in 13 Chüan, edited and compiled by Chang Poh-hang (張伯行) a scholar and statesman of the Kanghsi period. ※ *Read Pai-hsing here and throughout — ie bs.*

ambition from war to philosophy. He copied out the Chung-yung for Tsai, who at once gave himself up to the study of that work with insatiable eagerness. After this Tsai explored the books of the Buddhists and Taoists thinking to find in them the way of life. His labour was in vain, however, and after several years' study of them he went back to Confucianism, and searched the six classics.

Afterwards he went to the Capital and became a public teacher. The Yih-ching was his chief book for exposition, and in his discourses on that treatise he was wont to mix up theories drawn from heretical sources. As a Professor he compassed himself about with great awe and dignity, sitting on a tiger skin, the emblem of fierce majesty. But about 1056 the Brothers Ch'êng, his young nephews, came to K'ai-fêng-foo also to lecture on the Classics. Tsai went to hear them and was at once converted. He put aside for ever his heretical books, and threw away his tiger skin, advising his disciples to attend the lectures of Ch'êng Yi-ch'uan on the Yih-ching. Then he went back to his home in Shensi and continued his studies.

In 1057 Tsai became a Chin-shi, and was appointed at first to an office at Ch'i-chou (祁 州) in Chihli but soon afterwards to one at Yun-yen (雲 巖). He proved himself an official genial and benevolent, but at the same time thorough and earnest, and his administration was attended with good and lasting results. His next appointment was in connection with the military forces at Wei-chou in Kansuh, and in this he distinguished himself by his exertions for the people during a scarcity, and his wisdom and forethought. In 1069 he was promoted, and the illustrious Lü Kung-chu (呂 公 著) recommended him to the Emperor Shên-Tsung who summoned him to an audience. Tsai did not please the Prime Minister Wang An-shi, and he was sent away to a place near Ningpo to settle a jail commotion. Ch'êng Hao, as censor, objected to this appointment, but An-shi prevailed. When his work was finished Tsai returned to the Capital, but, his brother having become involved in political trouble, he soon after withdrew to Hûng-ch'ü. Here he had a small farm of poor land which with frugal management supplied all his wants. Ill health obliged him to leave this, and he settled at the foot of the Nan-shan, where he lived in a cottage with only books about him. His whole time was given up to study and the instruction of his disciples. Though his boyish shyness remained with him yet he was successful as a teacher chiefly through his kind, sympathetic manner, and his great love for wisdom. The disciples who were poor shared their Master's homely fare while they learned to aim at a higher knowledge and a nobler virtue than what the Sophists of those days taught.

After several years of this humble but happy life Tsai was recalled to office at the Capital, and his great aim now was to reform the State ceremonies. But in 1076 he had a strange dream which was followed by a severe attack of sickness. He resigned office, gave the Ms. of the Chêng-mêng—the great work of his life—to his disciples, and set out on the journey home. At Lo-yang he saw the two Ch'êng, and told them he was dying but that he hoped to reach Ch'ang-an (Si-an-foc). On arriving at Lin-t'ung (臨潼), however, his strength failed and it was seen he could not go any farther. That evening his attendant washed his face and hands, changed his clothes, and laid him in bed. When he came to see him next morning he was dead. There was no money in his box, nor had he enough property even to cover his funeral expenses. So when some of his disciples came from Ch'ang-an they had to bury him at their own expense. They laid him in the grave at Wei-Hsien, and conducted his funeral according to those ancient laws of which he had been so fond.

Tsai was posthumously ennebled as Mei-Poh or Earl of Mei, and received the epithet Ming (明) or intelligent. But he has always been best known as Hung-ch'ü, the designation given to him by his disciples. He was admitted to the Temple of Confucius in 1241, and his tablet shared the fate of Chou Tun-i as mentioned above.

The writings of Chang Hung-ch'ü are the Hsi-ming (西銘), Tung-ming (東銘), Chêng-mêng (正蒙), Ching-hsiao-li-k'u (經學 理窟), and a few miscellaneous pieces. The Tung and Hsi-ming, or East and West inscriptions were so named on the advice of Yi-ch'uan from their positions in the author's study. The former, called also the Pien-yü (破愚) or Piercer for the Simple, consists of only a few sentences. The Hsi-ming, known also by its first name Ting-wan

(訂頑) or Critic of the Stupid, is longer and more interesting. Such statements as—"All the world and I are brethren, all nature and I have the same origin," and "The halt, the sick, the forlorn are my brothers," have a rare liberality. Yang Kuei-shan found in them something very like Mêh-tzŭ's doctrine of "universal love," but Yi-ch'uan showed him there was a radical difference between the teachings of the two philosophers. The Chêng-mêng, which is partly based on the Yih-ching and Chung-yung, gives the author's theories as to the origin of the universe, with many curious physical and metaphysical speculations and with occasional criticisms on Buddhist and Taoist doctrines. The Hsiao-li-k'u is a longer work, but not so profound or so highly esteemed. It is largely taken up with the treatment of the ceremonial observances described in the old canonical works.

Chang was man of honest plodding industry, but without any native genius. He seems to have arrived independently at conclusions similar to those of Chou Lien-ch'i, and many things in the Chêng-mêng recall the T'ai-chi-t'u-shuo, and the T'ung-shu. Like Lien-ch'i also Chang is considered to have developed the teachings of Confucius and Mencius. His moral courage in renouncing heresy, and his long zeal in the cause of true learning have won from native authors many encomiums. The first lesson he taught his disciples was to control their feelings and regulate their conduct in strict accordance with the precepts of antiquity. His knowledge of truth was the result of enduring painful study, and of this his writings bear evidence. Compared with Ch'êng Ming-tao he was as Poh-yi (白夷) and I-yin (尹) were to Confucius.*

---

* See the Chang-Hung-chü-chi (張橫渠集), the Foochow edition; Tao-t'ung-lu (道統錄), Chüan 下; Hsing-li-hui-yao (性理彙要) Ch. 11.; Legge's Ch. Cl. II. p. 70.

77. Ch'êng Hao (程 顥). S. Po-shun (伯 淳).

Ch'êng Hao was born at Loyang in Honan in A.D. 1032. His father Hsiang (珦), who will appear hereafter, was an official of considerable learning and of an excellent reputation. The ancestors of the family belonged to Çhihli, but Hao's grand-father having been buried in the Prefecture of Honan, his descendants regarded themselves as Honan people. As a boy Hao was noted for his handsome, intelligent face, clear, bright eyes, and fine ringing voice. One day while he was still an infant, his grand-aunt took him in her arms for a walk, and on the way she dropt a bracelet. The loss was not discovered until her return home, and afterwards, when search was being made for the bracelet, the baby pointed to the place where it had dropt and where it was still lying. At the age of nine years he composed a moral distich which was highly praised. When twelve years old he was sent to school where he conducted himself like a man. About a year or so after this a high official named P'êng, seeing the unusual gravity and sobriety of Hao gave him his daughter in marriage. Then at the age of fourteen he was, along with his younger brother I-ch'uan entrusted to the care of Chou Lien-ch'i, to learn from that scholar the true meanings of the Classics and all his own system of philosphy. From the second time that Hao saw Lien-ch'i he conceived a great delight for the poetry of learning, and preferred the pleasures of the breeze among the rain-altars to the glory and pomp of office. So he read all kinds of books, and for nearly ten years went out and in among Buddhist and Taoist literature, coming back in the end to the orthodoxy of the Sages.

But his lot was cast in the troubled ways of public life, and he had to change the sweet quiet of philosophy for the bitter worry of office. At the age of twenty-five he took his Chin-shi, in the same year with Chang Tsai and the brothers Su (蘇), and was soon after appointed to office at Hu (鄠), a district town in the Si-an Prefecture. Here his tact and readiness of expedient soon made him a noted

man, and he came to have great influence. A temple in the neighbourhood had become famous by the possession of a stone image of
Buddha which on a certain day every year emitted rays of light from
its head. The miracle attracted annually crowds of men and women
who spent day and night in the temple very imperfectly distributed.
The consequences were very bad and official prohibitions were useless.
Ch'êng Hao asked the monk of the temple to send him this wonderful
head for inspection as he had not leisure to exmine it in the temple.
From that day on the image did not send forth any miraculous rays.
Ch'êng also kept the district of Wu from suffering by famine or
pestilence, and was in every way successful. His superior asked him
to what office he would like to be promoted, and Ch'êng replied—
"In recommending an official, regard should be had to his possession
of the requisite abilities, and he should not be asked what he wants."

The next place to which Hao was sent was Shang-yuan (上 元),
in the Prefecture of Kiang-nan (Nankin). Here he equalized the land-
tax, and did many other good things, even causing the little boys to cease
from catching birds with limed twigs. In 1067 he was transferred to
Chin-Ch'êng (晉 城), in Shensi, where he reformed the manners of the
people, trained teachers, erected schools, and made it a model town.
The people of this place loved and revered him as a father, and the
effects of his good government remained for many years. In 1069 he
was promoted to be a Censor, and the Emperor Shên-Tsung made of
him a confidential friend and adviser. Hao was conscientiously
opposed to the radical changes which were being made by Wang An-
shi, and he spoke against them courteously and moderately. But the
two could not continue to serve together and Hao applied for a
Provincial appointment. After some delay he was sent to Ch'ên-ning
(鎮 寧), a town to the west of Si-an, and in 1075 he was transferred
to Fu-kuo-Hsien (扶 溝 縣), in K'ai-fêng-foo. His just, humane,
and skilful administration won for him the affection of the people, and
the services he rendered when the Huang Ho caused alarm and disaster,
by bursting into a new course, were very conspicuous. Soon after he
retired to Loyang and devoted himself to study and teaching, as poor
as when he first went into office. He died in 1085 when an Edict

was on its way appointing him to an important post at the Capital.

The name of Ch'êng Hao in literature—given to him by his disciples—is Ming-tao (明道), his common designation. His posthumous epithet is Shun (純), or Pure. He was ennobled as Ho-nan-Poh (河南伯), and in 1241 he was admitted to the Temple of Confucius.

The only treatise ascribed to Ming-tao is the Ting-hsin-shu (定心書), which is said to be a work of a philosophical character, supplementary to the T'ai-chi-t'u-shuo of his illustrious Master. His State papers and other short writings togther with the records of his teachings are published with those of his younger brother.

The personal character of Ming-tao seems to have been one of peculiar beauty and excellence. He had the warm tender heart of an affectionate woman, with the chivalrous fortitude of a hero. The spirit of self-sacrifice was strong in him, and the soft kindliness of his nature was felt in the large family circle, and in the outer world of society. As a public servant he did with all his might whatever his hand found to do, and what his conscience told him was duty. He showed great tact, broad sympathy, and almost prophetic wisdom in his official actions and counsels. No one ever saw his face colour with anger, or heard him utter an unkind word, or knew him to neglect a duty. He never quailed or lost his merry humour, whether before the tumultuous rage of an excited rabble, the blustering of an irate chief, or the dooming wrath of a fickle monarch. When he doffed his robes of office he went back to his early love and studied the wise books of antiquity. But truth came to him by instinct rather than by study, and he was able to divine the deep meanings of the Sages because he had their spiritual gifts. Thus he came to give a new life and fresh brightness to the truth which evil ways and bad doctrines had nearly quenched. Purity and sincerity of mind and heart marked himself and he made the attainment of these the first essential with his disciples.*

---

* The Tao-t'ung-lu Chüan (下); Erh-ch'êng-wen-chi (二程文集). Ch. 1 &c. ;
 Hsing-li-hui-yao Ch. 11. Chu-tzŭ-ch'uan-shu (朱子全書). Ch. 53.

78. Ch'êng I. (程 頤). S. Chêng-shu (正 叔).

Ch'êng I was born A.D. 1033, a year after his brother Hao. He is said to have been a wise high-souled boy who would not do anything that was not quite correct. When thirteen years of age he became, along with his brother, a disciple of Chou Lien-ch'i, and remained with that teacher for two years. Having fiuished his education he turned to politics, and in his eighteenth year he sent in a Memorial to the throne giving excellent advice to the Emperor Jen-Tsung. In this document he compared himself to Chu-ko Liang, and prayed to be called to Court in order to have an opportunity of explaining his views more fully. This impudent Memorial was of course left unanswered, and the ambitious youth consoled himself with philosophy. But about this time Hu Yuan, in his capacity as Director of Studies, gave to the students as the subject of an examination essay—What was the learning which Yen Hui loved? Ch'êng I's essay on this occasion showed unusual abilities and led to his being employed by the Examiner as assistant. Then he became a teacher and soon had many disciples. He obtained his Chin-shi, but at the subsequent Palace examination in 1058 he failed, and thereupon resolved to abandon the prospect of an official career.

For many years he remained at home studying the Classics and composing his great commentary on the Yih-Ching. He had also u number of disciples some of whom afterwards became men of eminence. In 1085 Ssŭ-ma Kuang and others wrote a strong recommendation for the appointment of I to office, and Chu Kuang-t'ing (朱光庭), described him and his qualifications in terms of extravagant praise. He was nominated to office but declined, and when a better appointment was offered he refused it also because he had not been presented at Court. This difficulty was got over and a new office assigned him, but he wished to decline this also. His refusal was not accepted, however, and he went into office as Expounder of the Classics, in 1086. In this capacity he became preceptor to the young emperor Chê-Tsung. He showed himself a great stickler for ceremony and the old rules and customs, but above all for respect for the teacher. At the same time he did his duty with most conscientious faithfulness. But he interfered in government generally, regarding everything as belonging to his office. So he was always recommending the promotion or dismissal of officers about the Court. This conduct brought on him a great amount of enmity and hatred which he had neither the tact nor temper to dispel.

Moreover the priggish manner of the man, who could not sing on the day on which he wept, made him generally disliked. Some, like Su Tung-p'o, thought his gravity hypocritical, and a joke made by the poet led to a life-long feud between him and his friends on one side, and Ch'êng I and his friends on the other. Then he made enemies of the Ministers of the Presence by interfering with them, and a Censor denounced him to the Throne as mean, quarrelsome, and arrogant. The Emperor had to send I away, and he appointed him to the Imperial Academy at the Western Capital (Honanfoo). The change did not please I, but his father's death soon released him from office for a time though he could not get leave to resign. When the period of mourning was over he was prevented from obtaining employment at the Capital through the influence of Su Tung-p'o and another enemy who denounced him as resentful and insolent.

In 1097 he wished to retire from official life on account of the intrigues and party fighting which had grown up on his account. But he was sent to Fou-chow (涪州), a town of Chungking in Ssŭchuan, where he remained for three years. In 1101 he was recalled to Honanfoo and reinstated at the Imperial Academy. He looked so hale and fresh when he came back that his old friends and disciples were struck with wonder. But lapse of years had not conquered enmity and in 1103 he was again in disgrace. An Imperial Edict ordered his official papers to be destroyed and all his other writings to be submitted to the Censors' scrutiny. Ch'êng I now withdrew from public life and devoted himself to his Commentaries on the Classics. But in 1107 he was attacked by a sickness which proved to be his last. He had outlived most of his disciples, but Yin Shun (尹焞) and Chang Yi (張繹) were still with him, and to them he consigned all his writings

which were still in manuscript.   He was lying one day with his eyes
closed but suffering great pain.   Some of his disciples had called to see
him and observing his critical state they said—It is precisely now, Sir,
that what you learned when in ordinary health has to be used.   Looking
at them feebly for an instant and making a last exertion the dying man
answered—If principles are shown useful then they are wrong.   These
were his last words, and he died before the disciples had left his room.
He died as he had lived, self-reliant and independent.   His philosophy
taught that death and life are only ordinary events, changes which
occur in the orderly course of nature, and so for him death had no sting
nor the grave any victory.

   Ch'êng I was admitted to the Temple of Confucius in 1241 in the
reign of the Emperor Li-Tsung.   This monarch also conferred on him
a posthumous title and the epithet Chêng (正), Correct.   His name in
literature is Yi-ch'uan-Hsien-shêng (伊川先生), the Teacher from
the streams of Yi, and he is usually referred to simply as Yi-ch'uan.
Yi is the name of a town—Yi-yang—and a river in the west of Honan
near his native place.

   The great literary work of Yi-ch'uan was his Yih-chuan (易傳)
or Commentary on the Yih, to which he devoted the leisure of many
years, and in which he embodied much of the teaching of Chou Lien-
ch'i.   He made Commentaries also on the Ch'un-ch'iu and other
Canonical works.   Neither he nor his brother, however, published
anything, and it was only after repeated entreaties that Yi-ch'uan near
the close of his life entrusted his manuscripts to Chang Yi.   The sayings
and teachings of the two brothers have always been published together,
and this was evidently the desire of the younger.   Yang Shi, who will
appear below, put together his notes of their lectures and comments
for the use of the Fuhkeen people, and called his book Er-Ch'êng-ts'ui-
yen (二程粹言), the Pure Sayings of the Two Ch'êng.   But a
complete collection of all their Memorials, Discussions, and Miscellaneous writings, so far as they were preserved, was made by Chu Hsi
who edited them with notes and comments.   These have all been
republished as one work, with Chu Hsi's prefaces and additions, under
the title Er-Ch'êng-wên-chi.

The fame of Yi-ch'uan as a classical scholar and commentator is perhaps greater than that of his brother. He was careful and accurate and had a wide extent of learning. Both sought to revive the influence of old orthodoxy and to destroy the growing power of Buddhism and Taoism. Critics have found fault with much of their interpretation and arrangement of the Classics, but all must own that they gave a great stimulus to the profound and liberal study of these ancient treatises.

The character of Yi-ch'uan forms a striking contrast to that of his brother Ming-tao, though they admired and loved each other. The intense vanity, pompous and severe manner, and stern disposition of the former made him generally disliked. He could not pardon or over-look a fault, nor could he take a generous, liberal view of any question. Honest and upright in all his ways, of great learning and good abilities, he had no grace of manner or tenderness of heart. Stern and precise with his disciples he was regarded by them with respect and reverence, but they preferred the company of Ming-tao. The society of the latter was like the genial breezes of Spring, and his administration of office was like the enriching rain of Summer. The two brothers had the same high ideal of life, and accepted the same principles of philosophy, but their natural dispositions were very unlike. Ming-tao had genius, a taste for poetry, and a loving heart. Yi-ch'uan had industry, a desire to be right, and a self-sustained spirit.*

* See the Tao-t'ung-lu, Chüan 下 ; Er-Chêng-wen-chi (二 程 文 集); Er-Ch'êng-ts'ui-yen (二 程 粹 言); Hsing-li-hui-yao, Ch. 11.; Chu-tzŭ-ch'uan-shu, Ch. 53 ; Er-Ch'êng-yü-lu (二 程 語 錄).

———— ◆━●◆━◆ ————

79. Shao Yung (邵 雍). S. Yao-fu (堯 夫).

The family of Shao belonged to Fan-yang (范 陽) in Chihli, and Yung was born A.D. 1011, but the place of his birth is not recorded. The surname was originally Chi (姬), and his ancestors traced their history to the founders of the Chou dynasty. His father was a man of culture who enjoyed society and travelling, but did not go into public life. In boyhood Yung was noted as an ardent, high-spirited youth eager to make himself a name. His ambition was of a literary character and he read all kinds of books, and studied with the zeal and perseverance of a devotee. For several years he worked without a stove in winter, a fan in summer, or any sleeping-mat. Then he went on his travels in order to make the acquaintance of learned men and gain a wider knowledge.

He visited many places in the central and northern parts of the Empire, and then returned to Kung-ch'êng (共 城), in Wei-hui-foo (衛 輝 府), Honan. Here he resolved to settle down and renew his studies, his father and the rest of the family having already fixed their residence at this town. The Magistrate then stationed at Kung, Li Chi-ts'ai (李 之 才) was a great lover of learning and he soon came to know Shao Yung. The latter was happy in finding a master like Li, who was well versed in all the mystic lore of the Yih-ching, and Li gave his disciple the Commentaries which he had composed on the wondrous marks and symbolic lines of that work with their enigmatical interpretations. The teachings of this master decided the course which Yung's future studies were to take and also supplied him with much of the material for his works.

While his parents lived, Yung tended them with affectionate solicitude, supporting them by the labour of his hands. They were "a virtuous household, though exceeding poor," sometimes indeed in danger of starvation. Yet toil and privation never marred his temper or clouded the sunny cheerfulness of his nature. When his father died Yung buried him by the river Yi, and after the full time of mourning he changed his residence to the neighbourhood of Lo-yang. Here he came to know Fu Pi, Ssŭ-ma Kuang and other men of virtue and renown who were waiting for the evil days of Wang An-shi to pass over. His hut was a poor wretched thing which kept out neither rain nor wind, and some of his friends subscribed together and bought him a small cottage with a garden attached. To this little property he gave the name An-lo-wo (安 樂 窩)—Nest of quiet delight, calling himself the An-lo Hsien-shêng. Here "Satis beatus unicis Sabinis" he passed all the rest of his days, and his life was almost like a happy dream. By the fruits of his garden he was able to supply himself with food and clothes, and the society of books and friends gave him all that he needed more. Attempts were made to bring him into public life, and a good appointment was actually conferred on him, but he utterly refused to go into office, preferring " a philosopher's life, in the quiet woodland ways." He was wont to rise betimes and burn a piece of sweet-smelling wood in his room. Soothed by the fragrant incense to an aptness for quiet thought he sat down to study. During the day he read, or meditated, or wrote, or received enquiring disciples. But his studies were not confined to books, for he also observed the ways and workings of nature and then tried to find in his mind the laws and principles by which they proceed. His evening meal was taken about 5 o'clock and he always had three or four cups of wine at it—enough to exhilarate, but never to intoxicate. Afterwards, if alone, he hummed lays of the olden times or made verses fraught with quaint fancies and strange meanings. But if Szŭ-ma Kuang or some other kindred spirit came, he would sit the live-long night and talk over the signs of the times or a dark saying from the old Classics. When the weather was favourable, during Spring and Autumn, for he dreaded the extremes of Summer and Winter, he went for a drive in the city in a one-horse waggon. Every one knew him and knew the sound of his waggon, and when it was heard approaching all rushed out of doors to see him and give him welcome. " Our teacher has come," was the general cry, for no one addressed him or talked of him by name or surname. Some in order to lure him to stay with them made a room like his cottage and called it the "travelling nest," and at times he spent one or two days with these friends. The good all loved him, the bad owned his gentle influence, and little boys feared to be naughty lest Ssŭ-ma Kuang or Shao Yung should come to know. But indeed Shao Yung was credited with the gift of second sight, and he was supposed to know what was being done in many places and to see beforehand what was about to occur.

Moreover there came to the Nest some of the best and most eminent men of the time, men who were living in retirement at Lo-yang because they could not continue to serve a Sovereign who was bringing ruin on the Empire by following bad counsel. One might have seen there in the autumn evenings Fu Pi of courtly manners and rigid virtue —talking about his peonies or missions to the faithless Tartars, and Ssŭ-ma Kuang grave and self-possessed and rich in historic parallels. There too were Ch'êng Ming-tao of easy grace, and brilliant wit, and gentle manners—Yi-ch'uan stern and digni- fied having not yet learned "to tame the pride of intellect and virtue's self-esteem," Chang Tsai of wide sympathy and great learning, but shy and reserved, and haply many others. Some also came who had not yet achieved greatness, such as Yang Kuei-shan, the ardent student from far Fuhkeen and Hsie of Shang-ts'ai perhaps, already prognosticating his own dark destiny.

For about thirty years Shao Yung led this quiet happy life. But in 1077 sickness attacked him and he died, nursed to the end by his loving friends. They buried him beside his father, as he had asked, and, also in compliance with his request, Ch'êng Ming-tao wrote his epitaph. The posthumous epithet given to him was K'ang-chie (康 節), meaning perhaps calmly happy in self-control, and this became his usual designation in literature. In 1235 he was admitted to the Temple of Confucius, and in 1267 he was ennobled.

The greatest and best known of the writings of Shao Yung is the Huang-chi-ching-shi-shu (皇 極 經 世 書), meaning as explained by the author, the book of what is greatest, most central, most correct, and most transmutable. This treatise is curious, partly as an attempt to give number to all things or find it in all things. It is founded on the Yih-ching and carries out into detail the theories and principles of that work. But the author also drew largely from Chang Tzŭ-fang, Yang Hsüan and other sources, and he also worked much of it out of his own mind. The Huang-chi, says a native scholar, is not to be put in the same category with the Yih, for this gives the results of divination while that is merely a matter of calculation. It is not, however, all taken up with numbers, and much of it is really interest- ing reading, giving curious observations on natural phenomena, lessons from history, and thoughts on moral philosophy. The best parts are the Kuan-wu-P'ien, or Chapters on the study of Phenomena, but these are often referred to and printed as independent treatises.

The Yü-ch'iao-wên-tui (漁 樵 問 對), or a Dialogue between a

Fisherman and a Woodman, is a short treatise supplementary to the Huang-chi, but of a more popular nature. A woodman carrying a bundle of fuel is passing along a bank of the Yi river. He sees a man angling, lays down his bundle, and enters into conversation with the angler. The two men proceed to ask and resolve questions of practical and speculative philosophy, illustrating their opinions by examples drawn from their own industries. The angler, however, is much superior to the woodman, and when they are parting the latter says—'' I have heard of the Fu-hsi of antiquity, and I seem to day to have met him face to face.'' K'ang-chie was also the author of a volume of Poetry entitled—Yi-ch'uan-chi-jang-chi (伊 川 擊 壤 集), Collection of Yi-ch'uan Earth drummings, that is, Poems of Rural Life from the river Yi. These poems shows that their author loved natural scenery and enjoyed the changing beauties of the seasons with the cultivated taste of a genial philosopher. They are also said to be mystic and moral, and inspired to some extent by Lao-tsŭ and Chuang-tsŭ. Yung was evidently a reader and admirer of the former, and he was also a student of Buddhist literature. So the Ch'êng brothers were not quite correct, as Chu Hsi admits, when they said that his writings were pure Confucianism, for there is in them a little mixture of heretical theories. But still they are essentially orthodox, and they develope the teachings of the canonical books, specially the Yih-ching and Ch'un-ch'iu. Yung's notice of the soul going to Heaven, however, and of man being an incarnate spirit (or Ghost) tell of other teachers than Confucius and Mencius. For the old Sages he had an intense and geniune admiration, and his eulogies on Confucius in particular seem to be very extravagant.*

* See Hsing-li-ta-ch'uan (性 理 大 全) Chü 7 to 13; Er-ch'êng-wen-chi Ch. 3. Chu-tzŭ-ch'uan-shu Ch. 53; Sung-shi. Ch. 427.

THE HSIEN JU (先 儒), OR FORMER SCHOLARS.

THERE are at present Sixty-five of these, and they are arranged in rows on each side of the large hall of the temples outside of the Hsien Hsien, or Former Worthies. Every tablet bears the title or heading Hsien-Ju, or Former Scholar, which is to be understood before each of the following names.

———————

1. Kung-yang Kao (公 羊 高).

Kung-yang, whose name was Kao, is supposed to have belonged to the State of Ch'i (齊), and to have lived in the first half of the 5th Century B.C., though some bring him down to a time nearly two centuries later. But there is scarcely anything known about his origin and history. Tradition represents him to have been a disciple of Tzŭ-hsia (子 夏), one of the most learned of Confucius' disciples—the Pu Shang of the Twelve Wise Ones above, No 9—, and to have received from him orally the Ch'un-ch'iu (春 秋) or Annals of Lu compiled by Confucius.

On this work Kung-yang, with the help of several others it is supposed, composed a supplement or Commentary, and Ch'un-ch'iu and Commentary were communicated to his son P'ing (平). The latter transmitted them—still orally, according to tradition—to his son, from whom they were handed on down through several generations. At length in the reign of Han Ching-Ti (B.C. 156 to 140), the whole work was written out on bamboo and silk by Kung-yang Shou (公 羊 壽), and his disciple Hu-mu Tzŭ-tu (胡 母 子 都), It was made a special subject of study by Tung Chung-shu (董 仲 舒). whose name appears a little below, a celebrated scholar of this period and a friend of Hu-mu Tzŭ-tu. The success which it now had, led to its being adopted as a work of authority. Tung Chung-shu and others wrote on it, and it was admitted by Han Wu-ti into the Imperial Library. After this, however, the Commentary seems to have sunk into some obscurity, and it is not until the second century of our era that it again comes into distinction. It was now edited and published together with Confucius' text by a scholar named Ho Hsiu (何 休)— known also as Ho Shao-kung (何 邵 公)—with the title Ch'un-ch'iu-kung-yang-ching-chuan-chïe-ku (春 秋 公 羊 經 傳 解 詁). This edition has been often reprinted and it is still a standard work.

Kung-yang's Commentary, incorporated with the Ch'un-ch'iu, is one of the Thirteen Classics, and it was cut in stone along with the other Canonical works in the time of the T'ang dynasty. It is not so popular and does not hold so high a place among Chinese scholars as Tso's Commentary, and· Legge says of Kung-yang and Ku-liang, "There is really nothing in them to entitle them to serious attention." This seems to be a little too strong. Native critics regard the Tso-chuan as fuller of incidents and showing a better knowledge of the events of history, its author having had access to the State records.

The commentaries of Kung-yang and Ku-liang, on the other hand, are scanty and inaccurate as to narrative, but they are fuller and more precise as to matters of principle. Neither of the latter authors is supposed to have had access to the national archives, and hence they sometimes make mistakes as to names of persons and places, and as to matters of fact generally.

Some other historical writings are ascribed to Kung-yang besides the famous Commentary. Thus in the Han Shu we find mention of the Kung-yang-wai-chuan (公 羊 外 傳, in 35 chapters, and the Kung-yang-tsa-chi (公 羊 雜 集), in 83 chapters, but these works are not known at present.

In A.D. 647 T'ang T'ai-Tsung admitted Kung-yang to the Temple of Confucius and placed his tablet among the Associates. The successor of that Emperor, however, removed it a few years afterwards and placed it in the body of the hall. Its present place and title were assigned to it in 1530.

2. Ku-liang Ch'ih (穀 梁 赤), S. Ying-shao (應 邵.

The name of Kŭ-liang is given also as Shu (俶), and as Hsi (喜),
and his second name is also said to have been Yuan-shĭ (元始). Some
are even prepared to deny that there ever were such persons as Kung-
yang and Ku-liang.   Others think that these are different names for
one individual, but most writers are inclined to believe in the historical
existence of two men bearing respectively the above names.   It is
strange, however, that there is only one Ku-liang in history, and only
one family of Kung-yang, the extinction of which seems to have been
simultaneous with the publication of the commentary.   There is also
an unpleasant suspicion of allegory about the names borne by some
members of the Kung-yang family, such as Peace (P'ing 平), and
Long-life (Shou 壽). Still it is to be hoped that they are not to be
turned into solar myths.

As in the case of Kung-yang, very little is known about the history
of Ku-liang, and his fame rests entirely on the Commentary to the
Ch'un-ch'iu which bears his name.   He is said to have been a native
of Lu, and to have also been a disciple of Tzŭ-hsia, from whom it is
supposed, he received the words of the Ch'un-ch'iu accompanied by
Tzŭ-hsia's notes and explanations derived from the teaching of
Confucius.   Using these as his chief materials Ku-liang composed his
commentary.   This was handed down, in conjunction with the Sage's
text, through a succession of five persons until the time of Han Hsüan
Ti, who reigned from B.C. 73 to 48.   The text and commentary were
now written out on bamboo and silk, and the Emperor, who liked
Ku-liang's work more than the commentaries of Tso and Kung-yang,
admitted the former into the Imperial library.   But it was known to
scholars long before that time and in the reign of Han Wu Ti, B.C.
140 to 87—a learned official, Chiang-kung of Hsia-ch'iu (瑕 邱 江 公),
who owned the treatise, was able to discuss its merits compared with
those of Kung-yang's commentary.   The first to publish Ku-liang's
work, however, and to make it generally known was Fan Ning (范 甯)

—whose name appears a little below—a great scholar during the time of the Chin dynasty. The title given by Fan Ning to the treatise which he compiled was Ch'un-ch'iu-Ku-liang-chuan-chi-chie (春秋穀梁傳集解). In the time of the T'ang dynasty a scholar named Yang Shi-hsün (楊士勛) brought out a new edition of this work accompanying Fan Ning's notes and explanations with copious and useful comments. This edition has been reprinted several times, and is still the popular one.

According to some of the native critics, Ku-liang is clear in style but too brief in narrative, while Tso is sometimes condemned as prolix and superstitious and Kung-yang is declared to be critical and dogmatic. Some are inclined to think that Ku-liang derived the material of his work from Kung-yang, while others regard him as the older of the two. A theory also was maintained for a time that the two commentaries were the work of one person, but the critics of the Sung period decided against this theory mainly on the ground of differences in style. It has been opposed also by other scholars and the general opinion has always been in favour of three distinct commentators, Tso well versed in pageants and ceremonies, Ku-liang skilled in the classic usages and Kung-yang learned in the motives and designs of the Sage's remarks.

The tablet of Ku-liang was admitted to the Temple of Confucius in A.D. 647 and experienced a similar treatment to that of Kung-yang's tablet.*

· 3. Kao-t'ang Shêng (高堂生).

It is doubtful whether Kao or Kao-t'ang was the surname of this man, and whether his name was *Shêng* or *T'ang-shêng*, or *T'ang*. He is most usually quoted and referred to simply as Kao-t'ang Shêng. It is very uncertain when he lived as he is said to have been a disciple of Confucius, and also to have lived at the beginning of the Han dynasty, the latter being the generally received opinion. All authorities are agreed apparently that he belonged to Lu, and that he was a scholar

* For Kung-yang and Ku-liang see L. Ch. Cl. V. Proleg. p. 37: The Kung-yang-chu-su, (公羊注疏) Introduction; Ku-liang-chu-su, Introduction; Chu-tzŭ-ch'uan-shu, Ch. 36; Han-shu, chs. 30 and 88.

and official in that State, but very little is recorded of his life. The honorary title given to him in the Sung period was Lai-wu-Poh (萊 蕪 伯), that is Earl of Lai-wu, a town of Lu, at present in T'ai-an-foo in Shantung.

The fame of Kao-t'ang Shêng rests entirely on his connection with the Classic Books of Rites and Ceremonies. The Confucian literature had suffered very badly from the efforts of Ch'in Shi Huang Ti to have it all destroyed, and no part suffered so much as the Li (禮). When the Han dynasty was settled on the throne, every means was used to recover and collect the old Classics. Kao-t'ang Shêng had the good fortune to possess a manuscript of at least part of the work, or to know it by memory. This he communicated to Hsiao Fên (蕭 奮) of Hsia-ch'iu (瑕 丘), a town in his own native State. Hsiao Fên communicated it to his disciple Mêng Ching (孟 鄉), from whom it was transmitted to How Ts'ang (后 倉), and from this last it came down to Tai Tê (戴 德) and Tai Shêng (戴 聖).

Kao-t'ang's treatise became known as the Shi-Li (士 禮) or Official's Ceremonies, and it contained seventeen chapters. It is to some extent the same as the work which now bears the name Yi (儀)—Li. When a more complete copy of the Li was found in the ruins of Confucius' house, written in the obsolete seal characters, this latter was called the Ku-wên (古 文) or text in old writing. Kao-t'ang Shêng's edition was then spoken of as the Chin Wên (今 文), or text in the modern writing. But the latter was supposed to contain a purer text and hence it was called the Ku-ching (古 經) or old classic. It is very doubtful, however, whether the Shi-li is preserved in the Yi-li.

In A.D. 647 Kao-t'ang Shêng was made an Associate in the Confucian temples, but a few years afterwards he was removed to a lower position. His tablet was, until lately, 2nd on the West side, but recent additions to the "Scholars" have led to several changes of arrangement.*

---

* See Han-shu Ch. 30; Chou-li (Shi-san-ching edition.) Introduction; Chêng-yi-t'ang-Wên-chi (正 誼 堂 文 集) Ch. 8.; Wylie, Notes &c. p. 5.; Shang-yu-lu Chs. 22 and 7.

4. Fu Shêng (伏 勝). S. Tzŭ-chien (子 賤).

Fu's name is often found written Shêng (生), and this is the character used in the Han History, though, as Legge suggests, it is very likely simply equivalent to our Mr. or Teacher. He was a native of Ch'i-nan-foo in the north of Shantung. The dates of his birth and death are not known, but he lived during the latter part of the third and the first half of the second century B.C. attaining to the age of about 100 years. At the time of Ch'in Shï Huang-Ti he was already known as a great scholar. So when the edict was issued for the destruction of the Classics and the massacre of the learned he had to fly. Before leaving his house he hid in one of its walls the tablets on which the Shu Ching had been written out, apparently by himself. During the civil wars and general anarchy which brought about the extinction of the Ch'in and the rise of the Han dynasty he had no settled residence but wandered about from place to place.

When the Han Emperors recalled the scholars and sought out the surviving literature, Fu returned to his house. On digging out his tablets of the Shu he found them in a very bad state, only 29, or as some say 28, chapters being legible. These, however, he took as the basis of instruction and proceeded to teach the Shu in his native district. The Emperor Wên Ti, who reigned from B.C. 179 to 156, wanting to find a scholar able to arrange and edit this Classic could not for some time find any one to do the work. At length he heard of Fu Shêng and summoned him to Court for that purpose. Fu was, however, now more than 90 years old and could not go. A high officer was accordingly sent to Ch'i-nan, and he received either the original tablets or copies of them with Fu's comments and additions. It is related that when the Imperial messenger was receiving these, the old scholar spoke very indistinctly, and he had to call his daughter in to repeat his words. But she used the local patois, and the official, who belonged to Ying-chow in Anhui, could not quite understand her and lost about two or three words out of every ten that she uttered.

Another account represents Fu as retaining the whole of the Shu in his memory for 50 years, and at last writing it out for Han Wên Ti. But this refers perhaps only to the lost tablets, or, as has been suggested, he may have come to know all the work by memory from reading and repeating it frequently. Thus it is probable that when he was old and blind he taught entirely from memory, and that his disciples then committed his lessons to writing. The text which bore his name came to be known as the Chin-wen (今 文) or modern writing, to distinguish it from the Shu found in the wall of Confucius' house which was called the Ku-wen (古 文) or old writing. The former was written in the characters current at the time and the latter in those known as "tadpoles."

The great merit of Fu Shêng and that which gives him a place in the Temple of Confucius is that he saved a copy of the Shu Ching from the fires of Ch'in, and that he spread a knowledge of that work among the people of Northern Shantung where it had been, up to his time, almost unknown. Some of his disciples rose to distinction as expounders of this Classic, but Fu's text and teachings, with the exception of "some fragments," have long since perished.

In A.D. 647 he was admitted to the temples and made an Associate but afterwards met with the same fate as Kao-t'ang Shêng, and the others who came in with him.[*]

5. Tung Chung-shu (董 仲 舒). S. Chiao-hsi (膠 西).

Chung-shu was a native of Kuang-chuan (廣 川), a town in what is now the Prefecture of Ho-chien in Chihli. He lived in the second century B.C., and was one of the most renowned men of the Early Han dynasty. In youth he was a diligent student, specially of the Ch'un-ch'iu (春 秋) his early love for which he seems to have kept through all his life. He became a Public Instructor in the reign of Ching Ti, B.C. 156 to 140, and had many disciples. With these he was very precise and dignified, giving his lectures from behind a curtain, and exacting a strict attention to propriety. The new comers,

---

[*] See L. Ch. Cl. III. Proleg. Ch. 1. Sec. 2.; Shu-ching Vol. I. Preface with Kung Ying-ta's notes.; Han Shu Ch. 88.

moreover, were not admitted at once to his presence, but had to learn for a time under the older and more advanced disciples. So devoted a student was he that for three years he did not take a look at his own back garden.

From this quiet life Chung-shu was called to office by Wu Ti, who succeeded Ching Ti on the throne. He is represented as giving this Emperor plain and wholesome advice, drawing lessons from the records of the past and the sayings of Confucius to urge him to the adoption of vigorous measures of reform. The Emperor, without taking the advice to heart, took its giver into his favour, and appointed him to Chiang-tu (江 都), the modern Yang-chow in Kiangsu, at the same time making him preceptor to his brother the Prince Yih. Some time afterwards he lost the Imperial favour, and begged repeatedly to be allowed to resign. At last a rival, but inferior commentator on the Ch'un-ch'iu brought about his retirement through jealousy.

He now went back to his books and disciples, and spent the rest of his life, which was a very long one, in studying, teaching, and writing. His residence was for a time on the Kuei-yen (桂 殿) Hill, whence he is sometimes called Kuei-yen-tsŭ or the Philosopher of Kuei-yen. But he ended his days in peace among his kindred and was buried in the place of his youth.

Chung-shu seems to have made the Ch'un-ch'iu a life-long study, using as his help and guide the commentary by Kung-yang of which he was an able and eloquent defender. He himself wrote a work in sixteen chapters entitled Kung-yang-Tung-Chung-shu-chĭ-yü (公 羊 董 仲 舒 治 獄). The Han History mentions another work of his in 123 chapters, which was perhaps a collection of his State papers and miscellaneous writings. His best known treatise, however, is that which bears the title Ch'un-ch'iu-fan-lu (春 秋 繁 露), that is, Copious Dew from the Ch'un-ch'iu. This is a curious mixture of moral and metaphysical essays in seventeen ch'uan. Some of them are on subjects taken from or connected with the Ch'un-ch'iu, giving very fanciful interpretations to the bald paragraphs of that book. There are also prayers for rain and for the stopping of rain, and other curious pieces. This treatise is published in the collection known as the Han-Wei-tsung-shu (漢魏叢書), and has still many admirers.

Chung-shu has always had a high reputation among Confucianists. He was a strictly orthodox adherent of the Sage's own teachings, and opposed to that exercise of private judgment which led to schools and sects. He had all the abilities of a prime minister, says Liu Hsiang, and while not inferior to Yi-yin and Lü-wang he was superior to Kuan-chung and Yen-ying. Liu's politic son said this was going too far, and denied that Chung-shu came up to Tzŭ-yu and Tzŭ-hsia. But he was evidently regarded by the other Han scholars as the greatest of their number for this period. To him is ascribed the institution of upper schools or seminaries for advanced students with officials to superintend them. It has been said that Chung-shu and Yang Hsiung (揚雄) were the only two scholars among the ancients who combined solid learning with graceful accomplishments. Chu Hsi also says that Chung-shu was the purest of all the Hàn writers, that is, as to style.

His admission to the Confucian Temple took place in 1330, in the reign of Wên Ti of the Mongol dynasty.*

6. Mao Hêng (毛亨).

Mao Hêng was a native of Lu, and lived at the beginning of the Han dynasty in the early part of the second century B.C. But neither the dates of his birth and death, nor any facts of his life are recorded. The memory of his name rests entirely on his connection with the Shĭ-ching, or Book of Odes. This Classic had been handed down from Confucius' disciple Tzŭ-hsia through a succession of schoolars to Hsün Ch'ing (荀卿), commonly mentioned as Hsün-tzŭ, a celebrated philosopher of the Ch'in dynasty who survived to hold office under the first Han Emperors. Mao Hêng became a disciple of Hsün-tzŭ and obtained from him the tablets of the Shĭ. These he seems to have arranged and made into a book which was known as the Mao-hsĭ, containing 29 *Chuan*. He then wrote an illustrative and explanatory

* See Han-shu Chs. 56, 30.; Faber's Quellen zu Conf. p. 8.; Ch'un-ch'iu-fan-lu; Shang-yu-lu Ch. 13, Chu-tzŏ-ch'uan-shu Ch. 58. Ch'un-ch'iu-Kung-yang-chuan-chu-su (in Shi-san-Ching, ed. Yuan Yuan) Vol. I. Introduction.

commentary on the Classic, which was in 30 *chuan* and received the title Mao-shï-ku-hsün-chuan (毛 詩 詁 訓 傳).

Hêng's text and commentary became known to Prince Tê (得) of Ho-chien, known also as Prince Hsien, the greatest patron of learning at the time, who obtained them from Hêng and presented copies of them to the Emperor. At the same time the Prince handed over the treatises to Mao Ch'ang (毛 萇)—who comes in below—to look over and correct them. Ch'ang adopted the text and that still survives as the accepted standard. Hêng's commentary, however, was lost many centuries ago, and nothing is known of its merits. But it is not unlikely that it was largely used by Ch'ang in the composition of his two treatises on the Shï.

In order to distinguish between these two editors and commentators the writers of the Han period called Hêng, Ta-Mao-kung, (大 毛 公) and Ch'ang, Hsiao-Mao-kung (小 毛 公), that is, respectively, Great and Little or Senior and Junior Mr. Mao. This last word used alone generally refers to the later of the two.

Mao Hêng was not admitted to the honours of the Confucian temples until the year 1863.*

---

7. K'ung An-kuo (孔 安 國). S. Tzŭ-kuo (子 國).

K'ung An-kuo, a lineal descendant of Confucius, was a native of Lu. He lived in the second century B.C., and held office under the Emperors Ching and Wu of the Han dyansty. In early life he had the advantage of studying under Shên P'ei (申 培), usually referred to in literature as Shen-kung (申 公), one of the most famous of all the scholars who adorned the first reigns of the Han dynasty. Shên-kung was specially distinguished for his knowledge of the ancient classical literature, and he had an immense number of disciples. Under his teaching An-kuo studied the Shï and the Shu, though he is also said

---

* For Mao Hêng, see L. Ch. Cl. IV. Proleg. Ch. 1. Sec. 2 : Shï-ching (Shï-san-ching ed.) Intro ; Han Shu, Ch. 30.

to have gained his knowledge of the latter work from Fu Shêng, who
has occurred above. Subsequently he took office, and rose to high
position under the Emperor Wu, in whose favour he continued until
old age made him resign.

When Prince Kung of Lu found the old tablets of the Shu and
other Scriptures in the house of the K'ung family, he presented them
to the Emperor who gave them over to K'ung An-kuo. But as the
tablets of the Shu were all written in the obsolete "tadpole" characters,
An-kuo could not do anything with them until he obtained the portion
of the Classic which Fu Shêng possessed. By the help of this he
succeeded in deciphering his own tablets, and he wrote out their
contents in the characters current at the time. The work thus
transcribed was presented to the Emperor who ordered him to make
a commentary on the whole Shu, a task which An-kuo at once set
himself to accomplish. It was completed, but the family troubles of
the Emperor Wu which led to confusion in the country, prevented it
from obtaining immediate circulation. So it happened that neither
his text of the Shu nor his commentary on that work was much known
until the time of Ssŭ-ma Ch'ien. The Shang-shu-hsü (尚書序),
Preface to the Shang-shu, by An-kuo—known also as the Great
Preface, to distinguish it from that attributed to Confucius and called
the Small Preface—is a very interesting and well written document.
It gives a short account of the origin of the Shu and the discovery of his
tablets of that work with his subsequent labour on them. Native critics,
however, generally doubt its genuineness and refer its composition
to a period some hundreds of years later. It has also been much
disputed whether An-kuo was the author of the commentary current
under his name, and a decision is generally arrived at against its being
genuine. His edition of the Shu was lost long ago, though there is
still to be found what professes to be the "old text."

Besides his commentary on the Shu-ching, An-kuo wrote also a
commentary on the Classic of Filial Piety with the name Ku-wên-
hsiao-ching-chuan (古文孝經傳), and another on the Lun-yü
with the title Lun-yü-hsün-chie (論語訓解). The tablets of the
Hsiao-ching and the Lun-yü had been found with those of the Shu in

the ruins of his ancestor's house. He is said to have made, moreover, a collection of the sayings of Confucius.

K'ung An-kuo's tablet was admitted to Confucius' Temple in the year A.D. 647. Like many others it has had to cross over on account of new arrivals.*

---

8. Mao Ch'ang (毛 萇).

Next below Mao Hêng is the more fortunate scholar of the same surname, who received Hêng's work on the Shï-ching, and so entered into the fruits of his labour. Mao Ch'ang, whose name apparently is also written (長), was a native of Chao(趙), an old State comprising parts of the modern Shansi and Chihli. In the reign of Han Wu Ti, B.C. 140 to 86, he was Public Instructor at the Court of Prince Hsien of Ho-chien. While in that capacity he received from the Prince, according to one account, but according to another, from Mao Hêng himself, the latter's edition of the Shï and his commentary on that Classic.

Mao Ch'ang adopted Hêng's text, and he also composed a commentary on the Shï in 29 *chuan*, publishing at the same time his version of the text. There were at this period three other editions of the Book of Odes, which were called respectively the Ch'ï, Lu, and Han Shï. Prince Hsien, in order to do the great scholar at his court a favour, prefixed Mao's name to the edition of the Classic which he had prepared with great care and industy. Hence this edition, the only one which has survived, has always been distinguished as Mao-Shï. It is supposed to be nearer the original text consigned by Confucius to Tzŭ-hsia than was any of the others. Mao, it has been said, did not like to alter the text, and he preferred, moreover, to make his interpretation follow the context rather than the meanings of individual characters.

---

* See L. Ch. Cl. III. Proleg. p. 22.: Shu-ching (Shï-san-ching ed.) Vol. 1.; Chu-tzŭ-Ch'uan, Ch. 33; Han-shu, Ch. 88; Wylie, Notes &c. pp 3 & 6; L. Ch. Cl. I. Proleg. p. 13.

The commentary of Mao with his text of the Shĭ did not come into general use for about one hundred years. But from the beginning of the Later Han dynasty they rose into favour and popularity, and numerous critics and expositors have since that time exercised their learning and ingenuity on them.

It is not recorded in what year Mao Ch'ang was born or when he died, but he seems to have spent nearly all his life in Ho-chien. He was buried in Tsun-fu, a village in the Prefecture which still bears the name of that old principality.

In the year A.D. 647 he was received into the Confucian Temple as an Associate, but in the reign of the next emperor he was brought down to be among the Han "Scholars."[*]

---

9. Hou Ts'ang (后 蒼). S. Chin-chun (近 君).

Hou Ts'ang was a native of T'an (郯), a district in the South of the present Shantung. He lived during the 1st century B.C., and held office under Han Hsuan Ti who reigned from B.C. 73 to 48. In the early part of his life he became a disciple of the famous Hsia-how Shĭ-ch'ang (夏疾始昌), a man well versed in all the Classics, but specially distinguished for his knowledge of the Shĭ. The *Ch'i* edition of this Classic and Shĭ-ch'ang's teachings on it were communicated by the latter to Hou, who transmitted them in turn to three of his disciples. But it is for his labours in connection with the old documents containing the laws of rites and ceremonies and the precedents of former sages that Hou Ts'ang is chiefly celebrated. He received and studied the Book of Rites which Kao-t'ang Shêng had taught. Using this work as his basis apparently he, in conjunction with two other scholars, composed a treatise on the Li (禮). From the name of the room in which this treatise was written it was called Hou-shĭ-ch'ü-t'ai-chi (后 氏 曲 臺 記), Hou's Ch'ü-t'ai Record. This work was delivered to Tai Tê (戴 德), one of Hou's disciples, and from it and other writings Tê compiled the work which was afterwards called Ta-Tai-Li (大戴禮),

---

[*] See L. Ch. Cl. IV. Proleg. p. 11.; Shĭ-ching, Vol. 1; Han-shŭ, Ch. 88; Wylie, Notes &c. p. 3.

"Ritual of the Senior Tae," as Wylie translates the name. His treatise was subsequently revised and much abridged by his nephew Tai Shêng (戴聖), who produced from it the work known as Hsiao-Tai-Li or "Ritual of the Junior Tae." Such is the work that has come down to us under the name of the (禮記) Lè Kê "Book of Rites," and is now by imperial authority, designated one of the Five Classics."

Hou Ts'ang was admitted to the worship in the temples of Confucius in A.D. 1530, in the Chia-ching period of the Ming dynasty*

---

10. Tu Tzŭ-ch'ün (杜子春).

Tu Tzŭ-ch'ün was born in the latter half of the first century B.C., and lived into the second half of the first century of our era, having attained to an old age of more than 90 years. His native place was in Kou-shï (緱氏), a district in the West of the present Honan. He lived in the small town of Nan-shan (南山) and taught the Chow-Li (周禮), or Ritual of the Chow dynasty, among his fellow-townsmen. This work had been one of the last of the old books to be recovered, and the tablets of it which Prince Hsien obtained and which constituted the Imperial copy were in a wretched condition. Towards the end of the Early Han dynasty Liu Hsin took up his father's work of examining and editing these tablets. His work was not finished until after the rise of the Later Han, and it was not generally approved. Tu Tzŭ-ch'ün was a disciple of Liu Hsin, and as he himself owned a copy of the Chow-Li he was able to render his master great service in his work of editing. Besides he was one of the few scholars who could then read the old characters in which the tablets were written.

Tzŭ-ch'un published an edition of the Chow-Li, and the fame of his learing in that work attracted to him many disciples. Among these the most illustrious were Chêng Chung (鄭衆) and Chia K'uei (買逵). Tzŭ-ch'ün's text of the Ritual and his teachings on the book were communicated to these two scholars, who afterwards also wrote

* Wylie, Notes &c. p. 5.; L. Ch. Cl. IV. Proleg. p. 9; Shang-yu-lu, Ch. 16. p 52; Han Shu, Chs. 30&88.

commentaries. Chêng Chung's work did not meet with success, but Chia K'uei's became popular to some extent. It was used by another great scholar, Ma Yung (馬融) in the formation of his commentary, which was succeeded by that of Chêng Kang-ch'êng (鄭康成). Hence Tu Tzŭ-ch'ün has the merit of having preserved and first taught this very interesting old work—the Chou Li or Chow Kwan. The best native critics are agreed that this is a genuine book of the beginning of the Chow dynasty, and it presents us with a minute and valuable account of the internal organization and administration of the Government at that period.

Tzŭ-ch'ün is said to have written also on the Yih Ching and he was well known among his contemporaries as a man of great learning, but there is very little record of him apart from his connection with the Chou-Li. He was one of the company admitted to the honours of Confucian worship by T'ai Tsung in A.D. 647. Like the others, he was made an Associate, but the next Emperor removed him and placed him among the Han "Scholars." *

---

11. Hsü Shên (許慎). S. Shu-chung (叔重).

Hsü Shên was born in Shao-ling (召陵), a town in the South of the modern Honan. The History of the Han dynasty does not give the date of his birth and death, but we know that he lived in the first century of our era. As a youth he was of a pure and sincere disposition, and fond of study. The illustrious scholar, Chia K'uei (賈逵), a man of fine genius and great learning, became his friend and master. From him Shên received instruction not only in the teachings of the old books, but also in their style and language. Hence it came to be said that "K'uei and Hsü Shên of Ju-nan (the name of the district in which Shên was born) were masters in the old learning."

---

* See Biot's Tcheou-Li, Intro. p. XVIII.; Chou-Li (Shĭ-san-ching ed.) Vol. I; Ma Tuan-lin's Oyclô. Ch. 180.

Hsü Shên held office for a time "as an examiner of literature", and distinguished himself in this capacity by his efforts for the spread of education. He preferred, however, a quiet life, and retired to his home and studies. By genius and application he obtained a wide acquaintance with the old texts of the classical scriptures, and with the other standard works then in existence. He chose to go back to the original treatises rather than attach himself to any of the schools of interpretation which had arisen during the Early Han dynasty. The critical treatise which he wrote, entitled the Wu-ching-yi-yi (五 經 異 議) or Different Meanings of the Five Classics, gave him a popular reputation. So great became the fame of his learning as a classical scholar that there arose a saying among his contemporaries— The Five Ching have not two Hsü Shêns.

In his old age he compiled the Dictionary with which his name is more generally associated, and which has secured him an immortality of fame. The Shuo-wên or Shuo-wên-chie-tzŭ (說 文 解 字), that is, Character-Explainer, was left at his death not quite ready for publication, but his son Ch'ung (冲) put it in order and presented it to the Emperor An Ti in A.D. 121. Mayers says of this dictionary— "The original work was scarcely more than a list of characters, some 10,000 in number, accompanied in some instances by concise remarks." Chinese scholars, however, value it highly, and many of them have spent great learning and industry in confirming and illustrating its explanations and derivation. The editions of Tuan Yü-tsai (段 玉 裁), al. Tuan Mou-t'ang, and Kuei Fu (桂 馥) of the present dynasty are among the best.

In 1875 a Memorial was addressed to the Throne praying for the admission of Hsü Shên to the Confucian Temple. His merits are thus stated in this Memorial—"Hsü Shên came forward at a time when the words of the sages of antiquity had begun to be obscured under the commentaries of later writers, to establish the true meaning of their language. At about the end of the first century of the Christian era he composed the *Shuo Wên* dictionary, in 14 Sections, divided under 540 Classes, and containing 9,355 words. Subsequent writers of the Han dynasty extolled his learning; and in the Imperial catalogue of literature compiled in the reign of Kien-lung (in the last century), the value of his work is fully enlarged upon." The prayer of the Memorial was recommended by the Board of Ceremonies and Hsü Shên was soon after enrolled among the Han "Scholars" of the Confucian Temple.*

---

12. Ch'êng Hsüan (鄭 玄) S. K'ang-ch'êng (康 成).

Among the host of learned scholars and accomplished writers who adorned the two Han dynasties, Ch'êng K'ang-ch'êng was confessedly the greatest. He was born A.D. 127 at what was then called Kao-mí (高 密) of the Northern Sea, a town in the present Prefecture of Lai-chow in Shantung. He grew up a youth of a remarkably fine appearance, tall and stately, and of a genial disposition. In his native place he obtained an appointment as Petty Magistrate and Revenue collector, but soon threw it up in disgust to the great annoyance of his father. Official life did not please him, and he had recourse to literature and philosophy. He now read with eagerness the Yih Ching, the Ch'un-ch'iu with the commentaries of Kung-yang and Ku-liang, and all the extant works on Astronomy and Arithmetic. Not satisfied with the learning to be obtained at home, he went to the town of Cho (涿) in the present Shuntien-foo in Chihli to become a disciple of Ma Yung (馬 融). This haughty professor, surrounded by hundreds of admiring disciples, kept K'ang-ch'êng waiting three years for admission. When the latter had learned all he wanted from Yung, who came to love and esteem him, he returned to his native place for a time. Here he shut himself up to study, and wrote treatises on the Classics. His fame soon brought him disciples to whom he communicated in lectures his views on the ancient Confucian literature.

He again left his home and took office, but his heart was still set on study. Rebellion and anarchy were at this time distracting the

---

* Mayers Ch. Reader's Manual, p. 66.; Peking Gazettes for 1875 p. 129; Hou-Han-Shu, Ch. 79 (2nd part); Tuan Yü-ts'ai's Shuo-wen, Ch. 15 and Appendix; Kuei Fu's Edition; Appendix.

Empire and bringing the Han dynasty to extinction. It was the time of the famous Yellow-turbaned rebels. Once these rioters were invading Shantung when they met with K'ang-ch'êng. In compliance with the latter's request the Chief of the rebels "bid spare" Kao-mi, and he led his men by another way. So the town and surrounding district were saved from "ruin bare" by the merit of the genial scholar. Here he settled down in old age, and gave himself up to study and teaching, and intercourse with other scholars. He was a very jovial student, and had a great love for the pleasures of life. It was said of him that he could drink 300 cups of wine without becoming drunk.

In the spring of A.D. 200 he was seized with a severe illness which for a time confined him to his room. One night Confucius appeared to him in a dream and said—"Rise, rise—This year is in the sign of the Dragon, and next year will be in that of the Serpent." This he knew to be an omen of his approaching death. At this time war and rebellion were in all the land. There was no actual Emperor and several ambitious men were seeking to get the Throne. Among them was the famous General Yuan Shao (袁紹). He was now at Chi-chow (冀州), a town in what is at present the Chêng-ting Prefecture in Chihli with an army to oppose Ts'ao Tsao. He had known K'ang-ch'êng before, and he now ordered him to be brought by force to join the army at his camp. K'ang-ch'êng had no help for it, and set out on the journey, but on the way his sickness overcame him and he died near ₁Yuan-ch'êng (元城) in the modern Chihli in the sixth moon of that year, A.D. 200. He had requested that his obsequies should be celebrated without pomp or cost, but his coffin was followed to its place of rest by an immense concourse of friends and disciples.

K'ang-ch'êng wrote elaborate commentaries on the Lun-yü, the Yih, the Shu, the Yi-Li, the Li-chi, Chow-Li, Hsiao-ching, and two works on the Shi-ching of Mao Ch'ang. He wrote also a criticism on Hsü Shên's treatise on the Five Classics, and a vindication of the genuineness of the Chow-Li, besides treatises or essays on many other subjects. When his answers to Ho Hsiu's (何休) works on the Ch'un-ch'iu commentators appeared, Hsiu said—K'ang-ch'êng came into my house and took my arms to attack me. No one of the time matched K'ang-ch'êng in learning and power of expression. As Legge says, " the amount of his labours on the ancient classical literature is almost incredible." Later critics have found much to blame in his commentaries and expositions, but some of them remain the standard authorities. They display great learning, a wonderful command of language, clear thinking, and often sound judgment.

Ch'êng K'ang-ch'êng was made an Associate when admitted to the Temple in A.D. 647, but like the others so made at that time, he was brought down to a lower position in the course of a few years. In 1530 his tablet was taken away and put in the temple raised to his memory at his native place, but in 1724 it was reinstated in the Confucian Temple. His tablet is inscribed Ch'êng K'ang-ch'êng, because Hsüan (or Yuan) (玄) being the personal name of an Emperor could not be used. In books we often find this character replaced by Yuan (元), but Ch'êng is best known by his *tzŭ* or second name K'ang-chêng as above.*

---------◄•►---------

13. Chu Ko Liang (諸 葛 亮). S. K'ung-ming (孔 明).

Chu-ko Liang's family belonged to Lang-ye (瑯 琊), a district in the eastern part of the present Shantung, and he was born there in A.D. 181. His father, who was magistrate of the town of T'ai-shan (太 山) in the present Tsi-nan Prefecture of Shantung, died when Liang was only a child. He and his brother were taken charge of by their paternal uncle, and removed to the northern part of Hu-pei near the town of Hsiang-yang. On the death of their relative the two brothers, still little more than boys, took a small farm and built themselves a humble cottage.

Liang, or, to use his better known name, K'ung-ming grew up a tall, well-built youth of great strength and courage, though the villagers did not agree with him in his estimate of himself as being as great a

---

* For the life and works of Ch'êng K'ang-ch'êng see Mayers, Ch. R. M. p. 19 ; L. Ch. Cl. Proleg. I. p. 14 ; Hou Han-shu, Ch. 35 ;Shang-yu-lu, Ch. 19.

hero as Kuan-chung or Yo-yi. His days were spent in toiling on the farm, making and singing songs, and acquiring knowledge. He became known as a young man of great genius and extraordinary abilities, but was apparently not generally liked by his neighbours. One friend, however, was very fond of him, joined in his studies, and shared his opinions. This was Hsü Shu (徐 庶), the wise but ill-fated friend of of Liu Pei.

K'ung-ming had been leading this poor and simple life for some time, and had attained the age of 26 years, when the event occurred which began his fame. Liu Pei was now engaged in his long, hard struggle for the throne of his ancestors. His camp was at this time, A.D. 207, at Hsin-ye (新 野) on the borders of Hupei and Honan. One day Hsü Shu said to him—"Chu-Ko K'ung-ming is a couched dragon, why do you not go and see him?" Liu Pei had to go to this dragon's home three times before he was favoured with an interview. He at length induced K'ung-ming to join his fortunes, and the young recluse left his quiet, studious life for the bustle and tumult of unceasing warfare, and the worry of political intrigue.

He became to Liu Pei his bosom-friend and right-hand man—the very element of his existence. Kuan Yü and Chang Fei, the sworn brothers of Liu Pei, who had fought his battles and shared his fortunes for many years, were at first angry at the favour and influence which the country student quickly acquired. But soft words and long success turned away their wrath.

Liu Pei gained the Throne, but the Empire was divided and there was no peace in the land. It was the time famous as that of the Three Kingdoms, and the fair provinces of the Han and the Yangtzŭ were desolated by years of civil warfare. K'ung-ming continued to serve Liu Pei after the latter had become king. He moulded his sovereign's decrees, marshalled his armies, and led them to battle and victory. Liu Pei was succeeded by his wretched son and K'ung-ming remained faithful to his cause. He had now led the mixed, anxious life of State Counsellor and Field Marshal for many years. His name was feared by his enemies and regarded with awe and affection by his friends. In the opposing army of Wei was Ssŭ-ma Yi (司 馬 懿), a

worthy enemy, of skill and genius scarcely inferior to K'ung-ming.
It was when waiting impatiently for an engagement with this General
that K'ung-ming was seized with his last sickness. The gods would
not prolong his life and he died in A.D. 234. Before his death a star
was seen to fall from heaven into his camp, the testimony of nature
to the passing away of a great soul.

Of K'ung-ming's private life very little is recorded. He had a
wife who bore him one son. This wife's name was Huang, and she
was a plain and homely creature in appearance. She was very clever
however, and the rapidity with which she made bread was astonishing.
K'ung-ming found that she was skilled in magical arts and had small
wooden men to do her work. So he learned from her the way of
making these creatures, and thence proceeded to construct his famous,
" wooden oxen and self-moving horses. "

No man in all Chinese history is so thoroughly known among the
people and so generally a favourite as Chu-ko Liang. The San-kuo-
chi which tells of his " coming," his wise counsels, cunning stratagems
and brilliant victories is one of the most popular books in China.
Episodes from it are acted every day on the Stage. One cannot go
into a theatre, wherever a thousand Chinese are gathered together,
without seeing a drama performed in which K'ung-ming is the
principal character. You know him by his dress and appearance—the
sallow face and thin beard, the black robe of a Taoist alchemist with
the mystic Pa-kua wrought in gold on the back, the feather fan with
the Fêng-shui compass in its heart, and the old-fashioned cap. To
the many he is at once a cunning statesman, a great general, a prophet,
and a magician, and they never weary of hearing stories about his
stratagems and miracles.

But K'ung-ming has his place in the Temple of Confucius for
other reasons. He is here because at the call of duty he left the
study of ancient virtue in his cottage to practise it in every-day life—
because he came forth in a time of anarchy and lawlessness to give up
all his powers and energies for the fallen dynasty to which the empire
belonged by ancient right. It is acknowledged that there are stains
on his character and blemishes in his career, but the brightness of his

glory has largely dazzled them out of sight. He had the heart of a
Royal Minister of State, says one author, though his good principles
were not fully carried out. Even in early life when he used to sit
during the long evenings in his reed-hut, nursing his knee and making
whistling noises, he was already looking out into the future and
planning what was afterwards to be put into execution. His natural
genius is owned on all sides to have been remarkable, and his moral
courage and political fidelity were exemplary. Such as I-yin had been
to T'ai-chia and such as Chou-kung had been to Ch'êng Wang in old
times, such was Chu-ko Liang to Liu Shan, the heir and successor of
Liu Pei. It is remakable that up to the present time many of the
inhabitants of Ssŭchuan wear on their heads emblems of mourning of
Chu-ko Liang, and they speak of themselves as having turbans of
"heavenly mourning." The Burmese also worship the conqueror of
their ancestors. As a philosopher also K'ung-ming has some reputation
and he is tolerably well known as an author. He wrote a treatise,
illustrated by diagrams, on the Pa-ch'ên (八 陣), that is, the system
of marshalling in divisions, each consisting of eight companies or bat-
tallions arranged round or guarding a central point. This system,
founded on the mystic distributions of the Pa-kua, is of very ancient
origin, but it is supposed to have been first perfectly taught and turned
to practical account by K'ung-ming. It is said that in order to have
it carried out properly a very large force is required, but a small army
using it is supposed to have over a large army not using it an advantage
like that which science gives to one boxer over mere strength in
another. A small treatise in forty-six sections and having the name
Hsin-shu (心 書), or Book of the Heart, has also been commonly
attributed to K'ung-ming, but it does not appear on what authority.
The Book of the Heart is a very interesting little work, treating of
the character and duties of a good general, the faults and vices of a
bad one, and of the relations which should exist between officers and
soldiers and between the general commanding and his ruler. These
two treatises along with a small selection of letters, official documents,
and other papers of K'ung-ming have lately been collected and
published under the editorship of Chang Poh-han. The title of this

compilation is *Chu-ko-wu-hou-wên-chi* (諸葛武侯文集), and it
contains besides a Life of K'ung-ming with notices of his posthumous
fortunes and judgments passed on his conduct and character. It is a
useful and unpretending little treatise.

K'ung-ming was posthumously created Chung-wu-hou (忠武侯),
or the Loyal Military Marquis, and he is often designated simply Chu-
ko-wu-hou. He was admitted to the Temple of Confucius in 1724,
but he had been worshipped for many centuries before throughout the
Provinces in separate temples.*

14. Fan Ning (范甯) S. Wu-tzŭ (武子).

Fan Ning, a scholar and official of the East Chin dynasty, was
born A.D. 339 at Shun-yang-Hsien (順陽縣) in Nan-yang, a Prefecture
of the present Honan. In youth he was fond of study and he gained
a comprehensive knowledge of the old classical literature. The terror
which surrounded a great minister of this time known as the Ssŭ-ma
Wên (司馬溫) deterred Fan Ning from going into office. But after
the death of Wên and when more than thirty gears of age, he sought
employment and became magistrate of Yü-K'ang (餘杭), a town in
the modern Prefecture of Hang-chow (Chekiang). In this office, which
he held for six years, he was popular and successful and distinguished
himself specially by his efforts to improve the state of learning and
encourage education. Afterwards he was at the Capital and in high
office. But he tried to recall his sovereign to duty and honour and
induce him to dismiss his profligate Prime Minister. This last
succeeded in making the Emperor send Fan Ning away as Prefect of
Yü-ch'ang (豫章), the present Nan-chang-foo in Kiangsi. On the
eve of setting out Fan addressed a short but very pithy Memorial to
the Thone on the dreadful state, moral and physical, of the empire.
In this office also he was a patron of learning, but he was not very
fortunate and was accused to the Throne. He soon after retired from
office and returned to his old studies. He died in 401.

* For Chu-ko Liang's Life see Mayers Ch. R. M. p. 28; Stent in China Rev. Vol. V.
p. 211, &c.; Chu-ko-wu-hou-wên-chi.; San-kuo-chi; Chu-tzŭ-ch'uan-shu, Ch. 61.

Fan Ning was all through his life a diligent student and an enthusiastic teacher of old Confucianism. He wrote fiercely against Wang Pi (王弼), the young philosopher of the preceding century who struck out a new system of divination for the Yih, and against Ho Yen (何晏) of infamous memory in the History of the Three Kingdoms. Their guilt, he said, was greater than that of Chie and Chow (桀 紂) of the old dynasties. It is acknowledged that he was unjust and intolerant in his criticism of these two men. Fan Ning was opposed to magic and divination and all the vain heresies of his time. Like Kao-t'ang and Ch'êng K'ang-ch'eng he injured his eyes by too much reading, and he was cured by following the simple prescription which they had followed. The chief elements of this were to read little, go to bed early and rise early.

The work by which Fan Ning is known to posterity and which mainly gives him a place in this temple is his work on Ku-liang's Ch'un-ch'iu and commentary. The title of this treatise is Ch'un-ch'iu-Ku-liang-chuan-chi-chie (春 秋 穀 梁 傳 集 解), and as annotated by Yang Shi-hsün (楊 士 勛) of the T'ang dynasty it is still the accepted edition of Ku-liang's text and commentary. In the composition of his work Fan was assisted by his friends and disciples, and it was with him a labour of love and duty. He spent many years on it, and though critics have found fault with his quotations and illustrations, it has nevertheless always been held in esteem.

Fan Ning was admitted to the Confucian Temple as an Associate in A.D. 647. He also was reduced in the next reign to the rank of "Scholar." In 1530 his tablet was taken away from the Temple, but it was replaced in 1724.*

---

* See Ku-liang's Ch'un-ch'iu (as before) Vol I. Introduction.; T'ung-chien &c. Ch. 22; Chin-shu, Ch. 75, referred to by Legge Ch. Cl. V Proleg. p. 37.

15. Wang T'ung (王 通). S. Chung-yen (仲 淹).

Wang T'ung was born at Lung-mén (龍 門) now Ho-tsin in Shansi, in the year A.D. 584, being the fourth year of the reign of Sui Wen Ti. While he was an infant a soothsayer predicted that he would "penetrate the mind of all the world," and to help in the bringing about of this destiny his father named him *T'ung*, that is, pentrating. He became a precocious boy, devotedly fond of learning, and full of vanity and self-esteem. His father attended carefully to his education, and he had the best masters to teach him the canonical writings and other learning of the time. So given up to study was he at this period that he did not change his clothes for six years.

He had to put on clean clothes however, at the end of that time, for in 603 at the ripe age of nineteen years he resolved to try for office. Accordingly he prepared an exposition of his politics which he entitled T'ai-p'ing-shĭ-êr-ts'ê (太 平 十 二 策), that is, National peace in Twelve Essays. This he took with him to Ch'ang-an, the Capital, and presented it to the Emperor. It glorified the mild rule of example and principle, and denounced the stern government of force and cunning. But he had brought his jewel to the market, and had not waited for the coming of a purchaser. So his Memorial was cast aside.

The Imperial Court was a bad place—a scene of plotting and intrigue, and T'ung left it in disgust. A parricide mounted the throne, and the Capital, he saw, was not a fit place for a scholar who loved virtue and order. So he went back to his home between the rivers and made study and teaching the business of his life. His fame spread, and soon disciples from far and near crowded to hear him teach philosophy and expound the Classics. A friend in power wished him to take office but he declined. His father's hut, he said, sufficed to shelter him, his reedy fields procured him food, and study and conversation gave him all the pleasure he wanted. Several tempting offers were made to him afterwards, but he remained firm in his resolve to keep to literature and philosophy.

One night in the year 618 Yen Hui appeared to T'ung in a dream and said Confucius had sent him to say to T'ung—" Come home to your rest." This he knew was a sign to tell him of his coming death, and so it befell. A severe sickness came upon him, and he died on the seventh day from the night of his dream, aged thirty three years.

But in that short life time how much work was done ! For T'ung was not only the teacher of " more than a thousand" disciples; he was also a great writer. His works comprised Discourses on the Li, Supplements to the Shu and Shi, an amended edition of the Yuan-ching, and other treatises. These are all lost, though for a time they were universally admired. T'ung thought that the period of the Han dynasty compared not unfavourably with that of Yao and Shun, and he regarded himself as a new Confucius. His work on the Classics was compared with that of Confucius on them, and T'ung's editions were called the Wang-shï-liu-ching (王氏六經), that is, the Wangs' Six Classics. His Chung-Shuo (中說) he thought corresponded to the Lun-yü. T'ung did not see that though he might be compared to Confucius, yet he was to the Sage as an ounce to a pound, to use the homely Chinese figure.

Wang T'ung is in Confucius' Temple because he would not serve a bad ruler, but chose rather to live poor, studying and teaching the ways of good government and unchanging virtue. The rulers of the Sui dynasty were governing by laws, and punishments, and all kinds of force, and were trying to do away with the principles and teachings of Confucian philosophy. But T'ung by his writings and teaching gave these renewed life and vigour.

His disciples gave T'ung the posthumous title Wên-chung-tzŭ (文中子), and this is a common designation for him in books. His tablet was admitted to the Temple in 1530.*

* See T'ung-chien &c. Ch. 36 (Sui Wên Ti 3rd year) ; Hsing-li-hui-yao (性理彙要) Ch. 17 ; Shang-yu-lu, Ch. 9.

16. Luh Chih (陸 贄). S. Ching-yü (敬 輿).

Luh Chih was born in A.D. 754, the thirteenth year of the reign of T'ang Yuan (or Hsüan) Tsung, at Chia-hsing (嘉 興), a town in the Prefecture of Soochow. In the 18th year of his age he obtained the Chin-shī degree, and soon afterwards received an official appointment. On the accession of Tó Tsung in 780 Luh Chih came into favour with the Emperor and had rapid promotion. He was made a high officer of the Han-lin, attached to the household of the Heir apparent, and otherwise honoured. The Emperor was very fond of him and called him familiarly by his number in the family Luh Nine. In 791 he was made Vice-President of the Board of War, but released from his duties in the Palace.

This was the turn in the tide of Luh's fortune. He had rebuked the sovereign's vices and failings too plainly and freely. The Emperor had fallen from his early virtue and had become the weak slave of eunuchs and parasites. So he could not endure the stern chidings of his faithful Minister. In 795 he deprived him of his office in the Prince's household. A wicked minister named P'ei Yen-ling (裴 延 齡), who had been denounced by Luh but who was now a special favourite with the Emperor, saw the change in the sovereign's feelings, and accused Luh and others of arrogance and turbulence. The Emperor's rage now burst out against Luh and he wished to behead him, but at length contented himself with banishing him to Chung-chow (忠 州), in Ssüchuan as a subordinate Magistrate. In his exile Luh devoted himself chiefly to the study of medicine and compiled a work on the subject which was for a time in general circulation. But he did not write on topics connected with his life and opinions as he wished to let anger and malice die away from lack of fuel. Ten years he spent in this life of banishment as no prayers could prevail on Tó Tsung to order his recall. At last that wretched Emperor died in 805, and was succeeded by his son, Shun Tsung. One of the first acts of this weakling was to issue a decree recalling

Luh Chih to the Capital. But it was too late, for Luh had died before the decree reached his place of exile.

The Memorials which Luh Chih presented to Tĕ Tsung are still extant. They show a rare courage and fidelity in their plain, candid advice and criticism. "His Memorials," says Mayers, "have been handed down to posterity as models of style and intrinsic worth." He had more practical knowledge and a purer style than Chia Yi (賈誼), of the Han dynasty, but he had not Chia's genius nor had he the fierce daring of Chu-ko Liang. Luh's counsels to his sovereign were all founded in humanity and righteousness, and they might be summed up in these—to disperse wealth and gain the people, to keep away worthless men from his Court and put confidence in men of principle.

It is to his banishment that Luh Chih owes his fame, says the historian of the T'ang dynasty. He did not write any treatise on Confucian ethics or politics, and he was not a man of extraordinary learning. But he shed a glory on Confucianism by his life which was simple, pure, and noble. When in office he carried out his principles of duty and heeded not life. He spoke what was in his mind and he spoke it all. When cast aside he did not grieve but waited for his fate, keeping fast hold of duty and honour. Thus he showed himself to be indeed a "heavenly man," or, more literally, a subject of Heaven (天民).

The posthumous title conferred on Luh Chih was Hsüan-kung (宣公), and this is his usual designation in books. His political papers have been several times republished. They formerly bore the title Tsou-yi-han-yuan-chi (奏議翰苑集), or simply Han-yuan-chi. The Chêng-yi-t'ang edition, which is one of the best, is entitled Luh-hsüan-kung-chi (陸宣公集), and is in two small volumes.

The tablet of Luh Chih was admitted to the Confucian Temple in 1826 in the reign of Tao-kuang.[*]

---

[*] T'ang-chien &c. T'ang Tĕ Tsung; Hsin T'ang-Shu, Ch. 157; Hsing-li &c. Ch. 20; Luh-hsüan-kung-chi.; Mayers, Ch. R. M. p. 139.

17. Han Yü (韓愈). S. T‘ui-chĭ (退之).

Han Yü was born in the year A.D. 768 at Têng-chow (登州), a town in the Prefecture of Nan-yang in Honan, but his family belonged to Ch‘ang-li (昌黎), a town in Yung-p‘ing-foo in Chihli. He was the youngest of three sons and he lost both his parents before he was three years old, but only the death of his father who had been in office is recorded.

The little orphan fell to the care of his eldest brother, named Hui (會), and when the latter, having fallen into disgrace, was banished to Kuang-tung he took Yü with him. After a few years Hui died, and his widow went back to Honan. She brought up her brother-in-law with great care and affection, and watched over his education. The child was very fond of learning, and very clever, and he was also a boy of strong and lasting affection.

As he grew to manhood he longed for official employment, and soon after obtaining his Degree he was appointed to a small office. From this he rose gradually—not without checks—to very high posts. The Emperor T‘ang Tê-Tsung in 803 degraded and banished him to Yang-shan (陽山), a town of Lien-chow in Kwang-tung, for his Memorial against the collection of taxes in Chihli that year. Han Yü was a very honest and upright official, of uncompromising orthodoxy at least in theory. He was a thorough lover of the past, and a zealous maintainer of old customs and teachings, of too eager a spirit and too hot a temper.

His famous Fo-ku-piao (佛骨表), or Buddha Bone Memorial, presented to the Throne in 819, led to his banishment in that year to serve as Prefect of Ch‘ao-chow-foo in the East of Kwangtung. In this place he taught the rude natives the great doctrines of the ancient Sages, and drove away the scaly monster which harassed their river. Pity returned to the Emperor and he recalled his faithful servant at length to the Capital and reinstated him in office. But Han Yü had been delicate all his life, and he had grown prematurely old. Soon after his return to his beloved Capital he was attacked by a severe sickness and died in the year 823.

He was posthumously created Wên-kung (文公) and his common designations in literature are Han-wên-kung and Ch'ang-li-Hsien-shêng. He is famous as a Poet, Essayist, and Miscellaneous writer no less than as a Statesman and Scholar of the T'ang dynasty. But he is in the Confucian Temple because he stood out almost alone against the heresy of Buddhism which had nearly quenched the torch of Confucian truth. He defended orthodoxy against the world, as it were, and suffered for its sake. He did to the evil teachings of his days what Mencius had done to those of his time. As a public servant also he followed the spirit of the Sage's instruction, working good among the people, controlling or influencing the supernatural agents, and serving his rulers, even when bad, with all faithfulness.

The prose works of Han-wên-kung comprise his Memorials to the Throne, Philosophical Essays, Letters, Epitaphs, Sacred compositions, and Miscellaneous pieces. These are prized by all the Confucianists for their style and contents, and one author says we should wash our hands in rose-water before reading them. His Poetry has been often reprinted and edited with critical and explanatory notes. It is highly esteemed by native scholars who compare it to a lofty mountain, and say that it cannot be understood without notes. An excellent and useful edition of his collected poems is that entitled *Ch'ang-li-shǐ-chi-chu*, which gives the notes of Ho Yi-mên (何義門) and Chu Yi-tsun (朱彝尊) two great scholars of the present dynasty, and also supplies much useful information about the author and his times.

Han-wên-kung was admitted to the Temple of Confucius in the year 1084. He is worshipped also in the temple of Mencius.*

* A good and pleasantly written life of Han Yü by Dr. Chalmers is in Nos. 5 and 6 of the China Review Vol. I.; See also Chang-li-shǐ-chi-chu (昌黎詩集注); Legge Ch. Cl. II Pro. p. 92; Hsin T'ang-shu, Ch. 176.; Ch'ang-li-ch'nan-chi (昌黎全集).

18. Fan Chung-yen (范 仲 淹) S. Hsi-wên (希 文).

Fan Chung-yen came of an illustrious family which had formerly been settled at Pin-chow (邠 州) in Shensi, but had lately removed to the town of Wu (吳) in the Prefecture of Soochow. Here Chung-yen was born in the year A.D. 989, in the reign of Sung T'ai Tsung. When only two years old he lost his father, and soon afterwards his mother married a man named Chu (朱), and her son followed the surname of his stepfather. When he came to years of understanding he left his mother's house and went to live near Ying-t'ien (應 天) in Honan where he had some relatives. Here he gave himself up to study with unremitting zeal and devotion, though he had to work hard for a living. His favourite books were the old Classics and among these specially the Yih Ching, but he was also diligent in acquiring useful practical knowledge. For some time he was lodged by a Buddhist monk, but he had to bear great hardships.

In course of time, however, he obtained his Degree, and soon afterwards received a small official appointment. He now ceased to use the surname of his stepfather and returned to that of his father's family, changing his name at the same time. About this time his mother became again a widow and he took her to his home and nursed her all the rest of her days with loving devotion. On her death he observed the full period of mourning with all strictness and sincerity.

After this was over he returned to office and soon made himself conspicuous by his outspoken censures on the usurpation and extravagance of the Empress Dowager. Still the Emperor Jên Tsung, whose reign began in 1023, recognized in Fan Chung-yen a loyal servant, and advanced him to high places in the public service. But this sovereign was a weak man without any settled convictions, and he soon yielded to the solicitations of unprincipled advisers who sought Chung-yen's destruction. The latter was at length by the influence of one of these men degraded and sent away to Jao-chow (饒 州) in Kiangsi.

But Chung-yen was too good and too useful an official to be kept

long in the shade.   He was again promoted and entrusted with high
and important powers.   When the hordes of Kiang Tartars invaded
and devastated the eastern part of the Empire he was sent with a
force to drive them away.   He organized skilful measures of repression
and when they were successful he framed regulations, and drew up a
Treaty for the maintenance of order and peace between the Kiang
and the Chinese.   He had a long and distinguished career.   Skilful
in war and wise in council, fearless alike in word and action, he
fought against invasion from without and heresy and corruption within.
But his success against Buddhism was not great or encouraging, and
he was on one occasion reduced to silence in a discussion on Faith.
He would not believe in the miracles and other supernatural elements
of Buddhism because he could not see them.   Yet you believe, was
the crushing rejoinder, in the doctor's inferences from your pulse,
though you cannot *see* its dulness or its feverishness.

Chung-yen was still in active service in the year 1052 when an
attack of sickness proved fatal.   His death was greatly lamented by
all who had known or heard of him.   The Emperor sorrowed for him,
his fellow countrymen, for whom he had always wrought, wept for him,
and the rude Tartar hordes sent a large company to wail at his tomb.

The Emperor wrote an epitaph for the servant who had been so
true and devoted to him during life, but the best eulogy of Chung-yen is
in the plain record of history.   He was always firm of will but gentle in
manner.   So pious was he to his mother's memory that because she had
been poor he never through all his life indulged himself or his family
in any luxury.   He was kind and generous first to those of his own
household, and then to all with whom he came in contact.   Ever loyal
to his sovereign he was also faithful to the best interests of his country.

The sons of Chung-yen all grew up to honour, being the heirs of
their father's virtues.   He was posthumously rewarded with the
epithet Wên-chêng (文 正), and in the year 1715, he was admitted
to the worship of the Confucian Temple.   Even during his lifetime his
picture had been adored by the Chinese and Tartars who had come
under his just and gentle rule. *

* Mayers Ch. R. M. p. 38; Shang-yu-lu, Ch. 17.; Sung-shï, Ch. 311.

19. Hu Yuan (胡瑗). S. Yi-chih (翼之).

Hu Yuan was born in the year A.D. 993 at Hai-ling (海陵), in T'ai-chow (泰州), a town in what is now ,the Prefecture of Yang-chow in Kiangsu. Nothing is recorded of his family or his early years. In youth he went into seclusion at T'ai-shan, and gave himself up to study, leading the life of a poor anchorite of learning for ten years. Afterwards he became a teacher, and had many disciples whom he instructed in the ancient Classics and general literature. He tried several times to pass the examinations which qualified for office but always failed. At length, when he was more than forty years of age, he was brought to the notice of the Emperor Jên Tsung by Fan Chung-yen, who recommended him to the Emperor as a skilled musician. It was in this capacity that Yuan was first employed, but he was soon after sent to serve with Fan Chung-yen on the Eastern Border. This kind of work was not congenial to him and he resigned. Then he was appointed "Director of Studies" at Hoo-chow (湖州), in Chêkiang, and in this capacity he had remarkable success. The disciples who flocked from all quarters to receive his instructions were very numerous. These were all classed according to their courses of study. Some liked philosophy, some liked military tactics or the theory of war, some chose literature, and some the duties of practical life. The master in all cases directed his efforts to the development of the special tastes and talents of his scholars.

About the year 1045 Hu Yuan was appointed to the Imperial Academy and a like success followed him there. He had more disciples than the Hall would hold and he had to hire a neighbouring building. His teaching was much helped by his own good example, and his scholars were known by their orderly deportment and their superior manners. They loved and trusted their Master as a father or an elder brother, and he treated them as sons or younger brothers. He was very strict and precise with them, but he made out of them good men and useful officials. Among his disciples was a son of his early friend Fan Chung-yen.

The Emperor heaped honours on Yuan and wished to keep him at the Capital. But Yuan refused nearly all the honours, as his delight was to be among his books and disciples. About 1056 the Emperor made him " Doctor of the Court of Sacrificial Worship, " but Yuan was obliged to resign. He was now oppressed by age and sickness, and he obtained leave to go back to his home. The officials of the Court and his disciples gave him a farewell banquet, when he was setting off on his homeward journey. He reached his native place, but his ill health continued, and he died in 1059.

Hu Yuan knew the laws of ancient music and he was skilled in the art of casting bells, but his great fame was as a Classical Scholar, and a successful teacher. He was dignified and precise, but true and modest. The Emperor whom he served knew something of his worth, but could not gain his esteem and confidence.

The literary designation given to Hu Yuan after his death was An-ting-Hsien-shêng (安定先生), that is, the An-ting Teacher. This is perhaps his best known name among native Scholars. An-ting is a town of Pao-ning-foo in Ssŭchuan, where Yuan's learning became known and influential, and where he had served in the beginning of his official career. His tablet was admitted to the Temple of Confucius during the time of the Ming dynasty in the year 1530. *

20. Han Ch'i (韓琦). S. Ch'i-kuei (稚圭).

Han Ch'i was born in the year 1008 at An-yang (安陽), a town in the North of the present Honan. He grew up a clever but delicate boy, and was educated by his father. At twenty years of age he obtained his Degree of Chin-shĭ, and as the fact was announced a five-coloured cloud was seen below the sun. Soon after he was appointed to serve with Fan Chung-yen in subduing the enemies on the Eastern confines, and in reducing to order the districts comprised in the South of the modern Kansuh and Shensi. The success of these two was great and their reputation spread rapidly. They were

---

* See Hsing-li-ta-ch'uan (性理大全), Vol. 1. Introduction ; Shang-yu-lu, Ch. 2.; Shung-shĭ, Ch. 432.

constantly joined as the heroes of the Eastern Army who spread fear and terror in the minds of the enemy. They were sung of in ballads and their fame went over all the land making even the Emperor wonder.

Thus early in life did Han Ch'i achieve a reputation. He rose in office, and passed through a variety of positions. He was Prefect of Ting-chow (定 州) in Chihli, and won golden opinions from all for his success in relieving the people during a dreadful famine, and for his exertions to restore the literary examinations and advance the cause of learning generally. He held the office of Minister of State to three Emperors and was ennobled as Wei-kuo-kung (魏 國 公), Duke of Wei.

He is famous for the vigorous opposition he made to the efforts of the Empress Ts'ao to be associated with her consort in the administration of government. He also spoke wholesome but unpleasant words to that feeble creature, the Emperor Ying-Tsung about his duty to his mother, and gave him good counsel about the appointment of a successor to the Throne. But the crowning act of Han Ch'i's life was the forwarding of a Memorial to Shen Tsung, the successor of Ying Tsung, against Wang An-shi's scheme of government advances. This Memorial was presented in 1069 when Han Ch'i was holding a high position in Shensi. It sets forth in bold, clear language, brief and terse, the evils connected with this new system of raising the revenue, and begs that it be at once abolished. The Emperor on reading it said— "Han Ch'i is a true loyal servant, though abroad he does not forget the royal household." The counsels of Wang An-shi prevailed, however, and Han addressed a second Memorial to the Throne on the subject. In this he answered the great Minister's argument for his "new method," drawn from the Chou-li or Ritual of the Chou Dynasty, by boldly asserting that An-shi had tampered with the text of that venerable Classic. But his enemy was too strong, and Han asked to be relieved of his duties. He was accordingly sent in 1070 to Ta-ming-foo in Chihli.

He died in 1075, and on the night of his death a great star fell from heaven into his courtyard and frightened the horses in the stable.

When the Emperor heard the news he went apart and wept bitterly. He conferred on Han the posthumous title Shang-shu or President of a Board, wrote his epitaph, and decreed to him the epithet Chung-hsien (忠獻) which may be translated Loyal and intelligent. The title Wei-wang (魏王), Prince of Wei, was afterwards conferred on Han, but it has not taken the place of the older Wei-kung, and it is by this latter that he is best known in literature.

The political opinions and career of Han Ch'i led to his forming an acquaintance and friendship with several of the most illustrious men of his time. Fan Chung-yen has been already mentioned. Another intimate friend was Ou-yang Hsiu, a man equalled with him in fate and nearly equalled with him in renown. The great author and Statesman Ssŭ-ma Kuang also knew and esteemed him, and Ch'êng Ming-tao declared that Han Ch'i was clothed with righteousness.

He was man of a truly kind and amiable disposition. His face never betrayed any sign of emotion and nothing could ruffle his temper or interfere with his self-control. He bore with like equanimity the burning of his whiskers, the breaking of his exquisite jade cup, and the visit of a midnight murderer. "What have you come to do?," he asked this last as axe in hand the intending assassin came up to the bed on which Han was lying. "I have come to take your head," was the unpleasant rejoinder. "Who sent you?" asked Han, and on receiving the man's reply added—Take my head and go, but the murder was not committed.

As an official Han Ch'i was distinguished by a mild and humane administration of justice to the people, and a fearless, outspoken loyalty to the ruler. He was not an expert or polished writer, but he was an eminently useful public servant. His Memorials and other official writings were collected and published in 1514 by Tsêng Ta-yu (曾大有), a scholar and official of some eminence. A selection has since been made under the editorship of Chang Poh-hang and published with the title Han-Wei-Kung-Chi. This work contains a large number of Han's State papers and extracts from his official correspondence, of considerable interest for the light which they throw on the dark history of the time. It gives also a careful and minute account of his life and opinions which occupies *chüan* 10 to 20 both inclusive. The political writings of Han are still read and admired, not so much for their style as for their matter.

His sons after him walked in his steps and rose to merit and distinction. His tablet was admitted to the Temples of Confucius in 1852.*

---

21. Ou-yang Hsiu (歐 陽 修). S. Yung-shu (永 叔).

The parents of Ou-yang Hsiu belonged to Lu-ling (盧 陵), a town of Ki-an-foo in the Province of Kiangsi, and he was born in the year A.D. 1007. His father was an official of some distinction, but specially noted for his uprightness and filial piety. He had been left an orphan in early childhood, and he himself died when his son Hsiu was only three years of age. He left his boy to the care of his wife who fulfilled her trust with great conscientiousness. Though very poor she remained a faithful widow and devoted herself to the bringing up of her son. She gave him his early education, teaching him to read and write by means of characters traced on the ground with a reed, as she was too poor to pay for other writing materials.

From his early years Hsiu was noted as a boy thoughtful, studious, and quick to learn and understand. While still a youth, meeting accidentally with the writings of Han Wên-kung, he read and studied them with great eagerness and delight. They seem to have stirred up in him a literary ambition, and he aspired, we are told, to attain equality with their author. He passed the examination for the Degree of Chin-shĭ, taking the highest place, and soon after obtained official employment. His mother lived to see her cares and pains rewarded, and her hopes in process of fulfilment, as her son rose to eminence in the public service.

* Han-wei-kung-chi (韓魏公集); Sung-chi, Ch. 312; Mayers Ch. R.M. p. 46.; Hsing-li-hui-yao, Ch. 20.

Hsiu became the stanch friend and warm advocate of Han Ch'i (韓琦), Fan Chung-yen (范仲淹), and other faithful officials. For his spirited defence of Fan against a censor named Kao Jo-no (高若訥) he was sent away to I-ling (夷陵), the present I-chang-foo, in Hupeh. But he was soon promoted again, and rose to be one of the greatest of the great Ministers who surrounded the throne of Sung Jen Tsung. Afterwards he was accused of joining with Fan Chung-yen and others of his party to make a cabal for the monopoly of power. His official career was long and varied, but always marked by fearless integrity. He warned the Emperor Jen Tsung against the danger of dismissing good men from his councils, and of the risk to the Empire of not having a successor designated. He fought against the attempt of the Empress dowager to reign instead of Ying Tsung, and he opposed with all his energies the new measures of Wang An-shih. Seeing he could not prevail against this powerful statesman he implored again and again to be released from office. The Emperor, Shên Tsung, wished to retain his services, but Wang An-shih represented Hsiu as a dangerous man who would ruin the Empire if he were restored to office at the Capital. So the Emperor yielded in 1071 to Hsiu's urgent entreaty, and allowed him to resign with the honorary title of Junior Preceptor to the Heir Apparent. But his life was worn out and he survived only a few months. The historian of Shên Tsung's reign under the year 1072 records his death with due solemnity—" The retired Chancellor of the Kuan-Wên-Tien, Ou-yang Hsiu, deceased."

As an official Hsiu was distinguished for great abilities, wise counsel, and unswerving faithfulness to the Throne and the people. He was abused, defamed, and plotted against through all his career, but he took his trouble gently and preserved his soul in patience. It is not, however, only as a public servant that he has been esteemed and celebrated. In the accomplishments of learning and the practice of virtue, says the historian, he stood above all his generation. His first love was literature, and he was true to it through all his life. In the height of his glory while a Han-lin Chancellor he compiled, with the help of Sung Ch'i and other scholars, the Hsin-T'ang-shu or New

History of the T'ang dynasty. This was presented in 1060 to the Emperor Jen Tsung, having been undertaken by his orders. He compiled also in later years the Hsin-wu-tai-shĭ (新五代史) or New History of the Five dynasties, that is, the dynasties which came between the T'ang and the Sung. "Setting before himself" writes Wylie with respect to this treatise, "the Ch'un-ts'ew and Shĕ-ke as his models, he aimed at the lofty style of those ancient works, but he has laid himself open to the charge of sacrificing narrative of facts to elegance of diction." The Emperor Shĕn Tsung wished to have this work, but his order to seek it out was issued too late to reach the author. The Chi-ku-lu (集古錄) or Collected Old Records, is another work by Hsiu. In this book he has given a large number of old inscriptions and notices from tomb-stones, vases, and tablets with critical and explanatory comments. The Preface which he wrote to it, modestly and simply describes the nature and quality of the work. When in office at Ch'u-chow (滁州), a town on a tributary of the Yangtzŭ in the East of Anhui, he wrote under the *nom de plume* Tsui-wĕng (醉翁) or the Jolly Patriarch. He was in love with the quiet scenery of the place and the quaint simplicity of the people's manners. Memorials of their old Prefect, the Jolly Patriarch are still preserved by the inhabitants of this city. In wiser years he called himself Liu-yi-chü-shĭ (六一居士), the student 61 years old, and wrote under this title. He is known as Lu-ling-Hsien-shĕng (盧陵先生), the Teacher from Lu-ling, his native place.

All the writings of Ou-yang Hsiu have the charm of an easy graceful style, and clear precise language. He is learned, but he wears his weight of learning "lightly like a flower"; didactic, but he does his teaching gently and persuasively. His contemporary and friend, the poet Su Tung-p'o writes of him thus—"He discoursed on philosophy like Han Yü, on public affairs like Luh Chih, he wrote history like Ssŭ-ma Ch'ien, and he made poetry like Li Pai. These are not my words, but the words of all the world." This praise is excessive, and requires to be modified by the strictures of Yang Shĭ and Chu Hsi. The latter especially while admitting the genius of Ou-yang is severe on the faults of his life and philosophy. He did not believe in the "River Plan and Lo writing."

A posthumous title was conferred on Ou-yang Hsiu, and he was honoured with the epithet Wên-chung (文 忠), accomplished and loyal. Hence some collections of his miscellaneous writings have been published with the title Wên-chung-chi (文 忠 集). He was admitted to the Confucian Temple in 1235, but his tablet was afterwards removed. He was re-admitted, however, in the year 1530.*

---

22. Ssǔ-ma Kuang (司 馬 光) S. Chün-shih (君 實).

Ssǔ-ma Kuang was the second son of Ssǔ-ma Chǐ (池), an official of some distinction during the early part of the Sung dynasty. Kuang was born in A.D. 1019 at Hsia (夏) a town of Ho-nan-foo, on the borders of Shensi. The first instruction he received was from his father and elder brother who, he tells us, taught him to learn books by rote when he was only four or five years of age. Even as a boy he was distinguished by the gravity of manner and presence of mind which he kept through life. A story of these early years has been often told. One of his little play-fellows fell into a vessel filled with water and Kuang saved his life by breaking the vessel with a stone. An artist made the incident the subject of a picture at the time, and the four words which describe it are often given as a theme at the literary examinations. He was noted for his love of reading and desire for learning, and he is said to have been specially delighted with the Ch'un-ch'iu of Confucius when it was brought to him in the nursery.

In 1038 he was successful at the Chin-shi examination, and soon afterwards while still a very young man he entered the public service. His promotion was quick, and he soon distinguished himself by his wise and faithful counsels. Thus he rebuked the courtiers for congratulating the Emperor that an eclipse of the Sun was not visible at

---

* See Wylie, Notes &c. p. 13, 17. 18, 61 &c.; Sung-shǐ, Ch. 319; T'ung-chien &c. (Supplement.) Sung Reigns of Jen, Ying, and Shǎn.; Mayers Ch. R. M. p. 165; Hsing-li-hui-yao, Ch. 17.

the Capital. He also urged Jen Tsung to nominate his successor, opposed the attempts to set a side Ying Tsung, and when Shên Tsung ascended the Throne he presented a Memorial of seasonable advice. He was made a Chancellor of the Han-lin and a Minister of State. But he was an uncompromising opponent of Wang An-shi and all his measures, and so could not continue in service. When in the year 1070 the Emperor would not accept An-shi's resignation, Kuang refused the post of Chu-mi-fu-shi (樞 密 副 使) or Assistant Director of the War office. He declined to remain at the Capital in any position and was allowed to retire to Lo Yang with the title of Censor. But unable to have his way with the Emperor and unwilling to serve with men whose measures he condemned, he fixed his residence at this city as a private individual and forbore to interfere in State affairs.

In 1064 Kuang had compiled a History of China, during the period of the warring States and the Ch'in dynasty. This was presented to the Emperor Ying Tsung who was much pleased with it and ordered the author to continue his work. So Kuang applied himself to the composition of his general history of the Empire. Shên Tsung did all in his power to forward the work. The Imperial Library and the national archives were put at the author's disposal. Money and writing materials were supplied from the Emperor's store, and several scholars were appointed as fellow-workers. For nineteen years, including the long time that he was living in retirement at Lo-yang, Kuang devoted himself to the completion of his great work. At length it was finished, the title Tzŭ-chǐ-t'ung-chien, was given to it, and in 1084 it was presented to the Emperor. This History with the supplementary volumes comprised 354 chüan, and extended from B.C. 403 to the period immediately preceding the rise of the Sung dynasty.

By the people of Lo-yang, Kuang was regarded with great affection and respect. The women and children spoke of him by his name Chün-shi, and the peasants and rural patriarchs called him Ssŭ-ma-hsiang-kung (司 馬 相 公), or Mr. Minister Ssŭ-ma. In 1085 Shên Tsung died and his mother became Regent during the nonage of her grand-son, Chê Tsung. Kuang, urged by his own feel-

ings and the advice of Ch'êng Hao now resolved to go back to the
Court at K'ai-fêng-foo. His journey was one long ovation. The
people thronged the streets to see him pass and he could scarcely
proceed. At the Capital they beat their heads with joy and called
out one to another—the Minister Ssŭ-ma has come. "Go back no
more to Lo-yang," they cried, "but stay here to help the sovereign
and save the people." The Empress Regent took him into favour and
reinstated him in office. He applied himself at once to bringing about
the restoration of old institutions. But a fatal sickness attacked him
and he was laid on his bed. He lived, however, to learn that Wang
An-shi's most mischievous innovations were repealed, and so he felt
that he could sleep quietly in his grave. His last thoughts and
anxieties were about his country, but death came on him gently and
he was conscious of its approach. He died in 1086, and the inhabitants of town and country, wherever he was known, mourned for him
sadly. His coffin was treated with sacrificial reverence and some
had his likeness painted in order to do it worship. The posthumous
title given to Ssŭ-ma Kuang was T'ai-shi-wên-kuo-kung (太 師 溫
國 公), the Grand Preceptor, Duke of the State Wên, this being the
name of a district in Honan. The literary epithet added to his name
was Wên-chêng (文 正), accomplished and upright. His enemies rose
to power again and wreaked their vengeance on the dead. Kuang's
title and epithet were cancelled, his tomb levelled, and all indignity
heaped on his name. But their success was brief, and in 1129 his
honours were restored to Kuang, and he was joined with the Emperor
Chê Tsung in the worship offered to the latter. His tablet was admitted to the Temple of Confucius in 1267.

Beside his great History, Ssŭ-ma Kuang composed also the Chi-
ku-lu (稽 古 錄) or Record of Investigations into antiquity, which
goes back to very ancient times. He wrote also two valuable treatises
on subjects connected with etymology, and his miscellanies, or Wên-chi,
formed 80 *chüan* when collected and published. His usual designation in literature is Ssŭ-ma Wên-kung, but he is also often spoken of
of as So-shui-hsien-shêng (涑 水 先 生), the Teacher from So, the
name of a tributary of the Yellow River near his native place.

The character of Ssŭ-ma Kuang is singularly beautiful. He had no taint of meanness or selfishness in all his constitution. His elder brother had throughout life to take care of him as an infant, though he reverenced him as a father. His great delight was in study, and books were to him as pearls and gems are to others. Some regarded his writings as too speculative or ideal, and he accepted the term, saying that he wrote as he thought and felt. In his official capacity he was always dignified and upright, and in all things he showed a "public-spirited courage." The good of the people was ever before him whether he wrote history and branded heresy, or opposed invading hordes of Tartars, or denounced the unscrupulous innovation of ambitious statesmen.*

23. Yang Shi (楊 時). S. Chung-li (中 立).

Yang Shi was born in the year A.D. 1053 near Chiang-lo (將樂), a town in the Prefecture of Yenping in Fuhkeen. His ancestors had been settled there for a long time, and they had all been farmers. But Shi's father, a fond indulgent parent, resolved to make his son a scholar. In boyhood Shi was noted as unusually clever, and he grew up to be a man of a proud, independent nature, above all the meanness and trickeries of his time. He was very pious to his parents, and when his mother died, though he was at the time only a child, he mourned for her like a full-grown man. The dutiful services of a son were continued, moreover, to his stepmother.

He obtained his Chin-shi Degree about 1070, but declined the official employment which was soon after offered. The love of learning constrained him, and drawn by the fame of Ch'êng Hao (Ming-tao), he went to Ying-chow in Anhui where Ch'êng was serving, in order to become his disciple. A mutual attachment sprang up between master and scholar, and when the latter was leaving on his return home, Ming-tao said prophetically—"my teachings are going South." He afterwards became a disciple of Ming-tao's brother Yi-ch'uan.

---

* See Mayers Ch. R. M. p. 199 ; Wylie, Notes &c. p. 20, 8, 9. ; Remusat, Mel. As. T. 2. p. 149, Shang-yu-lu ; Ch. 21 ; Wên-kung-wên-chi (溫 公 文 集) Vol I. ; Tung-chien &c. Sung (Reigns of Jen, Ying, and Shên).

It was not until more than ten years had passed since Yang obtained his Chin-shi that he accepted office. He served for some time as Magistrate or Sub-Prefect in various places, and was subsequently transferred to Ching-chow in Hupeh as Director of Studies. But in the arts by which men rose to power he was to seek, and he felt more comfortable and independent in a humble position. His love was all for learning and his delight was to study and teach. So he came to have a school of many hundreds of disciples who flocked to him from far and near drawn by the fame of his learning. He refused several good appointments and always wanted to be free from public life.

The great Wang An-shi died in 1086, and his tablet was admitted to the Confucian Temple. But Yang Shi, who had opposed Wang in life, wrote such a vigorous protest that the tablet had to be removed. He refuted Wang's interpretations of the Classics, and helped largely in the complete overthrow of all the innovations of that once all-powerful Minister. These services are regarded as perhaps his greatest merit.

In his public capacity Yang counselled reform in the army, and unconditional opposition to the invading Kin Tartars. He consequently protested strongly against the Treaty of peace and the dismemberment of the Empire which took place in 1126. Notwithstanding the enmity of Wang An-shi's followers, he lived to fill several high offices. But the country seemed to him to be in a critical state, and as his counsels could not prevail he retired from office. He died in 1135, and though eighty two years old at the time, he had not lost his mental powers or his bodily vigour.

Yang Shi is said to have been of a quiet, amiable disposition but silent and reserved. Though endowed with uncommon natural abilities he did not care to shine in society or to win a passing glory among his contemporaries. Serving officially in a time of impurity he kept himself pure, taking no stain or dye from the coloured element in which he lived. His philosophical reputation is great, and he is regarded as the Father of the Fuhkeen School, having been the first to introduce into that Province the doctrines of Chow and the Brothers Ch'êng. Chu Hsi also was largely indebted to him for his acquaintance with the teachings of these philosophers. Yang expounded Mencius, the Chung-yung, and the Great Learning to his enthusiastic disciples in Fuhkeen, and made the study of the ancient Classics popular. He ran the risk, however, of bordering on heresy when he taught that *Jen* and *Yi* "Benevolence and Righteousness," did not exhaust man's moral nature. It seemed as though he would supplement the doctrines of Mencius by those of Lao-tzŭ and Chuang-tzŭ. So he is accused of having carried his notion of independence into the domain of philosophy, and of having in fact thought for himself.

Yang Shi was not an author, but his Memorials, Letters, and other short papers have been collected and published together with the notes of his teachings preserved by some of his disciples. The designation by which he is best known is Kuei-shan (龜 山), from the Shi-kuei-shan, a mountain in his native neighbourhood.

His posthumous literary title is Wên-ching (文 靖), or Wên-Suh (肅) according to one authority, that is, accomplished and self-possessed. In 1495 he was admitted to the honours of Confucius' Temple.[*]

---

24. Hsie Liang-tso (謝 良 佐), S. Hsien-tao (顯 道).

Of Hsie Liang-tso's life little is known, and neither of his birth nor death is date or place recorded. He is said to have been a native of Shang-ts'ai (上 蔡), in the Ju-ning Prefecture, Honan (though some authorities make this place to have been in Anhui), and he is generally known as Hsie of Shang-ts'ai. He was contemporary with Yang Shi, and these two, with Yu Tso and Lü Ta-lin, were known among the disciples of the Brothers Ch'êng as the Four Teachers.

Liang-tso early gave himself up to study, and attended the teachings of Ming-tao when the latter was in office at Fou-kow in the East of Honan. He was not quick or brilliant, but he was industrious and only too eager to store his mind with knowledge. Ming-tao warned him against the danger of trying to remember too much, and this put Liang-tso in a dreadful state of mind. Afterwards when he saw

---

* See Yang-kuei-shan-chi (楊 龜 山 集), Chs. 1, 6. &c.; Chu-tzŭ-chüan-shu, Ch. 54; Hsing-li-hui-yao, Ch. 12.; Tao-nan-yuan-wei (道 南 源 委). Ch. 1.

Ming-tao run over the columns of a History without making a mistake he left in a state of discontent. Then he became a disciple of Yi-ch'uan who seems to have had a high opinion of Liang-tso's character and abilities. It is said that once when he came back after a year's absence, Yi-ch'uan asked him what he had learned during that time. "Only to put away self-glory" replied Liang-tso, and then explained that this had been his besetting sin.

In 1085, moved by a rebuke from Yi-ch'uan, he tried for and obtained his Chin-shi, and soon afterwards was appointed to office at Ying-ch'êng (應 城), in the North of Hupeh. From this he was called to Court in 1110, but disgusted with its insincerity he withdrew and asked for the charge of a small provincial office. After some time he was sent to Lo-yang in charge of a government store, and while there he was, on a flying rumour, degraded and put in prison. The rest of his life remains untold.

Hsie wrote a work entitled Lun-yü-shuo (論 語 說), Remarks on the Lun-yü. This is said to have been popular for some time, but it has long been known only by name. Many years after Hsie's death, Chu Hsi, who had learned to admire him very much, took great pains in collecting all the extant fragments of his oral criticisms and teachings. These he arranged in a certain order and published with an explanatory Preface. This small book in three *chüan* has been often reprinted, and the edition published under the supervision of Chang Poh-hang, and entitled Shang-ts'ai-yü-lu contains nearly all that is known of Liang-tso's life and teachings.

As one of the editors of this work says, Hsie Liang-tso was an unlucky man. But he would not so have spoken of himself, for he believed in Fate or Providence, and held that all events are foreordained. He was a man of wide and very accurate knowledge, and his memory of history was remarkable. But he was unfortunate in life, and, to some extent, in reputation, for he was said to be tainted with heresy. One man saw in him traces of Lao-tzŭ's teachings, another found stains of Buddhism. But critics of more liberal minds regarded him as a pure Confucianist, and a thorough adherent of orthodoxy as taught by the Ch'êng Brothers. The Yü-lu shows that

Hsie had studied Buddhism well, and that he could point out wherein
it differed from Confucianism even in doctrines which seemed to be
common to the two systems. He pointed out errors in Buddhist
philosophy, helped to make the true teachings of the ancient Sages
known and understood, and suffered martyrdom in the days of evil
government. These are his great merits, and it was on account of
these that he was in 1850 admitted to participate in the worship
offered in the Temple of Confucius. *

---

25. Yin Shun (尹 焞). S. Yen-ming (彦 明) al. Tê-ch'ung (德 充).

Yin Shun came of a family which had already produced several
men who had become distinguished for their learning, and his father
rose to the position of a Secretary in the Board of Woods and Forests.
Shun was born at Lo-yang in 1071, the fourth year of the reign of
Sung Shên Tsung. He lost his father in early childhood and was
brought up by his mother, a wise and affectionate woman. In his
eighteenth year he joined the school of Ch'êng Yi-ch'uan, and
continued to be a disciple of that philosopher for nearly twenty years.
When he went up to the Chü-jen examination, he found that the
subject selected on that occasion as theme for the Essays, was the
proposition made at the beginning of Chê Tsung's reign to put to
death about 250 scholars and statesmen described by Wang An-shi
as factious intriguers. The friends of Wang An-shi were now in
power again, and they were trying to revive that statesman's measures.
Shun did not like the subject and he went away without writing an
essay. He then told his master that he would not go up to the
Chin-shi Examination, and his master advised him to consult his
mother in the matter. Her reply was—I know you as supporting me
by well-doing, not as supporting me from the emoluments of office.
So he made up his mind to abandon the prospect of a public career,

---

* See Tao-t'ung-lu (Supplement); Shang-ts'ai-yü-lu (上 蔡 語 錄); Chu-tzŭ-ch'uan-
shu, chüan 54.

and was soon after confirmed in this resolve by the charge of corrupt teaching being preferred against Yi-ch'uan, Chan Yi, and himself.

On the death of Yi-ch'uan in 1107, Shun became the chief of his school, and from this time devoted all his time and energies to study and teaching. For many years he led this retired life, greatly esteemed and reverenced by all with whom he came in contact. But his fame at length reached the Emperor, and in 1126, he was summoned to the Capital. He would not serve, however, and the Emperor gave him the title Ho-ching-ch'ü-shi (和 靖 處 士), The student of well-tempered, well-balanced mind, and allowed him to go back to his studies. Hereupon Hu An-kuo and several other high officials, presented a joint Memorial in which they expostulated with His Majesty for having allowed Shun to decline office. They described his learning as thorough, his virtue as perfect, his words and conduct as fit to be models, and his abilities as suitable for a high office. But the Emperor did not notice the Memorial.

The Tartars were now pushing on their conquest of China, and in 1127, they took Lo-yang. Shun's wife and one child were killed and he was carried away nearly dead. His disciples took him to a hill near Si-an-foo and he remained in that neighbourhood for some time. Then Liu-yü (劉 豫), who had gone over to the Tartars, tried, first by fair promises and afterwards by threats, to make him join the invading army. But Shun fled from the danger on foot and escaped into Ssŭchuan. At Fou-chow in that Province he remained for some time, the town being dear to him as a place where Yi-ch'uan had taught the Yi Ching. In 1136, he was induced to accept office, partly on account of the generous courtesy shown to him by the Emperor. But he had only reached Kiukiang when he heard of a Memorial by a Censor denouncing the teachings of the Brothers Ch'êng and praying that their promulgation be prohibited. So he remained there and sent a Petition to the Throne stating that he could not, if in office, conscientiously teach any other doctrines than those he had learned from Yi-ch'uan. The adherents of the latter prevailed, and Shun received a new appointment, but he loved retirement, and was with difficulty persuaded to take office. The Tartars about this time sued for peace and a Treaty, and Shun opposed by Memorial and letter the proposition for peace with a divided empire.

In 1140, old and nearly blind, he urged anew his prayer for leave to retire, and at last obtained his request. He went to live with his son-in-law who was in office at Shao-hsing in Chekiang, and here he died in 1142. The Emperor, Kao Tsung, who had been indulgent and liberal to him throughout, now provided that his funeral should be conducted with becoming solemnity. He was buried at a hill near the town of Hui-ki in the Prefecture of Shao-hsing.

Yin Ho-ching was the author of two or three works, of which the Lun-yü-chie (論 語 解), or Explanations of the Lun-yü, was the principal. It was undertaken by command of Kao Tsung and occupied the author for several years. He was old and feeble at the time and suffering much from ill health, but he thought it was his duty to do the work prescribed, and he laboured at it conscientiously until it was finished. After his death his few miscellaneous writings were collected and published, together with a number of documents bearing on his life and teachings. These form a small volume entitled Yin-Ho-ching-chi which was reprinted at Foochow some time ago.

Yin Ho-ching was not a man of brilliant genius or profound learning, but like Confucius' disciple Tsêng-tzŭ, as he owned, dull of intellect. He was a plain, blunt man whether in speaking or writing, with a firm will and a strong sense of duty. He dwelt much on the duty of keeping a feeling of quiet reverence, and he taught his disciples to put conduct before words. The doctrines of the two Ch'êng were preserved and transmitted by him, and their truth and orthodoxy defended. Faithful and upright in all things he refused office rather than side with a bad cause, and he preferred the risk of death before honour bought with shame.

His posthumous epithet is Suh (肅), Reverential, the name which according to Chu Hsi, best describes his character. In 1724, he was admitted to the Temple of Confucius. *

* Tao-t'ung-lu, (Supplement) ; Yin-Ho-ching-chi (尹 和 靖 集); Chu-tzŭ-chüan-shu, Ch. 54 ;

26. Lo Ts'ung-yen (羅 從 彥). S. Chung-so (仲 素).

Lo Ts'ung-yen was born in A.D. 1072, at a village near Nan-p'ing, a town in the Prefectural District of Yen-p'ing-foo, in Fuhkeen. It is recorded of him that in youth he had a determined will and was clever, but that he did not care to acquire the accomplishments which led to official employment. He became a desultory reader, and he seems to have led a quiet, aimless life until he was forty years of age. At this period he began to learn the philosophy of his fellow Provincial, Yang Kuei-shan, though he did not meet Yang until five years later when he visited him at P'i-ling in Kiang-su. This interview impressed him greatly with an idea of Yang's extraordinary learning, and he quickly became an earnest disciple and a thorough follower. Yang declared him the greatest among all his thousand disciples, and saw that his doctrines were safe in the keeping of Ts'ung-yen. One day in the course of a lecture on the first chapter of the Yih Ching, Yang stated that he had once heard Yi-ch'uan explain a certain passage in it admirably. Hereupon Lo sold his farm and set off for Lo-yang to obtain the explanation from Yi-ch'uan. The latter took much pains in expounding the passage, •but added nothing to what Yang had taught, and Lo went back to his home and resumed his studies. He was soon attended by a number of disciples, among whom the most eminent Li Yen-p'ing (Li T'ung).

When he was sixty years old the Chü-jen Degree was conferred on Lo Ts'ung-yen by Imperial favour, and he was appointed assistant to the Magistrate of Po-lo (博 羅) in the Prefecture of Hui-chow in Kwang-tung. But he had a great dislike for office, and preferred a quiet, meditative life in the cottage which he built for himself in the Lo-fou Mountains. He was on his way to his native place, according to one authority, when he died at Ting-chow (汀 州) in Fuhkeen. But according to another account he was in office at the time of his death, which occurred in 1135. His only son had died before him, and there was no one to take charge of the funeral. So his coffin

remained unburied for many years, and there was no one found
to do him reverence until 1213 when a stranger gave him his due
honour. The Emperor Li-Tsung, in 1247, conferred on him the
epithet Wên-chi (文質), accomplished and solid. But his usual
designation is Yü-chang-Hsien-shêng (豫章先生) from the old
name of Nan-ch'ang in Kiangsi. In 1614·he was admitted to the
Temple of Confucius.

Lo was the author of the Shêng-Sung-tsun Yao-lu (聖宋遵堯錄)
which is known, however, only by its shorter name Tsun-yao-lu. The
meaning of the title is, Record of the Deified Emperors of the Sung
dynasty who followed Yao. This treatise was finished in 1126, and
its author designed it to show that the disasters of the time were the
result of the apostacy of Shên Tsung and his successors. It contains
seven chapters giving a short account of the reigns of the first four
Emperors of this dynasty, and an eighth chapter which is supplementary.
The work was directed chiefly against Wang An-shi and Ts'ai Ching,
and the Emperors who were led by them, but it also gives interesting
notices of Han Ch'i, Ssŭ-ma Kuang, and other eminent statesmen.
The political maxim of the author is contained in these words—the
institutions of ancestors are not to be annulled, and their virtuous
influence is not to be relied on. This maxim is stated and illustrated
in another essay by the author, which is entitled Yi-lun-yao-yü (議論
要語). A few poems and one or two short papers are all the other
writings of Lo which remain. But he published also a collection of
notes of discourses by the Two Ch'êng on the Lun-yü and Mencius,
derived probably from Yang Kuei-shan. His chief merits as a
Confucianist are that he was a thorough disciple of this last, and that
by his teaching Yang's philosophy, he transmitted the true doctrines
of the Sages which had been revived by the Ch'êng. He taught
Li T'ung, and Li taught Chu Hsi, and so Lo was one of those
who trimmed and handed on the torch of truth which is the light of
the world.

Lo Ts'ung-yen was a patient and determined student who made
his own all that he read or otherwise learned. He propagated the
dangerous doctrine of calm reflection in private rather than the reading

of books and hearing of lectures. In teaching he had a quiet insinuating manner which was felt but not observed, as the airs of Spring quicken nature though no one knows how they work.*

---

27. Hu An-kuo (胡 安 國) S. K'ang-hou (康 侯).

Hu An-kuo belonged to a family of considerable reputation, his grandfather and father having both been men of distinction. The latter specially was celebrated not only as a scholar but also as a model of devoted filial affection. An-kuo was born A.D. 1074 at Ts'ung-an (崇安), a town of Kien-ning-foo in Fuhkeen. As a boy he was bright and intelligent but had a very hasty temper. His tutors were Chu Chang-wên (朱 長 文) and Chin Ts'ai-chi (靳 裁 之), friends of Yi-ch'uan, and it was with the latter of these that he first learned to study History.

An-kuo in 1097 went up for his Chin-shi examination. On this occasion all the candidate's essays were expected to advocate a return to Wang An-shi's policy and to abuse Ssŭ-ma Kuang and all his friends. An-kuo advocated the old policy and did not stigmatize Ssŭ-ma and his friends as intriguers and traitors. So though his essay was declared best he was put fourth on the list of successful competitors. But when the essays were read out to the Emperor he praised An-kuo's repeatedly, and caused the author to be placed third on the list. This was the beginning of his tribulation but also of his glory.

Soon afterwards he was sent to Hunan as Literary Chancellor. In pursuance of an Imperial Edict he recommended, while in this capacity, two learned men of Yung-chow for official employment. An adherent of Ts'ai Ching, the unprincipled, powerful Minister of the time, falsely charged these two men with being members of a cabal. Ts'ai made this a pretext for having An-kuo, whom he hated, seized and imprisoned. The Criminal Judge was ordered to examine him, and when nothing was found against him he was sent on to Hupeh for further imprisonment and examination. Though he was in the end

---

* See the Tao-t'ung-lu (Suppl.); Lo-yü-chang-chi (羅 豫 章 集); Chu-tsŭ-ch'uan-shu, Ch. 54.

acquitted and released yet Ts'ai caused him to be dismissed from the public service. In a very short time, however, he was reinstated in his office, and was soon after sent in a similar capacity to Ch'êng-tu in Ssŭch'uan. In 1113 his mother died and while he was still in mourning for her his father died. At the end of the prescribed term of retirement he did not return to office but lived privately. It was for the sake of his parents, he said, that he had gone into office, and now that they were no more he had no use for a large salary. Accordingly he resigned on the plea of ill health, and built a cottage near his parents' graves. Here he wished to pass his life, supporting his family by the produce of a small farm, and bringing up his children in the fear of dishonour and the love of wisdom.

In 1125 several fruitless attempts were made to bring An-kuo back to public life. At last, in obedience to an urgent Decree, he repaired to the Capital and had an interview with the Emperor. The language he used on this occasion was sharp and severe and his advice was bitter but wholesome. He talked through all a long summer morning until heat and shame made the Emperor sweat so profusely that his robes were seen to be saturated. But bad counnsellors stood round the Throne who plotted still for the ruin of An-kuo, and the Emperor could not keep his faithful servant at the Capital. The latter was of a weak and delicate constitution, and suffered from an infirmity in one foot. He entreated again and again to be allowed to return to private life, but he could not be spared.

When Kao Tsung succeeded to the unsteady throne of the lessening Empire he wished to have An-kuo as a Censor. The latter presented a long, plain-spoken Memorial in which he sternly criticised the pusillanimous, inglorious conduct of the Emperor in retreating to Hang-chow—leaving the North and West of the Empire a prey to the Tartars and his relatives in their possession. Yet Kao Tsung had great esteem and affection for An-kuo and made him an Expositor of the Classics. But since his counsels were not followed, An-kuo could not rest at Court, and always prayed for leave to go back to the fields. After several further vicissitudes of fortune he died while holding a high office in 1138.

The posthumous epithet conferred on An-kuo was Wên-ting (文定), that is, accomplished and resolved. The Emperor regretted his loss very much and made an exceptionally liberal allowance to his family, several members of which were already rising to honour and usefulness in the service of the State. The literary designation of An-kuo is Wu-yi Hsien-shêng (武夷先生), Wu-yi (Bohea) being the name of a range of hills near his native place. He was admitted to the Temple of Confucius in 1437, a time when his writings were very popular.

The youthful ambition of An-Kuo was to make himself a name as an author, and he lived to satisfy his ambition. The Ch'un-ch'iu-chuan, or Commentary on the Ch'un-ch'iu is his greatest work. Wang An-shi had declared the Ch'un-ch'iu uncanonical, and had consequently succeeded in having it struck out from the list of classical books used in the Palace and the National Academies. But An-kuo thought it a duty which he owed to his principles to show that it was a genuine work of the Sage who composed it as a guide and warning to all in authority. For more than twenty years he laboured at his task, setting aside Tso's commentary as obscuring the original, and searching out the hidden meaning of the Sage's statements. Legge says that it "is not intrinsically of much value, but it was received on its publication with great applause by Kaou Tsung, the first emperor of the southern Sung dynasty; and all through the Ming dynasty its authority was supreme. It formed the standard for competitors at the literary examinations." It fell out of favour with the present dynasty on the appearance of Mao Hsi-ho's pitiless exposure of its defects and errors in the treatise in which he makes An-kuo "his butt."

Another important work by our author was the Supplement which he compiled for Ssŭ-ma Kuang's History, and which was entitled Tzŭ-chi-t'ung-chien-chü-yao-pu-yi (資治通鑑舉要補遺) His miscellaneous writings are known by the name Wu-yi-wên-chi (武夷文集).

Hu An-kuo was a zealous, uncompromising Confucianist, not only in matters of faith and opinion but also in the practical duties of life. The brothers Ch'êng he regarded as the only true interpreters of the

Sage's principles. To talk, he says, of following Confucius but not the Ch'êng is like talking of going into a house but not by the door. Not so profoundly learned as Tung Chung-shu he knew to explain to others and apply in his own life what knowledge he gained. Whether in office or out of office he sought to serve his country's highest interests. He was true to his friends, loyal to his sovereign, and faithful in all the duties of life. In the mid-winter of trouble and disaster when all meaner things faded and died, he, like the pine or the cypress, stood alone firmly-rooted and flourishing.*

--------•◦►--------

28. Li Kang (李 綱) S. Poh-chi (伯 紀).

Li Kang belonged to the Prefecture of Shao-wu in Fuhkeen and was born A.D. 1083. His father K'uei (夔) was distinguished for his high attainments as a scholar and his excellent administration as an official. Kang obtained his Chin-shi in 1112, and soon after received an appointment. In a few years he had reached the Censor's office but, having incurred in that office the displeasure of a Minister of State, he was degraded. In the year 1119 a serious flood caused alarm at the capital, and Kang presented a Memorial to the Throne, in which he dwelt on the flood as a sign from Heaven that the native rebels and foreign enemies should be dealt with in earnest. The Emperor was displeased and sent him away to Sha-Hsien in Yen-p'ing-foo, as a Collector of Customs.

He was recalled to the Capital, however, and in 1125 we find him there as a Sub-Director of the Court of Sacrifices. This was a year of great anxiety and distress in the western parts of the Empire. The Kin Tartars broke their Treaty and crossed their boundary. Hui Tsung appointed the Heir apparent Governor of the capital and proposed to remove the seat of Government. Kang, in a Memorial which he wrote with blood drawn by pricking his arm, urged abdication as absolutely necessary. The Emperor was convinced and resigned in

---

* Sung-shi, Chüan 435; Legge Ch. Cl. 5 Proleg. p. 137.; Shang-yu-lu, Ch. 2.; Hsing-li-hui-yao, Ch. 12.

favour of his son who reigned in his stead as Ch'in Tsung. Kang, having gained the favour of this Emperor, soon rose to high position. He counselled war to the death with the Tartars, and opposed vehemently all propositions which involved the dismemberment of the empire. Consistently with this he also used all his efforts to prevent the abandonment of K'ai-fêng-foo as the capital. In 1126 he was dismissed from office in order to please the Tartars. Hereupon a deputation of more than a thousand men presented a petition to the Emperor praying for his recall to office. The Emperor granted their request and Kang was soon again in power. He commanded the forces at the defence of the Capital and beat the Tartars with great slaughter.

On the accession of Kao Tsung in 1127 he was against his will made a Minister of State. It was represented to the Emperor that this appointment would displease the Tartars who hated Li Kang and feared him greatly. After a short time the Emperor, who was always halting between two courses, yielded to his bad advisers, degraded Kang, and sent him away from the Capital. The story of Kang's life from this time forward is sad and painful. He was tossed about from office to office, all the time seeing his hopes dashed, his counsel set at naught, and his labours fruitless. He died while in official exile at Foochow, and the historian thus solemnly records the event—Died, Li Kang, Duke of Lung-hsi and Grand Secretary of the Kuan-wên Hall. He had been made Duke of Lung-hsi in recognition of his services in Honan, and his zealous efforts to have the country about the Huang Ho at first defended and afterwards recovered from the Tartars. The Emperor was much distressed when he heard of the death of Li Kang and ordered a liberal gratuity to his family, giving him also the posthumous title of Junior Peceptor. The epithet conferred on Kang was Chung-ting (忠 定), Firm in loyalty. His tablet was not admitted to the Temple of Confucius until the year 1851.

Li Kang was the author of several treatises, the most important of which were his Commentaries on the Yih Ching and the Lun-yü. He wrote also several political works bearing on the history of the troubled time in which he lived, and some Poems and Essays.

The fame of Li Kang, however, does not rest on his literary works, but on his life. And the record of this shows us a man of a thoroughly patriotic spirit, forgetful of all private wrongs, and possessed with a love of national honour. Though thwarted by personal enemies, betrayed by the Emperors he served, and subjected to insults and persecution, he never failed in his duty or swerved from his loving allegiance. As a child clings fondly to the skirts of its mother even though she chide it in anger, so, writes, his biographer, Li Kang, in the midst of all the wrongs done to him, never wavered in dutiful affection to his country. He would have no truce with the forsworn invaders while they were on Chinese soil. Rather lose the empire city by city—village by village—and die nobly on the field of battle than gain a shameful life and an inglorious throne by cowardly submission.. Though bred to letters and philosophy and all unused in the arts of war, he was ready not only to join the ranks against the invaders, but even to take the lead and fight to death for the altars of the Gods and all that makes Fatherland. His country's disgrace was his burden of sorrow, and the one great aim of his life was to have that disgrace removed. Thus more than the fame of his learning, his good administration, or his splended feats of war, is the memory of his perfect self-forgetfulness in the presence of public duty.*

---

29. Li T'ung (李 侗) S. Yuan-chung (愿 中).

Li T'ung was a native of Khien-poo (劍 浦), a town in the Prefecture of Yen-p'ing, and was born A.D. 1093. In youth he was noted for his cleverness at school and his excellent conduct to his parents and bad elder brother. As he grew up he enjoyed festive society, and when he had taken too much wine at dinner used to mount a horse and have a gallop of eight or ten miles. But when

* Sung-shi, Chüan 358-9; T'ung-chien &c.   Sung Hui Tsung, Ch'in Tsung, Kao Tsung.; Shang-yu-lu, Ch. 14.

he came to years of discretion he abandoned this sort of life, and began to study philosophy. At the age of 24 years he became acquainted with Lo Ts'ung-yen and joined his school. Having read the Tsun-yao-lu of Ts'ung-yen, he studied with him the Ch'un-ch'iu and other Classics and soon became the chief member of the school.

Li T'ung now made up his mind to keep away from public life, and so did not present himself at any of the examinations for literary Degrees. He built a small, rude cottage in the country and went to reside there with his family. Here he spent a life, quiet and uneventful, in study and teaching, and intercourse with a few friends. He was poor but happy, caring neither for riches nor glory. Of his disciples the most celebrated was Chu Hsi, whose father was a friend of Li T'ung and sent Hsi to study the Classics with him. Li soon discerned the genius of his disciple and evidently enjoyed the task of expounding to him his favourite work, the Chung-yung. Hsi continued to receive his instructions down to the end of Li's life, and was content to travel many miles in order to get a lesson. The fame of the disciple in this case made the fame of the master.

In 1163 Li T'ung died rather suddenly, leaving two sons who were already rising to honour in the State. His posthumous epithet is Wên-ching (文 靖), but his usual literary name is Yen-p'ing. He was admitted to the Temple of Confucius along with his master Lo Ts'ung-yen in 1617 (or 1614 according to some authorities).

Li T'ung did not write any treatise and it is to Chu Hsi that posterity is indebted for a record of his teachings. Chu preserved and published the written answers which he had received in reply to questions or doubts chiefly on the Four Books, the Shu and the Ch'un-ch'iu. He also collected all the notes he found of Li's sayings and wrote his life. These are all to be found in the Li-yen-p'ing-chi (李 延 平 集) along with contributions from several other scholars.

Li T'ung was of a quiet and gentle disposition, very precise and methodical, but very warm-hearted. He was never in a hurry or excited, and he was simple in his tastes. His cottage was well managed, and his wife was neither to be seen nor heard, though she brought up her family with credit and kept everything in good order.

She and her family were often stinted in food and clothes in order that help might be given to the needy among their relatives and fellow-villagers. Li mixed a little in society, but he was not in any degree a man of the world, and he seems to have taken little interest in public affairs. As a philosopher his great merit is to have communicated to Chu Hsi the teachings derived from Lien-ch'i and the two Ch'êng through Yang Kuei-shan and Lo Ts'ung-yen. He taught his disciples to seek for truth rather in their own minds than in the writings of others. Strictly orthodox, he disliked controversy and did not care to talk about the errors of Buddhism, though he turned Chu Hsi and others from reading its literature. His own favourite study was the internal basis of the emotions or the condition of mind in which these are latent. The theme of his meditations was taken from the Chung-yung—"while there are no stirrings of pleasure, anger, sorrow or joy, the mind may be said to be in the state of Equilibrium. When those feelings have been stirred, and they act in their due degree, there ensues what may be called the state of Harmony. This Equilibrium is the great root *from which grow all human actings* in the world, and this Harmony is the universal path *which they all should pursue*." He placed self-improvement and the attainment of moral excellence before intellectual acquirements. Yet he was well read in philosophy and the ancient Classics, and knew them with the understanding and the heart. Though a plain man of the country, he had genius and learning, and fixed principle. He was, said a contemporary, like an ice vase or an autumn moon, bright and clear without a speck. But some of his characteristic theories have been censured as too closely resembling those of the contemplatist Buddhists, a charge to which he would have strongly objected.*

* See the Li-Yen-p'ing-chi (李延平集) ed. Chang Poh-hang.; Chu-tzŭ-ch'uan-shu, Ch. 54; Legge Ch. Cl. I p. 248.

30. Chang Chih (張栻). S. Ching-fu (敬夫).

Chang Chih was a native of Mien-chu (綿竹), a town of Ch'êng-tu-foo in Ssŭchuan, and was born A.D. 1133. His father Chün (浚), usually known by his title Wei-kuo-kung (魏國公), or Wei-kung, was a distinguished general and statesman, an enemy of Ch'in Kuei, and a persevering opponent of all who proposed peace with the invading Tartars. He was a man of dashing pluck and enduring courage, a wise and patriotic official, and a good scholar. Chih was his younger son and he loved him wisely and well, teaching him early to prize humanity, public duty, loyalty and filial piety.

Chih was in boyhood wise and thoughtful beyond his years, and was endowed with a rare genius. The preceptor in philosophy to whom his father consigned him was Hu Hung (胡宏), known as Hu Wu-fêng (胡五峯), a son of Hu An-kuo, and himself a scholar of no mean fame. From Hu he gained a knowledge of the ancient Classics and of Confucian ethics as expounded and developed by Chou Lien-ch'i and the two Ch'êng. Chih was a youth of quick parts, fond of study and reflection, and his master saw in him a future hero of orthodoxy.

But he had to take his part in the affairs of life, and he began service as a subordinate in a yamên, a position which he obtained through the influence of his father. On the restoration of the latter to favour in 1163, Chih served with him as aid-de-camp and confidential secretary. But next year his father died, his last moments being embittered by thoughts of the nation's disgrace. I have not been able, he said on his deathbed to his sons, to regain the Western Provinces or wash off the shame brought on our former Emperors, so bury me not by the side of my forefathers, but lay me at the foot of Mount Hêng (衡)—the sacred mountain of Hunan. His order was obeyed, and Chih remained near his tomb for several years. It was here that in 1167, occurred the most important event of his life, the visit of Chu Hsi, who, led by the reputation of Chang, came to see him at home.

The conversation of the two students soon turned of course to the wisdom of the ancients, and they kept up an argument on the Chung-yung for three days and three nights. Then they climbed Mount Hêng together, discussing by the way the pressing subjects of contemporary politics but more the patient themes of immortal philosophy.

In the meantime Chang presented a Memorial to the Throne in which he urged a renewal of war with the Tartars, and the adoption of a firm determination to drive them all out of the Empire. He had inherited his father's brave, proud spirit, and his deadly enmity to the Tartars, without the stain of prejudice which tarnished his father's glory. His Memorial was not heeded, but some time after he was appointed to a high office at Court. Within a year, however, he was dismissed from this office and sent to Yuan-chou in Kiangsi in 1172. He was restored to the Capital for a time, but was again removed to the Provinces. His last office was that of Prefect at King-chou in Hupeh, and he died in 1180. The Emperor lamented his death as a loss to the public service, and Chu Hsi lamented it as a loss to true learning.

The last act of Chang Chih on his deathbed was to write a Memorial to Hsiao Tsung advising His Majesty to keep only good men about him, and to have likings and dislikings only of a public and disinterested nature. At the time of his death he had the title Compiler of the Right Wên-Tien. His posthumous epithet is Hsüan (宜), or Diffusive, and his literary designation is Nan-hsien (南軒). In 1261, (or 1241, according to some authorities) he was ennobled and admitted to the Temple of Confucius.

Chang Nan-hsien was an author of some popularity and of good reputation. Among his writings were treatises on the Lun-yü, Mencius, the T'ai-chi of Chou-tzŭ, and Chu-ko Liang. But of these he had finally revised and corrected for publication only the first—the *Lun-yü-shuo*. The others were copied and circulated by his disciples without his sanction or approval. After the death of Chang his unpublished Manuscripts were given to Chu Hsi who prepared them for publication, adding his own letters from Chang and whatever Memoranda he could procure from others. These are all contained in the Chang-nan-hsien-chi, a compilation edited by Chang Poh-hang.

As an official Chang was thoroughly loyal and public-spirited. He never failed or feared to do his duty to his Sovereign, trying to rouse him to a course of virtue and honour. To the people whom he was sent to govern he was just and generous. Everywhere he sought to give them peace and comfort and to stimulate in them a desire for education.

His philosophical teachings, which are considered links in the chain of transition from Chou-tzŭ and the Ch'êng, were for some time highly prized. Chang learned the truths early and he did not tarry to teach others what he learned. His mental powers were great, and he saw quickly and clearly into the deep mysterious thoughts of the old Sages. He adopted Mencius' views about human nature, and developed his teachings about humanity and public duty ("Benevolence and Righteousness"). He also took up Mencius' doctrine of the opposition between personal gain and public duty, and maintained its universal application. But his philosophy, though grand and noble, was like the skeleton framework of a house, wanting the details which fit it for practical uses. Chu Hsi, who could not, however, always agree with him, writes of him in terms of hearty admiration, and perhaps Chang's fame rests largely on the fact that he was a friend and teacher of that philosopher. *

---

31. Lü Tsu-ch'ien (呂 祖 謙). S. Poh-kung (伯 恭).

Lü Tsu-ch'ien was born at Kuei-lin-foo in Kuangsi in 1137, but his family belonged to Kin-hua-foo in Chekiang. He was a descendant of Lü I-chien (呂 夷 簡), a famous statesman and scholar in the reigns of Chên Tsung and Jen Tsung, of the Sung dynasty. His grandfather and father were also officials of some repute, the former having held a high position at the Capital. Tsu-ch'ien received his

---

* See the Chang-nan-hsien-chi (張 南 軒 集); Hsing-li-hiu-yao, Ch. 12; Chu-tzŭ-nien-p'u (朱 子 年 譜) Ch. 1. Shang-yu-lu, Ch. 88 and 22.

early education at home where he had access to a collection of the
writings of the Honan philosophers. When he grew up he studied
with Lin Chĭ-ch'i (林 之 奇) and other men of learning, and was a
quick and clever student.   .

His first official appointment was obtained through the merit of
his father, but he afterwards became a Chin-shi and was thereupon
made a Director of the Official Examinations. In a few years his
mother died and he was consequently obliged to retire for a time into
private life.   The leisure thus forced on him was turned to good
account, for he continued his studies and became a teacher, many
disciples being attracted to him by the fame of his learning.   On his
return to public life he was made a Public Instructor and State
Annalist.   While thus in office at the Capital he urged the Emperor
Hsiao Tsung to encourage orthodoxy and to concert vigorous measures
for the recovery of the lost Provinces.   His father's death obliged
him to go again into mourning, and at the end of the usual period of
retirement he returned to office.   Though the Emperor did not follow
his counsel yet he was pleased to honour him notwithstanding some
envious opposition.   But ill health, from which he seems to have
suffered nearly all his life, obliged Tsu-ch'ien to resign office about
the year 1178.   He now retired to his home in Kin-hua-foo, and
continued his literary work.   His most intimate friends were Chu
Hsi and Chang Ch'ih, and they were called the Three Eminent men
of the South-east.   In 1181 he died, while still bearing the title of
State Annalist, and was honoured with the epithet Ch'ĕng (成),
Perfect.   The name given to him by his disciples was Tung-lai (東 萊)
and this has continued to be his literary designation.   In 1261 the
Emperor Lí Tsung ennobled him and caused his tablet to be placed
in the Confucian temples.

Lü Tung-lai was a great writer and a scholar of immense
reading.   In philosophy he adhered thoroughly to the school of which
Chou Lien-ch'i, Chang Tsai, and the two Ch'ĕng were the chiefs.
It was at his suggestion, and partly perhaps with his help, that Chu
Hsi wrote the Chin-ssŭ-lu (近 思 錄) which gives the principle writ-
ings of these four philosophers, with notes and explanations.   Lü

Tung-lai compiled the Huang-ch'ao-wên-chien (皇朝文鑑), Literary Mirror of the Imperial Dynasty, that is, the Sung. This work is a collection of documents bearing on the history of the dynasty during the period preceding the accession of Kao Tsung in 1127. It was compiled by order of the Emperor who gave it the above title when it was presented to him in 1177. The merits of the Wên-chien are disputed, Chang Ch'ih declaring it useless for practical purposes, while Chu Hsi gives it high praise.

The Lü-shi-chia-shu-tu-shi-chi (呂氏家塾讀詩記) in thirty two *chuan* is a much more famous book. Dr. Legge translates the title—" Leu's Readings in the She for his family school " and says— " It gives not only the author's view of the text, but those of 44 other scholars, from Maou down to Choo, very distinctly quoted." The Ta-shi-chi (大事記), a book of historical criticisms, is also a work of note by Tung-lai, but this and the previous treatise were left by him in an imperfect condition. He wrote also a critical commentary on the Yih Ching and several works of a political and historical character. His treatises were popular for a time and some of them are still much read. Besides the above, there is a collection of his miscellaneous short writings made by his brother.

Lü Tung-lai was in youth of a peevish, exacting disposition, but he was converted by the following words of Confucius which he read while confined to bed by sickness—' "He who requires much from himself and little from others, will keep himself from *being the object of* resentment." ' His conversion was sincere and lasting, and he became a man of a quiet genial temper. His short life was much troubled by ill health, but his conduct in office and at home was throughout exemplary. His writings are of unequal merit, for he had the ambition to be a universal scholar and at the same time a philosophical critic. Some one once happened to say to him that he did not know men. Nettled at this he resolved to point out the secret motives of conduct —the genuine and fictitious feelings—of the historical personages about whom he wrote, and herein, says Chu Hsi, he was wrong. He had great powers of mind, but he read too much and studied too little. Hence his style is not always good and his errors are many. Too

impetuous and too eager to excel, he marred his best works by faults
of ambition and affection. But he was a thorough and consistent
follower of Confucius, teaching and illustrating the Sage's doctrines
in his books and embodying them in his public life.*

---

32. Luh Chiu-yuan (陸 九 淵) S. Tzŭ-thing (子 靜).

The family of which Luh Chiu-yuan sprang was one in which
virtue and learning had long been fostered in quiet seclusion. But
the Luhs could boast of a remote ancestor who had been a Minister
of State during the T'ang dynasty. His descendants had lived in
peaceful retirement on the patrimonial property down to Ho (賀), the
father of Chiu-yuan. Ho was noted in his native village as a man
of solid learning and a good life. "Heaven thinks of the virtuous
man," and so Ho was blessed with six sons, five of whom became men
of eminence. The family lived at Chin-ch'i (金 谿), a town of Foo-
chow-foo in Kiangsi, and it was here that Chiu-yuan was born in the
year 1139. At the birth of this last, however, the stars fought, and
he had a narrow escape from a destiny of rural oblivion. A neighbour
unblessed with any children begged for the baby as soon as it was
born, that he might have a son to cherish him in old age and perform
the yearly rites of remembrance at his grave. The father agreed to
the request, but the elder brother, Chiu-ling, interceded, and finally
took possession of the infant.

At the early age of about three years Chiu-yuan showed signs of
thoughtful activity. One day he asked his father in what way heaven
and earth were limited. At this question his father only smiled and
had not what to answer. But the child pondered over this, his first
difficulty in philosophy, until he forgot to sleep and eat. Even in
these young days his conduct was noted as unlike that of ordinary
children, and he grew up to be a youth of great affection and enthusiasm. Four of his brothers had also names beginning with *Chiu*,
and as the five were all young men of unusual abilities and learning
they were called the Five unofficial scholars *Chiu*.

---

* Sung-shi, Chuan 434; Ma Tuan-lin, Chuan 248; Chu-tsǐ-ch'uan-shu, Chuan 59;
  Legge Ch. Cl. IV. Proleg. p. 173; I. p. 163; Shang-yu-lu, Chuan 15.

In 1172 Chiu-yuan became a Chin-shi, and soon after began to teach philosophy. He met Chu Hsi in 1175 and had long discussions with him, for he differed from Chu on some important points of scholarship and opinion. Afterwards in 1181 he went to visit Chu at the White Deer Cavern in order to obtain from him an epitaph for his elder brother Tzŭ-shou. In the meantime he had been appointed to a subordinate post at Ching-an, a town of Nan-ch'ang-foo in Kiangsi. Then his mother died, and at the end of the time of mourning for her he was transfered to Ts'ung-an a town of Kien-ning-foo in Fuhkeen. While here he was summoned to Court and refused to go, but afterwards he accepted office in the Imperial Academy at the Capital. He now tried to fulfill a dream of his youth, which was, to find men and means to recover the Provinces conquered by the Tartars. He also delivered a long moral lecture to the Emperor Hsiao Tsung, who rewarded him for it by promotion. But a Censor objected and Chiu-yuan was sent away to T'ai-chow in Chekiang. He did not stay there, however, but went to his native place, and resumed his teaching in philosophy. Hundreds flocked to his house and came day by day to hear him read and expound the dark sayings of old. His disciples embraced all ages, from youths flushed with their first success in leaning or puzzled by their first doubts and difficulties, to old men leaning on staffs and dull with long years of painful study. He had great success as a teacher, rousing his disciples to think for themselves and calling forth their latent capacities.

In 1190 Chiu-yuan was recalled to public life, and appointed Prefect of Ching-mên (荆門) in Hupeh. His administration at this place was a marvel of success. He changed the bad coarse manners of the people, decided lawsuits with a justice prompt and cheap, reformed the revenue system, gave the city a wall and attracted to it artisans and traders. He had always loved and served his elder brother, Chiu-ling, and wife, as father and mother, and he now brought them to spend a few months with him at Ching-mên. Chiu-ling, like all others, witnessed to the purity and excellence of his rule. And not men alone but Heaven also testified to the might of his virtue, for when a drought had been sent or snow withheld and

Chiu-yuan prayed, Heaven relented and yielded the boon desired.

He was recommended for promotion but preferred to remain as he was. In 1199 one day he told the members of his family that he was about to die. Soon after he had to pray for snow, and the day after he prayed the snow came. Chiu-yuan then bathed and put on a change of clothes, knowing that his end was near at hand. He sat down and awaited the event in reverent composure and died two days after at noon. The epithet Wên-an (文安), Culture-repose, was conferred on him posthumously, and his literary designation is Hsiang-shan. He had called himself the Hsiang-shan-wêng (象山翁), or old man of Hsiang-shan, a town in the Prefecture of Ningpo. In 1530 his tablet was placed in the Temple of Confucius.

Luh Chiu-yuan, even though requested by his friends, did not write any treatise. Yet some productions of his pen must have been published during his lifetime, for Lü Tsu-ch'ien knew his Essay at an Examination from its resemblance to other writings of "Little Luh" which he had read previously. A few years after his death all his writings were collected by his son, edited by a few of his disciples, and published with the title Hsiang-shan-chi (象山集). This collection consists of Letters, Memorials, Introductory Notices to Books, Poems, and other miscellanies. The Hsiang-shan-wai-chi and Yü-lu are also included under the general title given above.

As a philosophical thinker Chiu-yuan holds a distinguished place, though some of his opinions are considered high and metaphysical. In early life he rejected Ch'êng Yi-ch'uan as misinterpreting Confucius, and he regarded even the disciple Yu-tzŭ (有子) as heterodox. He was first awakened to a sense of the narrowness of his views by reflecting on the two words Yü-ch'ou (宇宙), the former denoting all space and the latter all time. He now found that he should concern himself only with universal truth and right which hold good at all times and in all places. Perfect truth, he now held, was to be attained only by internal processes of the mind and not by any amount of reading and hearing lectures and investigation of external subjects. Man, he taught, is highest among all the creatures, and he is highest only by his mind. He dwelt much on the greatness and importance of this, meaning by mind the Tao-hsin (道 心), or mind purified and enlightened and so brought back to its native perfection.

The controversy between Chu Hsi and Luh Chiu-yuan is a very important affair in modern Chinese philosophy, and is usually referred to in literature as Chu Luh-t'ung-yi (朱 陸 同 異), that is, Chu and Luh's agreeings and differings. In the year 1175 Lü Tung-lai invited the two brothers Luh Chiu-shun and Chiu-yuan to meet him and Chu Hsi at the Ngo-hu-ssŭ, near Hsin-chow, in Kiangsi. Chu Hsi and Chiu-yuan had never met and Lü thought that by a friendly personal discussion certain differences of opinion in philosophy which existed between them might be removed. The only persons who took an active part in the conversations on this occasion were Chu Hsi and Chiu-yuan, the latter being well supported by his elder brother. Chu maintained that in education there should be first learning and afterwards thought, but that both these were necessary. Luh on the contrary held that thought should precede learning and that the latter was not indispensable. The latter regarded man's mind as the universe in which thought should be exercised and taught that books were useless as a means towards self-perfection. To the expression "self-conquest" Luh gave a transcendental meaning and said it did not refer to the controlling and subduing of human passions and appetites. Chu Hsi maintained that man could never attain to truth and wisdom by the unaided efforts of his own uneducated mind and that the moral nature could not be renovated or kept perfect without the help of learning. Luh, on the other hand, held that man could, by solitary meditation, overcome the influences of the senses and attain of himself to a clear perception of what is true and right. The one thus inculcated a practical system of morality and philosophy, and the other taught an ideal perfection of the individual soul to be reached by solitary and absorbed reflection.

In Chou Lien-ch'i's teachings Luh Chiu-yuan objected to the expression Wu-chi (無 極), and his letter to Chu Hsi on this subject is still extant. It drew forth a reply which is perhaps the clearest and best account of the T'ai-chi or "Ultimate Principle" to be found in all Chinese literature. Luh, moreover, was disposed to doubt the genuineness of the Appendix to the Yih Ching as the work of Confucius, thought that Mencius came off badly in his arguments with Kao-tzŭ, and held some other rather independent opinions. It is plain that he did not lack much of being a heretic, though he and his followers have strenuously denied the charge of a Buddhistic leaning which Chu Hsi brought against his teachings. It was mainly on account of the evil consequences which he saw would follow from the spreading of Luh's opinions among unthinking disciples that Chu opposed them with all his energies. They were very near, he thought, to the theories of Buddhist mystics and would certainly bewilder and lead astray all who adopted them. So it came to pass, for some of Luh's disciples found themselves adrift on an ocean of uncertainty without compass or guide of any kind, and others made an unsatisfactory compass between Confucianism and Buddhism.

Luh himself seems to have modified some of his views and when he visited Chu Hsi at the White Deer College in 1181 he was received as an orthodox friend. Chu collected his disciples together and invited Luh to lecture to them. After some coaxing he consented and delivered an admirable exposition of a saying of Confucius thus translated by Dr. Legge, "The mind of the superior man is conversant with righteousness; the mind of the mean man is conversant with gain." Yet Luh never abandoned his early opinions, though his elder brother went over to the modest views of Chu Hsi. The one great blemish in Chiu-yuan's character was his great self-conceit, and this perhaps was the great obstacle to his conversion. No contemporary equalled him in genius, in power of thought, and in eloquence of exposition, and he was conscious of his superior endowments. In office, in the lecture-room, and over the wine he always regarded himself as a superior man and acted on the assumption that he was such. He made personal application of the statement that any man may become a Yao and thought himself, says one critic, equal to the great Sages of antiquity.

Luh Chiu-yuan has been regarded by his followers as a faithful adherent and developer of Mencius and a disciple of Chou Lien-ch'i and the Ch'êng, but his doctrines have long been regarded by the majority of Confucianists as a source of grave and wide-spreading errors. Some of his followers carried to excess the theory of self-development by quiet reflection allowing nature to have free course. These indeed became Buddhists in everything but name and did serious damage to the cause of orthodoxy while still professing to be its adherents. The master would certainly not have approved of many of the tenets and practices of these disciples, but he does not seem to have studied the possible or actual results of his teachings.*

<hr />

33. Yuan Hsie (袁 燮). S. Ho-shu (和 叔).

Yuan Hsie was a native of Yin (鄞), the Hsien in which Ningpo lies. The date of his birth is not given, but it was probably about A.D. 1150, or perhaps a few years later. As a child he was quiet and thoughtful, content to sit all day gazing into a basin of water placed before him by the nurse for his amusement. In due time he became a Chin-shi, and was appointed Magistrate of Kiang-yin (江 陰), in Kiangsu. While in this office he caused full and minute plans and maps to be prepared of all the divisions and sub-divisions of his District, giving the names, occupations, and other particulars of the inhabitants. At this period the western part of Chekiang was afflicted by a severe famine, and Yuan Hsie was ordered to devise means for the relief of the sufferers. Then he was commissioned to be an Inspector of the sea coast of Kiangsu and Chekiang, but the deaths of his parents took him away from office for several years.

The Emperor Ning Tsung on his accession to the Throne in 1195, made Yuan a Grand Secretary, but when Chu Hsi and his friends and doctrines were proscribed he sent in his resignation. In 1208, he was appointed Prefect of Nan-ch'ang-foo in Kiangsi, and soon after he was recalled to the Capital. He was made a Professor in the Imperial Academy, Reader in Classics to His Majesty, and a

* Sung-shi, Ch. 434; Chu-tzŭ-ch'uan-shu, Ch. 60; Chu-tzŭ-nien-pu, Chs. 2, 3.; Chu-tzŭ-yü-lei, Ch. 7.; Wang-hsiao-chĭ-yi (王 學 質 疑), appx.; Wang-Yang-ming-chi, Ch. 5; Wylie, Notes &c. p. 185; Wên-an-kung-chi (文 安 公 集).

Vice-President of the Board of 礼 Rites. To the Emperor Yuan Hsie spoke words of encouragement and advice rather than stern reproof, but he vehemently opposed all the peace-policy of Shi Mi-yuan (史彌遠), a man of little principle or honour but of great ambition. The friends of this Minister prevailed on the Emperor to dismiss Yuan Hsie, and he was consequently ordred to go to Wênchow as Prefect. He withdrew from public life, however, and went home where he died about the year 1220, but the date is not recorded.

The literary designation given to Yuan Hsie by his disciples was Chie-chai (潔齋), and the posthumous epithet with which he was honoured is Chêng-hsin (正獻), or orthodoxly intelligent. In 1868, his tablet was admitted to the Confucian Temple on the Petition of a Governor of Chekiang.

Yuan Hsie was the greatest among the disciples of Luh Chiu-yuan, whose theories about the training of the mind and its consequent powers he adopted. His chief works are the Chie-chai-chia-shu-shu-ch'ao (潔齋家塾書鈔), in 12 chüan, and the Chie-chai Mao-shi-ching-yen-chiang-yi (毛詩經筵講義). The latter treatise was written while he was in office at the Capital in the Emperor's household, and it was intended for His Majesty's edification. The author uses certain odes of the Shi as texts on which to deliver lectures, and in his comments he draws parallels between the state of affairs described in the odes and that of his own times. The miscellaneous writings of Yuan are contained in the Chie-chai-chi, and it is in this and the Shu-shu-ch'ao that his expositions and illustrations of Luh's philosophy are to be found. He is said to have written also a book on the Li or Classic of Rites, and he helped to edit and publish the literary remains of his Master.

Yuan Hsie was a zealous student, a wise and faithful official, and a clear, graceful writer. He had no eccentricities of opinion, but was an orthodox and consistent follower of Confucius in his life and philosophy. *

---

* Sung-shi, Ch. 400.: Wên-miao-ssŭ-wei (文廟祀位). Appendix.

34. Huang Kan (黃 榦). S. Chĭ-ching (直 卿).

Huang Kan was the son of Huang Yü (瑀), a learned and distinguished official under Sung Kao Tsung. He was a native of Foochow, and was born in the year 1152. In early youth he lost his father, and some time afterwards he went to see Liu Ch'ing-chĭ who advised him to become a disciple of Chu Hsi. Being a very filial son he first consulted his mother and having obtained her consent he went northward to find Chu. His first interview with that teacher enraptured him, and he at once gave himself up to study with intense ardour. For some time he did not lie down on a bed, but when wearied out rested himself for a few hours on a chair. By his zeal and application and excellent conduct he quickly won the esteem and affection of his master. The friendship thus begun was strengthened by a marriage alliance, Chu Hsi giving him his second daughter in marriage.

At the beginning of Ning Tsung's reign, 1195, Huang was appointed to a petty office at T'ai-chou in Chekiang, but his mother's death, which occurred soon afterwards, caused him to retire for a time from public life. He built a shed near his mother's grave and while keeping mourning there, he was visited by numerous disciples to whom he expounded the ancient Classics. Then his great master died, bequeathing to him the charge of his philosophical manuscripts and of his disciples. Huang had often worked with Chu, searching out references for him and correcting errors, and he had also largely contributed to the master's commentary on the Li. He kept the full period of mourning for Chu, and when that was over he was sent in 1203, to a subordinate post at Shi-mên-Hsien, in Chekiang. Afterwards he was appointed Magistrate of Lin-chuan, in Kiangsi, and subsequently sent to An-fêng in the same Province. While in this last office he was ordered to proceed to Ho-chow to try a man for murder. The witnesses and the accused were examined before him but the guilt of the latter could not be proved. Huang after having thought much over the case dreamt that he saw a murdered man in a well. Next morning he called for the accused and told him he had committed the murder and had thrown the victim into a well. The criminal was overwhelmed with confusion and immediately confessed his crime.

Huang was next sent, in 1206, to Han-yang, in Hupeh, as Prefect, and here he won golden opinions from all for his prompt and excellent measures to relieve the people during a famine. He also built schools, taught philosoply, and in every way encouraged learning among them. Some time afterwards he was made Prefect of An-ch'ang-foo in the South-west of Anhui. At this time the Tartars were at Kuang-shan in the South-east of Honan, and it was feared they would soon attack the defenceless city of An-ch'ang. But Huang infused into the people a spirit of energetic resistance, built a strong wall round the city, and manned it with efficient soldiers. By day he laboured incessantly at his official duties, and at night he expounded History and the Classics. When the defences were finished, on the 15th day of the first moon, he had a great illumination and all the people made merry. They deputed their oldest inhabitant, a widow of five score years, to return thanks to the Prefect. The old woman attended by her two sons and all her grandchildren went to the residence of the Prefect, who received her with great courtesy and offered her presents, which the spirited old woman, however, refused. An-ch'ang survived a flood and the invasion of the Tartars, and the inhabitants said it was through "Father Huang" they were saved from both.

Disgusted with the cowardly and debauched state of the army, he retired into private life and resumed his studies. But before doing so he wrote an earnest, touching appeal to the General against the selfish wantonness displayed in the camp, and warning him against the disasters which would certainly follow his conduct.

Being now free from office he made a journey to the Lu-chan, and with some friends wandered over places among the mountains hallowed by the memory of his master. He remained for some time and expounded philosophy in the White Deer College.

The Emperor appointed him Censor and summoned him to the

Capital, but enemies prevailed and the Decree was not issued to Huang. So he went back to Kien-ning with his wife and eldest son and settled down there—the successor of Chu Hsi in the school which the latter had founded. Disciples came to him from all quarters, so that he had to hire rooms in a monastery to lodge them. But he enjoyed his release from office only for a short time and died in 1221.

The literary designation of Huang Kan, is Mien-chai (勉 齋), and his posthumous epithet is Wên-suh (文 肅), that is, of cultured reverence. In 1724 he was admitted to the Temple of Confucius.

Huang is said to have composed some commentaries on the Classics, but the only one which is mentioned is that on the Li. His Letters and Miscellanies were collected and published under the title *Huang-mien-chai-chi*. Most of his letters are either on philosophical subjects or on events in which he was concerned. His glowing Eulogies on Chu Hsi, Prefaces and Postscripts to books, and official papers make up the principal portion of the rest of the work. His claim to a place in the Temple does not rest on his writings, however, but partly on the integrity and patriotism of his official career, he having been pure, brave, and disinterested in a time of general corruption and depravity. But it is rather as the friend and helper of Chu Hsi and the teacher of his doctrines that Huang is honoured among Confucianists. His fame brought disciples from remote parts of the Empire and these carried back to their homes the new views of the old learning and a lively interest in orthodox philosophy.*

———————•◦•———————

35. Ch'ên Shun (陳 淳). S. An-ching (安 卿).

The birth place of Ch'ên Shun was Lung-k'i (龍 溪), a town in the Prefecture of Chang-chow near Amoy, and he was born in the year 1153. In youth he was an eager and ambitious student, of an independent nature and not caring much for the ways of his neighbours. While he was studying with a view to the official examinations a friend told him that the Sages' learning was not contained in

———

* Huang Mien-chai-chi (黃 勉 齋 集) ed. Chang Poh-haug.; Hsing-li-hui-yao, Ch. 12; Tao-nan-yuan-wei (道 南 源 委) Ch. 3.

the books he was reading, and gave him a copy of the recently published Chin-ssü-lu by Chu Hsi. Hereupon Ch'ên gave up all idea of an official career and resolved to devote himself to philosophy.

In 1190 Chu Hsi came to Chang-chow as Prefect and Ch'ên at once became his disciple, introducing himself by a moral poem. He became a zealous student and continued with Chu all the time the latter was at Chang-chow. Then he began to teach at that place and soon had many disciples. After several years he went to visit Chu who was then living at home and suffering from the malady which was soon to prove fatal. Ch'ên showed him the fruits of his labours, and Chu commended them, but advised him to study less abstruse subjects and learn the simple rules of every day philosophy. In 1216 he went up to the Capital to a special Examination, and next year he received a subordinate appointment, but died before he could take office.

The literary designation of Ch'ên, given to him by his disciples, is Pei-k'i (or Ch'i), (北溪) and he was admitted to Confucius' Temple in 1724. He wrote commentaries on the Chung-yung and other Classics, and a large number of short treatises. His disciples collected their notes and records of his teachings and published them under the title *Yun-ku-lai-k'ou-chin-shan-so-wên* (筠谷瀨口金山所聞), known generally by its short name Yun-ku-so-wên. His miscellaneous writings were edited and published after his death by his son. Among these are the *Hsiao-tao-t'i-t'ung* (學道體統), which he composed to refute the teachings of a popular heretical professor, and the *Tzŭ-yi*. It is perhaps to this latter Mr. Wylie refers when he writes—"The term (性理) *Sing lè* as a designation of mental philosophy, was first used by 陳淳 Ch'in Chun, one of Choo He's disciples in the 性理字義 *Sing lè tszĕ é*."

Ch'ên Shun was not a man of extraordinary genius or distinguished by any great public services. In his private character he was modest, amiable, and benevolent, and his piety to his mother was celebrated. Though he did not seek for a name and lived in contented retirement yet his fame became spread abroad over all the country. He was an insatiable reader, and a most enthusiastic disciple of Chu Hsi, who said it was a matter of congratulation that his principles would be taught by Ch'ên in the South. He taught also the doctrines of Chou and the two Ch'êng, as the true interpretations of the ancient Classics, but he gave many of them new applications and developments. He distinguished between T'ien-li (天理), or Conscience, and Jen-yü (人 欲) or Desire, and he regarded this T'ien-li as identical with Jen (仁) or perfect human virtue. Though he declared that there was nothing high or subtle in his doctrines and that they were for daily life, yet they have been ·pronounced to be too abstruse and speculative. He explained the T'ai-chi as *Li*, or spirit, that which has revolved in the universe from all eternity, dispersed and collected alternately in the unceasing succession of natural phenomena. In the moral world the whole heart of the Sage is its perfect potentiality and its active operation is seen in his conduct responsive to all the changes of nature. This doctrine, which has been often enunciated by other Confucianists, may be better understood as stated in detail by a modern English poet, as follows :—

> " To every Form of being is assigned
> An *active* Principle ; howe'er removed
> From sense and observation, it subsists
> In all things, in all natures; in the stars
> Of azure heaven, the unenduring clouds,
> In flower and tree, in every pebbly stone
> That paves the brooks, the stationary rocks,
> The moving water, and the invisible air.
> Whate'er exists hath properties that spread
> Beyond itself, communicating good,
> A simple blessing, or with evil mixed ;
> Spirit that knows no insulated spot,
> No chasm, no solitude ; from link to link
> It circulates, the Soul of all the worlds.
> This is the freedom of the universe ;
> Unfolded still the more, more visible,
> The more we know ; and yet is reverenced least
> And least respected in the human mind,
> Its most apparent home. "*

* Tao-nan-yuan-wei, Ch. 3 ; Sung-she, Ch. 430 ; Wylie, notes &c., p. 69.

36. Ts'ai Ch'ên (蔡 沈). S. Chung-mo (仲 默).

The family of which Ts'ai Ch'ên came was one which had already in several generations produced men of great learning and abilities. His father was Ts'ai Yuan-ting (蔡元定)—who will appear hereafter —a celebrated scholar and philosopher, and a friend and adherent of Chu Hsi by whom he was greatly esteemed. Ch'ên was born at Kien-yang-chow, in the North of Fuhkeen, the home of the family for many years, in 1167. He was the youngest of three sons and was distin-guished in boyhood by his sedate and manly bearing, his filial conduct, and his love of study. Following in the footsteps of his father, he became a disciple of Chu Hsi and chose the peaceful life of a private student. But when Ts'ai Yuan-ting was banished to Tao-chow in Hunan for his adherence to Chu Hsi's doctrines, Ch'ên went with him. They went on foot all the way, traversing the unfrequented parts of the Two Kuang and Hunan for some hundreds of miles. Their days of sadness among strangers and their lonely wanderings among the hills and streams, which called up memories of the places of their youth, were solaced by the sweet uses of philosophy.

In 1198, his father died, in exile, and Ch'ên had his remains carried home. He followed the coffin on foot all the way from Tao-chow to Kienyang, refusing, on his father's account, a present of money sent to him by a friend. He was now about thirty years of age; and putting away all thought of trying for office he retired to the heart of the Chiu-fêng (九 峯), mountains. Here he settled for life and gave himself up to study, taking the ancient sages as his masters. Many disciples came to him and he took a pleasure in explaining their difficulties and teaching them the deep things of philosophy. He died in 1230, leaving two sons who also became famous, the elder as a scholar and philosopher and the younger as a statesman.

The posthumous epithet of Ts'ai-ch'ên is Wên-chêng (文 正), that is accomplished and orthodox. From the name of the mountains among which he chose to live he was called Chiu-fêng Hsien-shêng, and this is his usual literary designation, though he also called himself Wu-yi (Bohea), from the hills of this name in his native neighbourhood. In 1437, he was admitted to the Confucian Temple and was further honoured with a title of nobility.

Ts'ai Ch'ên was at one time ambitious to excel as a poet and composed some pieces in the manner of the best T'ang poets. But the high place he holds among Confucianists is due to the work which he performed for the Shu-ching. When he had buried his father before going into seclusion he returned to Chu Hsi and attended him, as has been stated, in his last illness. When Chu found that he could not revise and correct the text of the Shu and furnish it with a commentary he entrusted the work to Ts'ai. The latter spent nearly ten years at the task thus bequeathed to him, and in 1209 the work was completed. The title of the book is *Shu-ching-chi-chuan* (書 經 集 傳), Collected Comments on the Shu-ching. It is still the standard edition of that Classic, and, as Dr. Legge says, "is universally studied throughout the empire." The explanations it gives are clear and precise and its style is a model of excellence.

Another great work of Ts'ai Ch'ên is the *Hung-fan-huang-chi-nei-p'ien* (洪 範 皇 極 內 篇), that is, Inner pages of the Great Plan's Royal Pole. The title is derived from a section of the Shu which is headed Hung-fan, or the "Great plan," and the name of one of the classes into which this is divided. The Hung-fan-huang-chi is the Lo-shu, or Writing of the River Lo, which is the Pole-star or standard for all arrangements of number. The work is entirely about numbers, showing in a fanciful manner how these enter into all things and regulate the affairs of men and nature. It is a sort of appendix to the Yih Ching, carrying out into elaborate detail calculations supposed to belong to the vague theories of that book. In the early part it is philosophical and some what Pythagorean, but afterwards it looks like a Chinese Bradshaw. The general theory of the book and its calculations were obtained from his father who committed to Ch'ên the task of making these into a treatise. *

* For Ts'ai Ch'ên and his works see Shu-ching-chi-chuan, Preface &c., Ch. 4., p. 20; Sung-shi, Ch. 434; Tao-nan-yuan-wei, Ch. 3.; Hsing-li-ta-ch'uan, Ch. 24; Legge, Ch. Cl. III; Proleg., p. 35; Hsing-li-hui-yao, Ch. 12.

37. Chen Tê-hsiu (眞 德 秀). S. Ching-yuan (景 元), al. Chin-hsi (景 希), al. Hsi-yuan (希 元).

Chên Tê-hsiu was born in the year 1178, at P'u-ch'êng (浦 城), a town of Kien-ning-foo in Fuhkeen. His education was begun when he was in his fourth year and at that early age he showed signs of unusual genius. At the age of fourteen he lost his father, and his mother, though poor, had to undertake the education of her son. But a fellow townsman, admiring the cleverness of Tê-hsiu, took him into his family, educated him with his own sons, and ultimately gave him his daughter to wife.

In 1199, Chên was made a Chin-shi and after passing another examination with great success he was appointed to office. Having been summoned to the Capital to serve in the Imperial Academy he was in 1208 made a Public Instructor, and in this capacity he memorialized the Throne on the subject of renewing war with the Kin Tartars. Next year he was made a keeper of the National Archives and was further honoured. Wicked fellow-officials could not brook his virtuous presence and sought to ruin him. Their malice he bore patiently but he asked permission to retire. His services could not be dispensed with, however, and he was retained at the Capital. The use of Government paper money, which had been introduced in the reign of Kao Tsung, was now the subject of much complaint and no one dared to accuse the officials to the Emperor. Chên, however, ventured to do this and stated in detail the grevious malpractices which had grown up in connection with the use of the Govenment Notes. Soon afterwards he was sent to congratulate the new King of the Tartars on his accession to the Throne, but he went only a part of the way and returned distressed at the state of affairs in the provinces. Rich fields, he told the Emperor, were left neglected and waste, fine stalwart men were idle, there were no drilled troops and no preparations of defence. He implored His Majesty to have the lands brought back to cultivation and to appoint an officer with general control in the districts which feared invasion.

Afterwards he was by his own request, sent away from the Capital and placed in charge of a large and important Circuit in the South of Kiangsu and Anhui. While in this office he distinguished himself by his zealous and skilful administration. He personally superintended the government of Kuang-tê (廣 德) and T'ai-p'ing (太 平), and delivered the people of these two cities from a dreadful famine. Then he was sent to Ch'üan-chow (Chinchew), in Fuhkeen, as Prefect. Here he worked hard to improve the moral and material condition of the people. He lightened the imposts on foreign vessels frequenting the port and raised their number by this means from three or four in a year to more than thirty. He discouraged litigation, took active measures to suppress piracy and to put the sea-coast in a state of defence.

In 1222 he was made Prefect of T'an-chou, in Hunan, with an honorary title, and here also his administration was marked by wise and generous measures for the good of the people. On the accession of Li Tsung, in 1225, he was called to the Capital and appointed a Secretary in the National Academy. But enemies plotted against him and charged him with having favoured the Emperor's brother, Ch'i Wang, who had been put to death on a false accusation. Chên was degraded, and his enemies, made bold by his disgrace, asked for his banishment. To this the Emperor would not consent and Chên was allowed to go to his home. Here he composed the Tu-shu-chi (讀 書 記), or Record of Study for the use of his disciples. In 1233 he was restored to office and sent again to govern Ch'üan-chow, where his return was greeted with manifestations of universal delight. From this place he was removed to Foochow, and soon after the Emperor summoned him back to the Capital and made him President of the Board of Ceremonies. He now presented to the Emperor a treatise which he had composed while out of office, entitled Ta-hsiao-yen-i (大 學 衍 義), an Illustrative Exposition of the Great Learning. A severe illness now attacked him and he was obliged to resign. In 1235 he died, retaining his mental faculties to the end and waiting for death with calm composure.

The Emperor was much distressed when he learned of the death of Chên, and he decreed him a posthumous title and the honorary

epithet Wên-chung (文 忠), accomplished and loyal. His lit
designation is Hsi-shan (西 山), Western Hills, and he was enn
and admitted to the Confucian Temples in 1437.

In philosophy Chên Hsi-shan was a thorough follower and lee
expositor of Chu Hsi's teachings. He was the author, or compile
several treatises, some of which have been considered of great v
The Tu-shu-chi and Ta-hsiao-yen-i have been already mentio
Of the former Mr. Wylie states—"it was left in a rough manus
form at his death, and was arranged for publication by his pupil T
Han, in 1259. It treats chiefly of mental philosophy, and the char
and doings of eminent ministers from the Hëa down to the time o
Five dynasties." The Ta-hsiao-yen-i was intended to be a so
manual for Emperors and high officials. It shows that the lea
principles of the Great Learning are the same with those taught b
Shu, Mencius, and orthodox philosophers down to Chou Lien-ch'i,
that good rulers had always conformed to them while bad rulers
violated them. It "is an illustration," says Mr. Wylie, "
historical examples of the doctrines of the *Ta hëŏ*, classified under
leading heads, which are further subdivided according to subjects

Chên compiled also the Wên-chang-chêng-tsung (文 章 正 宗
Correct Progenitors of Elegant Writing. The essays which com
this treatise are derived from old but uncanonical works and
arranged under four heads—Imperial Decrees, Political Discuss
Historical Documents and Poetry. He wrote also a critical examine
of the History of the T'ang dynasty, the Hsin-ching (心 經) or Cl
of the Mind, and several other short treatises. His Memorials to
Throne, Letters, and other Miscellanies have been collected
published with the title Chên-Hsi-shan-chi (眞 西 山 集).

Chên Tê-hsiu was a tall man, with a broad forehead, a
complexion, and a stately dignified bearing. He had great n
courage, a patient temper, and a generous, self-denying disposi
In all the offices he held he did conscientiously what he saw to be his
to the ruler and the people. In politics and philosophy alike, he
a sober practical reasoner. One of his favourite doctrines was
present action in politics should be regulated by past experience,

so it behoved those in authority to be well versed in the history of former times. In philosophy he taught, like Chu Hsi, that ecstatic meditation or absorbed reflection could not of itself bring the mind to perfection, and that in order to attain this the help of books and teachers was needed.[*]

---

38. Wei Liao-wêng (魏 了 翁). S. Hua-fu (華 父).

Wei, whose name is sometimes given as Liao-wêng and sometimes as Hua-fu, was born in 1178, the same year as Chên Tê-hsiu, at P'u-kiang (浦 江), a town of K'iung-chow in the west of Ssŭchuan. His father's surname was Kao (高), but he was in childhood adopted by a man named Wei and hence he has always been known by that surname. As a boy he was noted for his grave manner and studious disposition. He distanced his elder brothers at school, and from his quickness at learning and his very retentive memory he was called by the villagers Shên-t'ung (神 童), the marvellous boy. When fourteen years old he published an Essay on Han Wên-kung which showed by its polished style that he had a genius for authorship. At the examination for the Chin-shi which he passed in 1199, he had the courage to advocate Chu Hsi's teachings which were at the time proscribed with penalties.

The first office which Wei Liao-wêng held was that of a Sub-Prefect at Hsi-ch'uan (西 川), in his native Province. In 1202, he was summoned to the Capital and made a member of the Imperial Academy, and soon after he received further honours. At this time a powerful and unscrupulous minister named Han T'ê-tsao (韓 侂 冑), was urging a renewal of hostilities with the Kin Tartars. For this the nation was notoriously in an unfit condition, and a war would produce only general misery and still further degradation. Few, however, ventured to oppose the minister, and among them was Wei Liao-wêng. He presented to the Emperor a short and pithy Memorial in which he set forth with great force the circumstances which made

---

[*] Chên-Hsi-shan-chi; Wylie, Notes &c., p. 69; Ma Tuan-lin, Ch. 219; Tao-nan-yuan-wei, Ch. 4.

war impossible. Soon after he requested a Provincial appointme and was sent to Chia-ting-foo in Ssŭchuan. From this he went hon to nurse his parents, but after the execution of Han Tê-tsao he w again summoned to the Capital. When his actual father died buried him at the foot of the Pai-ho Shan, the mountain of the Whi Stork Genius. Here he built first a hut and afterwards a college a remained at the place for some time. But he did not spend his tin idly for many disciples came to him daily, whom he taught t learning of the ancient sages as restored and developed by the t Ch'êng and Chu Hsi. Thus he introduced the study of orthod philosophy into that part of the Empire. His own masters were I Kuang (輔廣), and Li Fan (李燔), two disciples of Chu Hsi, and now transmitted their teaching to his disciples first at Chia-ting a afterwards at Han-chow (漢州). He was sent to this latter tov when his years of mourning were over, and he did much to reform t manners of its rude and turbulent people.

But a bridge fell within the bounds of his jurisdiction and ma persons were killed by the fall. This event led to his degradati and dismissal to a titular post at the Wu-yi Hills in Fuhkeen. So afterwards his former rank was restored and he was sent to Mei-ch (眉州), in Ssŭchuan. Then he was promoted to be Criminal Judg and shortly afterwards Grain Commissioner also for the T'ung-ch (潼州), Circuit in the same Province. About this time he obtain from the Emperor honorary epithets for Chow Lien-ch'i and the t Ch'êng, as a means of encouraging learning.

In 1222, he was recalled to the Capital and soon rose again in favour. But shortly after Li Tsung ascended the throne in 1225, became the victim of false charges and was sent to Ching-chow (州), in Hunan as Sub-Prefect. At this place he was attended crowds of disciples who came to him from all parts of the surroundi country, and here he wrote his Chiu-ching-yao-i (九經要義 Essential explanations of the nine Classics. In 1231, he was ag summoned to the Capital and honoured with high offices. He rose be President of the Board of Ceremonies and a Chancellor of t Imperial Academy, but his enemies were very powerful. They w able to have him sent away from Court and kept in the Provinces, and he died in 1237, while serving at Foochow.

The Emperor, who had always parted with him reluctantly, was greatly distressed at the sudden news of his death. He decreed him posthumous honours and the epithet Wên-ching (文 靖). The literary designation of Wei is Ho-shan, from the name of the mountain near Chia-ting in Ssŭchuan. In later times he was ennobled and in 1724, he was admitted to the Temple of Confucius.

Wei Liao-wêng was the author of several works which show wide learning, a good style, and soundness of faith. Tho Ho-shan-chi-chiu-ching-yao-i (鶴 山 集 九 經 要 義), which has been mentioned already by its short title, gives a selection of the best explanations of the Nine Classics arranged according to subjects. This was compiled with the view of removing doubts and perplexities caused by the apparently conflicting commentaries of different expositors. He wrote also treatises on the Yih, the Li, and other canonical works chiefly of a critical and exegetical nature.

As an official Wei Liao-wêng had that moral courage which prompts to do right in scorn of consequences. He recommended and denounced men regardless of the power which might be arrayed against him. To the Emperor he always spoke out his mind fearlessly, pointing out the course of honour and duty, and exposing the evil courses which were fraught with disaster. To the people whom he was sent to govern he was always beneficent in a large and liberal sense. He took measures to save them from oppression and misrule, to make their manners gentle, and to elevate their moral condition.

As a philosopher he was a follower of Chu Hsi whom he admired with a frank and outspoken enthusiasm. He introduced into Western Ssŭchuan the teachings of Chou Lien-ch'i and the two Ch'êng. The Memorial in which he set forth the merits of the three last is still extant. It and the Preface which he wrote for the Biography of Chu Hsi are in the collection of his smaller pieces called the Wei-Ho-shan-chi (魏 鶴 山 集). He had a great reverence for the old institutions and ceremonies and taught his disciples to study them diligently. *

* Sung-shi. Ch. 437; Hsing-li-hui-yao. Ch. 13 : Shang-yu-lu. Ch. 17.

39. Ho Chi (何 基). S. Tzŭ-kung (子 恭).

Of the life of Ho Chi very little is recorded. He belonged to Wu-chow (婺 州), in the Kin-hua Prefecture of Chekiang, and was born in 1188. His father, whose name was Poh-hui (伯 熭), was an official and in the early years of Chi came to Lin-ch'uan in Kiangsi as an Assistant Magistrate. His superior at that town was the celebrated philosopher Huang Kan, and Poh-hui sent his two sons to study with him. Ho Chi was a youth of good parts and steady application and Huang Kan foresaw that he would become an ornament to the orthodox learning.

After having studied the philosophy of Chu Hsi and the ancient Classics Ho Chi retired to his home to pursue his investigations alone. His reputation for learning soon grew and he had many disciples. Offers of employment in the public service were repeatedly made to him, but he declined all, even those which were of an easy and agreeable nature. He lived to the age of eighty years and died in 1268. The Emperor Kung-Ti in 1272, conferred on him the posthumous epithet Wên-ting (文 定), Accomplished and Resolved, showing by this act that in the midst of all his troubles he did not forget to honour deceased men of worth. In 1724, his tablet was added to the number of those in Confucius' Temple.

Ho Chi wrote illustrative commentaries on the Ta-hsiao, Chung-yung, Tso-chuan, Yih-ch'i-mêng, T'ung-shu, and Chin-ssŭ-lu. In minuteness and thoroughness he resembled the Han scholars, but all his philosophy was based on that of Chu Hsi. He was a great reader and made marginal notes in all the books which he read. For the Shi-ching he had almost a religious respect. Before taking it up he swept from his mind all disturbing elements, and then sat down and hummed over a few odes in a quiet leisurely manner. He was eminently orthodox without any ambition to get a name by peculiar views or interpretations. Among his disciples the greatest was Wang Poh who was most persevering in his efforts to acquire clearness and certainty of knowledge.

The Wên-chi (文集) or Miscellanies of Ho Chi make thirty *chuan*, and his Wên-pien (問辨) or Discussions with Wang Poh make eighteen more. He was a man who courted obscurity, who talked little and smiled rarely, but had a patient, amiable temper. His views on the ancient Classics were broad and comprehensive, and he showed that those works were illustrative of each other.

The literary designation of Ho Chi is Pei-shan (北山), North Mountain.*

———————•—•—◆—•—◆——————

40. Wang Poh (Pai and Peh) (王柏). S. Hui-chǐ (會之).

Wang Poh, who was born in 1197, belonged to the town of Wu-chou in Chekiang, the native place of Ho Chi. His grand-father Wang Shi-yü (王師愈) had been a disciple first of Yang Kuei-shan and afterwards of Chu Hsi, Chang Ch'ih, and Lü Tsu-ch'ien, and had risen to a high position in the public service. His father also, Han (瀚), was a scholar and official and was stationed for some time at Kien-ch'ang-foo in Kiangsi. He died while Poh was in his boyhood and the latter was left to the care of his oldest brother. This brother *also* was ~~also~~ a man of learning and a disciple of Chu and Lü, and all the other members of the family seem to have had a similar taste for literature and philosophy.

In his youthful years, however, Poh had an ambition to be a military hero and aspired to the fame of Chu-ko Liang. So he called himself Chang-hsiao (長嘯), Long whistle, meaning thereby to dub himself a mighty man of war impatient of obscurity. Chu-ko, before the coming of Liu Pei, used to sit idly by the fire in his mountain cot, nursing his knee and uttering long; low whistling sounds. He was longing for the time to come when he would go out into the world and win a deathless fame by great deeds. Poh wished to be like him and the name was the symbol of his ambition.

* Sung-shi. Ch. 438; Shang-yu-lu, Ch. 7.

But ~~he~~ when reached the age of thirty he was converted by passage in the Lun-yü in which Confucius explains to Fan Ch' t perfect virtue is—"in retirement to be sedately grave ; in the mana ment of business to be reverently attentive." Hereupon he tur his thoughts to learning and made the attainment of wisdom his an tion. He now discarded Long-whistle as a name unbecoming reverent deportment of a disciple of Confucius and chose insl Lu-chai (魯 齋), Lu-study, to show that he had become a follo of the Sage. His chief master in philosophy was his fellow tov man Ho Chi. With him he studied the Classics and from hin learned the tenets of Chu Hsi as these had· been communicated to by Huang Kan. He was an eager student, but always troublod v doubts and difficulties and rather impatient of authority. The gei unquestioning spirit of his master must have been sometimes tried his disciple coming back again and again with new doubts or 1 phases of old doubts. Ho taught him to acquire fixed convictions a habit of reverent attention, and Poh became not only a lear man, but also an independent thinker and an acute critic.

He did not go into office or take any part in public affairs, devoted all his energies to literature and philosophy, leading a qu happy life among his kindred and disciples. It was his daily cus to rise early and, after morning worship, to attend to family conce before going into his study. Though affectionate and tender-hear he was very precise in his conduct towards the little ones of the ho With his disciples also he was precise and he made them put mourning-clothes on the death of the Emperor Li Tsung. The ciples were very numerous, and he directed his instructions to ther such a manner as to rouse them to think for themselves. Hc modified his teaching to suit their varied capacities, in all ca however, making the Great Learning the first book of study.

In 1274 Waug Poh was suddenly attacked by a sickness wl proved fatal. When he perceived that death was near at han< signed for his wife to leave the room, and allowed only some of young relatives and disciples to remain. Then he adjusted his and robes aud sat down to await the end in calm composure.

posthumous epithet Wên-hsien (文 憲), Pattern of literary culture, was confered on him by the same Edict which gave one to Ho Chi, and master and disciple were admitted together to the Temple of Confucius. Lu-chai, the name adopted by himself, is Wang's usual designation in literature.

The honours paid to Wang Poh are on account of the great services which he rendered to the cause of Confucian learning, and the amount of literary work which he accomplished is enormous. He wrote critical or explanatory commentaries on several of the Classics, the works of Chou, the two Ch'êng, and Chu Hsi, and on the early books of History, besides several volumes of Poetry, Essays on Etymology, and other treatises. It is by his labours on the Classics, however, that he is best known. Though in the main a disciple of Chu Hsi, he differs from him on many points and boldly forms individual opinions. He did not accept the theory that the 5th chapter of the Great Learning was lost, and he restored the old division of the Chung-yung into two sections, making the 21st chapter in the present arrangement the heading of the second section. He regarded the exposition of the Great Plan in the Shu-ching as the teaching of old sovereigns and not the words of the Viscount Ki. In the Shi-ching he rejected many of the poems and altered the positions of some contending that all the 305 pieces now composing the work are not those selected by Confucious. Many of them, he thought, were country ballads which the Han editors took to fill up gaps in the canonical works, as the six odes now wanting were once furnished by a Han scholar. Among the pieces rejected by Wang Poh were the licentious songs of Ch'êng and Wei. He is regarded, however, as too bold a critic and too speculative a thinker, and his judgments have not a great influence among modern scholars.*

* Sung-shi, Ch. 438 ; Shang-yu-lu, Ch. 9.; Legge Ch. Cl. IV. Proleg. p. 174.

41, Wên T'ien-hsiang (天文祥) S. Sung-jui (宋瑞) an
shan (履善).

Wên T'ien-hsiang was born in 1236 near Chi-shui (吉水
town in the Prefecture of Chi-an-foo in Kiangsi.   In the Di
Government school of his native place were pictures of Ou-yang
and two other famous men each of whom had in his title the
Chung (忠), Loyal.   T'ien-hsiang used to contemplate the port
and say—" I shall not be a man of any worth if I am not worshi
after death among these men," thus unwitingly hinting at his
fate.   In 1254 he went up for his Chin-shi examination, and
account of the unusual excellence of his Essay the Emperor awa
him the highest place.   The subject given was the way to attain
keep a good and successful government—and Wên, who had
suffering from intense nervous excitment, wrote as if by inspira
The thoughts welled up spontaneously in his mind, and flowed
his pen in correct language and proper succession so that he did
need to make a draft or re-write his Essay.   The Examiner con
ulated the Emperor on having got a man whose spirit divined
and wrong and whose heart was set on loyalty.

Shortly after this Wên's father died, and at the end of the
of mourning for him he was appointed to a subordinate post at N
hai in Chekiang.   The Mongols were now advancing rapidly in t
conquest of China, and in 1260 a degraded minion named T'
Sung-ch'ên urged the Emperor Li Tsung to retire from Hang-cl
This advice was at once opposed by Wên who begged that T'
be put to dead.   This petition he repeated when advanced to k
Secretary in the Board of Punishments, but without success.   F
the Capital he was sent to Kiangsi as a criminal judge, and he
denounced with all his energies the infamous Chia Ssŭ-tao who
councelled flight and surrender.   In 1273 Wên was transferred
Hunan, and next year sent to Kan-chow in Kiangsi as Prefect.

On the accession of the Emperor Hsien, in 1275, an Edict was issued for a levy of forces, and Wên, sad at heart, exerted himself to raise an army in Kiangsi. He soon collected about 10,000 men, Chinese and *Man* savages, whom he sent away for the defence of the Capital. But in order to do this he had to use up all his private resources and work himself almost to death. The existence of the dynasty, however, was at stake, and he had a chivalrous sense of duty. To his friends he was wont to say—"Who joys with another's joy mourns with his sorrow, and who lives by another also dies for him." Soon afterwards he was sent to govern Soochow, and submitted to the Emperor a plan for dividing the provinces which remained into four military circuits with a commander-in-chief at the head, but his plan was rejected as impracticable. Ch'ang-chow, in Kiangsu, was now invested by the Mongols and Wên sent four detachments of troops to drive them away. Of these forces three were cut to pieces, the fourth went over to the enemy, and Ch'ang-chow was taken. Wên was now ordered to abandon Soochow and come to the defence of the country about the Capital. He was next made an Assistant Minister and sent to treat with the Mongol. General Bayen. But his proud manner and menacing language made Bayen think it advisable to make him prisoner and send him to Peking. On reaching Chinkiang, however, he managed to escape with several others and fled to Chên-chow (now Yi-chên in the Prefecture of Yang-chow). Here he was at first taken for a traitor and narrowly escaped beheading, but after some thrilling adventures he at last reached Wên-chow in safety.

The throneless Court was now at Foochow, and Wên was sent to levy forces in Kiang-si, but soon after he had his camp at Changchow in Fuhkeen. Here even in these days of disaster and despair he had the spirit to behead an official named Wu Hsüan, who, having surrendered, came to advise Wên to do likewise. He had about this time one or two petty victories but they were of no avail, and in 1277 he was utterly routed by Li Hêng, at Hsing-kuo-Hsien, in Kiangsi. His wife and children were captured and sent away to Peking, but one of his sons died on the way. He himself was saved by a friend assuming his name, and he made his way to Kuangtung. In 1278 he received from his sovereign—the child Prince at Yaishan—the empty honour of Shao-pao, Junior Guardian, and the title Hsin-kuo Kung (信 國 公). Having raised a body of troops he now went to Chaoyang in Kuangtung, but his army was defeated and he was captured at Wu-p'o-ling. On being taken to the tent of the successful General he refused to do him obeisance, and the General, Chang Hung-fan, treated him with all courtesy. He was kept on board ship and taken to the attack on Yai-shan, but he refused to write and advise Chang Shi-chie to capitulate.

At the beginning of 1279 Wên was sent as a prisoner to Peking, the Capital of the Grand Khan now Emperor of China. As he passed his native place on the way, he was overcome with grief and could not eat for several days. On his arrival at Peking he was brought before Marco Polo and other Ministers of the Emperor, who tried to bring him to submission but were silenced by his arguments. For more than three years he was kept a prisoner, though treated with much respect and indulgence. About the end of that time a Buddhist monk at Foochow saw an ill omen in the sky, a madman elsewhere called himself a Sung Prince, and rumour hinted at Wên T'ien-hsiang as concerned in a conspiracy. The Emperor sent for him and offered to make him a Minister of State if he would consent to serve. This Wê refused to do, and at the urgent request of his courtiers Kublai ordered him to be put to death. But he called Wên before him again and said—What do you want? "By the goodness of the Sung Emperors I was their Minister," replied Wên, "and I cannot serve a second dynasty—grant me only to die and it will suffice." The Emperor relented and wished to recall his order but it was too late. When the executioner arrived Wên retained a perfect composure and merely said—"My work is finished." Then having made obeisance twice towards the South received his doom which the historian thus records under the 19th year, of the period Chï-yuan, of Yuan Shi Tsu (1282). "In the 12th moon, was beheaded the Sung Junior Guardian, Privy Councillor and Hsin-kuo Kung, Wên T'ien-hsiang." His clothes were searched for papers, but all that was found was a slip on which he had written—Confucius says, Perfect private virtue, Mencius says,

Acquire public virtue, but private virtue is attained by carrying public virtue to its completion. If this is learned from the reading of the sages' books there will scarcely be shame either in life or after death. (The words are 孔曰成仁孟曰取義惟其盡所以仁至讀聖賢書所學 何事而今而後庶幾無媿) His body was given to his wife and she burst into tears as she looked on his face which still bore its living expression. It must have pleased him—if aught avail the dead—that his body was carried to his native place and laid beside that of his mother which arrived from Chaoyang in Kuangtung at the same time.

The literary designation of Wên T'ien-hsiang is Wên-shan (文山), and his admission to the Temple of Confucius took place in 1843. A few of his essays, letters, and other short pieces have been collected and published with the title Wên-shan-wên-chi. In these is included the "Song of Perfect air" which he wrote in prison. It shows his proud spirit and his longing to be with the dead—the noble martyrs for principle whose names were recorded in history. Life had lost all charms for him now that his native land was swayed by barbarians—the ox was stalled with the charger and the fowl was on the roost of the Phenix.

Wên T'ien-hsiang was in early manhood robust and handsome, with fine bright eyes and a clear complexion. He was a poet, a good scholar, a fluent graceful writer, and an eloquent talker. But zeal for the Sung dynasty was his consuming passion, and he sacrificed health, property, and life for the cause which he held so dear. His devotion to the dynasty was of the most purely disinterested and chivalrous nature, and he furnishes a perfect example of that loyalty which first stirred his youthful ardour. Mr. Lister applies to him the words which the "affable archangel" uses about the seraph Abdiel. But surely he forgot at the moment Chang Shi-chie and Luh Hsiu-fu who also were "faithful found among the faithless."

> Among innumerable false, unmoved,
> Unshaken, unseduced, unterrified."

A more modest parallel for Wên T'ien-hsiang might be found among the Highlanders who remained loyal to the Stuarts in the 18th Century.

Chêng-wên (正 文) is the posthumous epithet of T'ien-hsiang.*

————————•◦•——————▼

42. Luh Hsiu-fu (陸 秀 夫). S. Chün-shi (君 實).

Facing Wên T'ien-hsiang is his friend Luh Hsiu-fu, who, born to a like fate, has had a like renown. Luh was a native of Yen-ch'êng (鹽城), a town of Huai-an-foo, in Kiangsu, where he was born in 1236, the year also of T'ien-hsiang's birth. In 1238 his father removed with the family to Chinkiang, and here Hsiu-fu received his education. He was steady and intelligent and his teacher pointed him out among his hundred scholars as an extraordinary boy. In 1260, he became a Chin-shi, and soon after the illustrious General Li T'ing-chĭ (李庭芝) selected him to be confidential secretary. He continued for several years in the service of Li in the various offices through which the latter passed. His manner was grave and reserved, and he had no enjoyment in gaiety and dissipation or even in the society of his fellow-officials.

At this period northern Kiangsu—known as Huai-nan—was celebrated as the birth-place and resort of learned men, and for this reason it had received the designation Little Court. It was said that among the scholars of this region few were equal to Luh Hsiu-fu in mental abilities and attainments. His chief Li recommended him strongly for official employment and in 1275 he entered the public service under the hapless sovereign Ti-Hsien (Kung-Ti). His promotion was rapid for he became a Minister of State in the same year. But soon afterwards he had the misfortune to disagree with the Prime Minister, Ch'ên I-chung and was dismissed from Court and sent to Chao-chow, near Swatow. Chang Shi-chie, however, remonstrated warmly with Ch'ên who was obliged to have Luh restored to office in the following year, 1277.

---

* See Wên-shan-wên-chi (文山文集); T'ung-chien, &c.; Chuan 22, 23 (of the Sung and Yuan Supplement); Mayers, Ch. R. M. p. 254; China Review, Vol. III. p. 257.

From this time he clung to the broken fortunes of the Sung dynasty with heroic loyalty. The Emperor had done a deed of unknown shame in making himself the vassal of the barbarian invader. His son was declared Emperor with the style Tuan Tsung, and the noble-minded Yang-kuei-fei helped her son in government. She styled herself merely "slave" at audiences and the rigour of state ceremonies was now much relaxed. But Luh retained always the grave, respectful demeanour due to an Emperor in the full enjoyment of power. The Court had been driven from place to place through Chekiang, Fuhkeen, and Kuangtung. In the course of his flight the young Emperor died from cold and fear in 1278. Hereupon the other officials proposed to disperse, but Luh induced them to remain. They declared Tuan Tsung's brother Emperor and styled him Ti-Ping, Yang-kuei-fei continuing to act as Regent for her son who was only eight years of age.

Huang Fan-chung, the Commander-in-chief of Kublai's Chinese forces, was now pressing hard on the Sung Emperor and his adherents. These were taken in 1278, by Chang Shi-chie and Luh to Yai-shan, a natural stronghold near Hsin-hui in Kuangtung. Here they remained for some months and Luh kept life and spirit in the hunted exiles now at bay. He even taught the young sovereign the Great Learning, thus fitting him to die, for had not the Master said that if one learns truth in the morning he is fit to die in the evening. The story of the capture of Yai-shan has been often told and is well known. When all was lost and hope was dead Luh forced his wife and children to throw themselves into the sea. He then proceeded to the vessel which had been set apart for the child-Emperor and said to the latter, "Public affairs having come to this crisis, it is Your Majesty's duty to your country to die. The disgrace brought by Kung-Ti is very great, and Your Majesty may not again bring shame." Then he took the child on his back and plunged into the sea.

Thus perished, in the spring of 1279, the "last champion" of the Sung dynasty and with him the last representative of that dynasty. An inscription was cut on a rock at Yai-shan stating that there the General Chang Hung-fan had exterminated the Sung. But an indignant censor afterwards erased the inscription and wrote up instead—" Here died Luh Hsiu-fu, a Minister of State under the Sung dynasty. " His tablet was placed in the Temple of Confucius in 1859. *

43. Chao Fuh (趙 復). S. Jen-fu (仁 甫).

The date of Chao Fuh's birth is not known, but it is probable that he was born about the year 1200. His family had originally belonged to Yün-mêng-Hsien (雲 夢 縣), a town of Tê-an-foo in Hupeh. For some time, however, they had been settled in a hamlet situated at a short distance to the South from Tê-an city. As this hamlet was inhabited mainly by people of one surname it came to be known as Chao-chia-chou.

Fuh grew up a tall, handsome youth with bright, intelligent eyes. He was reserved in manner and very fond of his books, but he read only orthodox authors, "setting his mind on opening up peace by royal principles. " In manhood his filial piety and virtuous life, his scorn for those who had made themselves rich and great by bad means, and his dignified bearing and genial courtesy to others, were felt as a penetrating influence in the village.

Between 1225 and 1234, he obtained his Chü-jen and Chin-shi Degrees in succession, but did not seek for or receive any official appointment. His love was for learning and philosophy and he opened a school for students at the foot of the Wên-pih Peak near his native place. For the use of his disciples he prepared two works, the Hsi-hsien-lu (希 賢 錄), and the Shi-yu-t'u (師 友 圖). His lectures were attended by youths who came from all parts of the surrounding country and some from long distances.

But this quiet state of affairs was rudely subverted by the Mongol invasion which reached Tê-an in 1235. The enraged Khan had given orders that the inhabitants of cities taken should be put to the sword, but that the Professors of Confucianism, Buddhism, Taoism, Divination, and Medicine should be exempt from this order. Such persons were

---

* Sung-shi, Ch. 151.; T'ung-chien, &c. Ch. 22; (Supp. Sung and Yuan); Knang-tung-hsin-yü (廣 東 新 語), Ch. 2; China Review, Vol. III, p. 257.

to be taken alive and sent to the Khan's Court. So when Tê-an fell
and a general massacre had taken place, Chao Fuh found himself in
the list of the saved. But he did not-like this and wanted very much
to die and be laid with his parents and kindred. He became the
prisoner of an officer named Yao Ch'ü (姚 樞), who treated him
with all gentleness and courtesy. But Chao was bent on dying and
during the night he stole away from his keeper's tent resolved to
drown himself. Yao, finding that his prisoner had fled, mounted his
horse and hastened to seek him, riding over the ghastly corpses which
lay scattered over all the country. It was a clear moonlight night
and he soon descried Chao kneeling on the bank of a stream with hair
disheveled and hands raised up to Heaven. He brought him back to
the tent and gently soothed him to bear his desolate lot.

Chao was taken to the seat of the Khan at Peking, and before
leaving the camp he gave all his manuscripts into the charge of Yao.
At the capital he refused all offers of official appointment, specially
that of being guide to the Mongols' army, and the Khan, pleased at his
loyal constancy, allowed him to live at large. In 1238 his two friends
Yang Wei-chung and Yao Ch'ü built a College which they named
T'ai-chi-shu-yuan. The College contained a Hall of Worship to
Chow Lien-ch'i with potraits of his six most celebrated followers.
They invited Chao to teach in this College and he gladly consented.
He caused the works of Chow to be engraved on the walls of the temple,
and taught with great ardour and brilliant success the philosophy of
the two Ch'êng and Chu. For the use of his disciples he also composed
the Yi-lo-fa-hui (伊 洛 發 揮), and the Chuan-tao-t'u (傳 道 圖).

In 1242, Yao Chü, won over to philosophy form war and politics,
retired to his native city Su-mên, now Wei-hui-foo, on the borders of
Chihli and Honan. Here also he built a College and introduced the
writings of Chao Fuh and his great masters. Soon afterwards he
induced Chao, who had resigned his post at the Capital, to come and
teach for a time in this College. He went back to his native place in
1251, and resisted all attempts to induce him to take service under
the Mongols. But he could not rest at home for his relatives and the
friends of his youth were gone and the place was no more a home.

So he wandered about from place to place, visiting occasionally an old acquaintance of congenial sympathies. It is not known when or where he died or where he is buried, for he had resolved that no one should plant a tree or raise a stone to mark where he was laid. His choice was the "secretum iter et fallentis semita vitæ."

The literary designation of Chao Fuh is Chiang-Han, for Chiang-Han-shang-Hsien-shêng (江 漢 上 先 生), the Teacher from above the Yangtzŭ and Han. To show his allegiance to the native sovereigns he often styled himself Ch'ien-hsiang-kung-Chin-shi (前 鄉 貢 進 士), or Chü-jen and Chin-shi of the previous dynasty. In 1724, his tablet was admitted to the Temple and in utter disregard of his life and principles he was treated as first of the Yuan scholars.

Chao Fuh wrote commentaries on the Yih and other Classics besides the treatises already mentioned, and some poetry. The Chuan-tao-t'u is a table illustrating the "transmission of truth" from Fu Hsi down to Chu. The Hsi-hsien-lu gives lessons from the lives of Yi-yin and Yen Yuan, and the Shi-yu-t'u is an account of the 53 illustrious disciples of Chu Hsi. The Chao-tzŭ-yen-hsing-lu contains these short treatises, a few poems by Chao, and all that has been discovered about his life and work. It is the production of three men surnamed Ch'ên (陳), and apparently brothers, and is a recent publication.

The great merits of Chao are that he remained steadfast in loyalty to the native dynasty, and that he introduced and spread a knowledge of Chow, Chang, the two Ch'êng and, above all, Chu Hsi into the parts about Peking. He taught the Yih with the commentary on it by I-ch'uan, and all the other canonical works according to the readings and interpretations given by him, Ming-tao, and Chu Hsi. Hence it came to pass that the founder of the Yuan dynasty made Chu Hsi's editions of the Classics the text-books for the official Examinations. Moreover Chao had an immense number of disciples who carried his teachings to their homes. Some of these rose to eminence and fame, the most distinguished being Hsü Hêng, who appears below, though it does not appear that Hsü enjoyed the advantage of hearing Chao's discourses. *

---

* The Chao-tzŭ-yen-hsing-lu (趙 子 言 行 錄).

44. Hsü Hêng (許 衡). S. Chung-p'ing (仲 平).

The home of the family to which Hsü Hêng belonged was at Ho-nei (河 內), a town in the Prefecture of Huai-ch'ing (懷 慶) in Honan. He was born, however, in the year 1209 at Hsin-chêng (新 鄭) in the Prefecture of K'ai-fêng, his father having fled thither from the troubles which had come upon his native place. The education of Hêng was begun when he was six years of age, and he surprised his teacher by asking—"For what purpose do I read books"? "To obtain your Degree," said the teacher. "And is that all?" replied the precocious child, an answer at which the teacher marveled. The latter foresaw that Hêng would become a great man and he insisted on resigning his situation, declaring himself not competent to teach the young prodigy. For Hêng was an unusually clever, studious boy, always wanting to comprehend thoroughly whatever he read. A second and a third teacher were engaged in succession, but they also found themselves unfit for their office, and Hêng was at last left to educate himself. He hungered and thirsted for knowledge and eagerly de-voured all the information he could obtain. The troubled state of the country had made books very rare, and he was poor, so, like Chao Fuh, he had to copy out the works which he wanted to study. At some distance from his home there lived an astrologer who had a large and miscellaneous library, including copies of the Classics with commentaries. Hêng, having obtained leave to stay with the astrolo-ger for some time, read and copied out many of his books. His reading about this time embraced almost every department of Chinese learning —philosophy, history, law, astronomy, engineering, Buddhism, Taoism, and other subjects.

The alarm of war drove him away and he went first to Tsu-lai-shan in Shantung where he found a copy of Wang Poh's treatise on the Yih Ching. From Tsu-lai he went to Ta-ming-foo in Chihli where he remained for three years, continuing his multifarious studies and teaching. Hearing that there was peace in Huai-ch'ing he resolved to go to that place, but at Wei-hui-foo he made the acquaintance of Yao Ch'ü (姚 樞). In 1243 he fixed his residence at Wei-hui and became a disciple of Yao, who taught him what he himself had learned from Chao Fuh. This was the turning point in the life of Hsü Hêng. He read and made copies of the works of the two Ch'êng and Chu Hsi which Yao possessed, and became an enthusiastic follower of the last. All other learning was now laid aside, the unprofitable books were burnt, and he studied and taught only Confucianism as expounded by Chu Hsi. He now led the life of a rural philosopher and tilled a small farm for the support of himself and family, helping occasionally the needy among his disciples. In the midst of toil and poverty he set an example of honesty and integrity, and his household was a pattern to all around.

In 1255 he was brought to the notice of Kublai who was at the time devising measures for the restoration of order in Shensi. He appointed Hsü Director of Studies at Si-an-foo, but Hsü declined the office on the plea of not having passed the usual Examinations. But he was induced to go to Si-an and introduce a system of education. In this he was very successful and schools were quickly established in many towns. Kublai's army, however, in 1259 proceeded with the conquest of China, and Hsü, to the great distress of the people of Shensi, resigned and went home to Huai-ch'ing. But next year, on the accession of Kublai, he was called to office at Peking. His old teacher Yao Ch'ü was also now in office at the Court and Hsü joined him in opposing the counsels of harshness and severity which an unprincipled Minister was urging on the Khan. Hsü was promoted to be a Libationer in the Imperial Academy, but soon afterwards he resigned office on account of ill health.

In 1267 he was again at the Capital holding a high position. He had now to oppose the grasping ambition of a Mongolian Minister, and failing in his efforts he importuned the Khan for leave to resign. In 1271 Kublai instituted a College for the education of Mongolian boys in the manners and learning of China and he made Hsü the Principal. This was congenial occupation and he gave himself up to the work with great fervour, but he had to resign in 1273 and go to his native place. Three years afterwards the Khan called him again to Court in order that he might adjust the Calendar, making him Grand Secretary and President of the Astronomical Board. Hsü was engaged on his task in conjunction with another man of science and produced the well-known treatise Shou-shi-lih (授時歷), the Season-communicating Calendar. In 1280 the Khan again reluctantly gave him leave to resign and he went home to Huai-ch'ing. He was now old and broken down with long sickness, and he did not survive many months. One day in the year 1281 he was sitting at his cottage door humming some pretty verses in which Chu Hsi expresses his happiness in the enjoyment of beautiful moonlight scenery. When he finished these verses his spirit passed calmly and gently away.

Hsü Hêng had said to his son—"My life has been embarrassed with an empty name, and I was unable to keep out of office. When I am dead do not ask for a posthumous epithet or make a formal epitaph. Write only the four words—Here lies a Hsü—that inscription will enable my descendants to recognise my resting place." His son kept the commandment, but Hsü was not allowed thus to pass into oblivion. His death was attended with portents from Heaven, for a great wind arose which tore up trees, and the sky thundered and lightened that evening. His disciples came from far and near to weep at his funeral, and not they alone, but rich and poor, old and young of Huai-ch'ing all came to weep at his door. The Emperor Ch'êng Tsung in 1298 conferred on him the epithet Wên-chêng (文正), and Wu Tsung ennobled him as Wei-kuo Kung (魏國公), his native place having once formed a part of the State of Wei. In 1313 he received the crowning honour of being received into the Temple of Confucius. From the name which he gave his retreat at the Tsu-lai Shan he was called Lu-chi (魯齋) by his friends and disciples, and this is his usual designation in literature.

The services which Hsü Hêng rendered his country were very great. His pure character and varied accomplishments made him a favourite with the Mongolian rulers and so enabled him to do much good. He rebuked the vices of the Court with fearless honesty, and raised his voice and used his pen in the cause of peace and order. He taught and practised the sober lessons of a plain philosophy in the midst of superstitious barbarians and faithless renegades. To him, says a native author, may be applied the words of Mencius—"a depraved generation cannot confound him who is complete in virtue." That his principles did not prevail was the fault of the times, and truth, like the Sun, is sometimes behind a cloud and sometimes suffers eclipse. As a teacher he revived the study of Confucius and Mencius, but specially of Chu Hsi in Honan and Shensi. His Primer in Philosophy was the Little Learning of Chu, and when his disciples had mastered that he introduced them to the Four Books. To Chu he is said to stand in a like relation to that in which Mencius stands to Confucius.

The miscellanies of Hsü have been collected and published along with his Life and other notices of him in a work entitled Hsü-chai-chi. The official and other writings preserved in this compilation afford interesting and pleasant reading. Hsü had a clear, simple style and a homely, straight-forward way of expressing himself. Some of his illustrations are quaint and striking, as when he explains the position of a Secretary of State by comparing that official to a comb or spoon. His Discourse on the essentials of good government is sound Confucianism and his Lecture on the Great Learning gives a popular exposition of that work in the language of every day life.*

45. Chin Li-hsiang (金 履 祥). S. Chi-fu (吉 父).

The family of which Chin Li-hsiang came was one in which virtue and learning had been hereditary for several generations. It had long been settled at Lan-k'i (蘭 溪) a town on the Tsien-tang river in the Kin-huo Prefecture of Chekiang, and here Hsiang was born in the year 1232. His education was begun by his father and elder brother, and he early showed himself to be possessed of genius and capable of

* Hsü-Lu-chai-chi (許 魯 齋 集); T'ung-chien &c., (Supplement) Ch. 223.; Chao-tzŭ-yon-bsing-ln, Ch. 下 ; Ch'ou-jen-chuan 疇 人 傳 Ch. 24.

application. As he grew up he took in a wide course of study, including astronomy, geomancy, ceremonial observances, taxation, military tactics, and meteorology. In manhood, however, he neglected these and applied himself to philosophy, particularly that taught by Chou Lien-ch'i and his followers. For some time he was a disciple of Wang Poh and Ho Chi, and from the latter he learned to study and admire the writings of Chu Hsi.

At this time the Sung dynasty was plainly doomed to pass speedily away, and Chin resolved not to seek for official employment. But when news came in 1269 that Siang-yang and Fan-ch'êng in Hupeh were closely besieged by the forces of the Khan he could not refrian from offering advice. Accordingly he drew up a Memorial to the Throne in which he proposed that a fleet should be sent by sea with a large force to attack Chi-chow in Chihli not very far from the Capital. The besieging army would thus be drawn away to defend Peking and the surrounding country. The Memorial described minutely the course which the fleet should take, the cities and towns at which it could call, and the islands it would pass. Unfortunately the proposition came too late for the Sung Emperors, but the Memorial was remembered long afterwards and found useful and correct.

In 1275 a titular post was offered to Chin which he declined. War was now raging over all the country and the house of Sung was near its extermination. Chin fled from the fury of the ravaging armies and went into seclusion in the Jen Hills near his native place. Here, when peace came, he was able to lead a simple, happy life. He loved to wander alone among the crags and dells of the hills and enjoy the changing phases of nature. His life, however, was not that of an ascetic for he had many disciples and mixed much with the people of the neighbourhood. On one occasion he learned of a mother and son who had been condemned to exile in places far apart. Without disclosing his name he paid the redemption money for both, and had the pleasure of seeing the son rise to eminence, but neither mother nor son ever knew who was their redeemer. In the latter part of his life he became the head of a College near Kin-hua, and had numerous disciples, the greatest being Hsü Ch'ien whose name will shortly appear. Little more is known about his life, and he died in 1303.

From the name of the hill at which Chin lived he was called Jen-shan (仁 山) by his friends and disciples. The last Emperor of the Yuan dynasty gave him the posthumous appellation Wên-an (文 安), Cultured Repose, that is, scholar in private life. His tablet was placed in the Temple in 1437.

The critics of his time used to say that Chin Li-hsiang combined in himself the moral virtues of Ho Chi and the intellectual endowments of Wang Poh. His greatest literary achievement was his addition to the T'ung-chien-kang-mu. The name of this work is T'ung-chien-ch'ien-pien (通 鑑 前 編), and it embraces the period from Yao down to Wei-Lie Wang, of Chow, where Ssŭ-ma Kuang's History begins. The Tso-chuan, Wai-chi, and other works which treated of these early times did not draw their information from canonical writings and so Chin considered them to be deficient in authority. His Ch'ien-pien is the result of a careful study of the ancient Classics helped by the Huang-chi-ching-shi, of Shao, and the Huang-wang-ta-chi, of Hu. It was given in manuscript to Hsü Ch'ien who revised and corrected it for the use of the disciples, and it was not actually published until 1330. Besides this great work Chin wrote also commentaries on the Great Learning, the Chung-yung, and the Shu, and a critical examination of the Commentaries on the Lun-yü and Mencius. These also were given over to Hsü Ch'ien and circulated in manuscript among the disciples for many years. His Miscellanies were collected and published with the title Jen-shan-wên-chi (仁山文集). He explained and developed the theories of Chu Hsi, and by his writings and his determined choice of obscurity he reflected a lustre on Confucianism.*

---

* Shang-yu-lu, Ch. 13 ; T'ung-chien &c. (Suppl.) Ch. 24; Do. Ch'ien-pien, Introduction.

46. Wu Ch'êng (吳 澄). S. Yu-ch'ing (幼 清).

Wu Ch'êng, was born in 1247, near the town of Ts'ung-jen (崇 仁), in the Fu-chow Prefecture of Kiangsi. His natal village was situated between the Hua-kai and Lin-ch'uan Hills, and an expert had declared that the locality would produce a remarkable man. This turned out to be Wu whose birth was preceded by two portents. An old man saw an unusual vapour settle on the house of the Wu family, and an old woman dreamt that something came wriggling down into the pond beside her house. These were both satisfactorily accounted for next morning by the announcement that the Wu family had been increased, by the birth of a son.

The genius of Ch'êng displayed itself very early, for in his third year he was able to remember and repeat old poetry which he heard recited. In his fifth year he could not be kept from his books and used to sit up all night reading. His mother feared he would injure himself and gave him a short allowance of oil, but when she fell asleep he replenished his lamp. This enthusiasm for learning continued and when he was nine years old he was always among the first at the public examinations of the village school. He now began the study of the Great Learning and worked at it for three years. In a similar thorough manner he read the Lun-yü, Mencius, and the Chung-yung. But when he went up for the Chin-shi Examination he failed to obtain the Degree.

In 1276 he went to reside near Lo-an, also in the Prefecture of Fu-chow, and here he published his edition of the Hsiao-ching or Classic of Filial Piety. At this time also he revised and corrected the current editions of the Yih, Shu, Shi, Ch'ün-ch'iu, Yi-li, and Li-chi. Having been recommended for official employment he was about to receive an appointment when he declined on the plea of the old age of his mother. By the advice of the censor who had recommended Wu the Emperor Kublai sent an officer to obtain copies of the works which Wu had finished for the use of the Imperial Academy.

In 1295, he was made official Preceptor at Nan-ch'ang-foo in his native Province, and some time after he was nominated to a post in the Han-lin-Yuan. Arriving at the Capital after long delay he found the post filled, and at once went back to Kiangsi. Here he was appointed Director of Studies, but at the end of three months he had to resign on account of sickness. The next appointment held was that of a subordinate in the Imperial Academy which was conferred on him in 1308. Here he revived the system of instruction which had been introduced by Hsü Hêng, and discharged his duties in a most thorough and conscientious manner. Every day he received the students one by one, and answered their questions or explained their difficulties, suiting his teaching to the disciple's capacity. After several years he resigned and many of the youths of the Academy accompanied him to Kiangsi. In 1321, he was made a Secretary of the Han-lin, and in 1323 he was ordered to write a Preface for certain Buddhist Scriptures which Ying Tsung caused to be written out in gilt letters as a work of merit. Wu, however, in a firm but courteous manner refused to send down his name to posterity in connection with such a work. Next year the Emperor T'ai Ting, opened the Classical Hall, and appointed Wu with certain others to lecture in it to the Prince and the young nobles of his Court, on the T'ung-chien, the Great Learning and other treatises of History and Government.

A few years afterwards Wu resigned and went back to his native place. In 1330 the post of Director of Studies in Kiangsi was conferred on his son that the latter might be enabled to maintain his father. One day next year a great star was seen to fall to the North-east of Wu's house, and next day he died. The historian records the event thus; "In the 6th moon, (of the Chī-shun 2nd year, 1331) the Han-lin Secretary, Wu Ch'êng died." In the case of Hsü Hêng the title was omitted, and the historian has been justly censured for his imperfect appreciation of Hsü's merits. The same honour was plainly due to both.

Posthumous preferment was decreed to Wu Ch'êng and he received the title Lin-ch'uan-chun-kung (臨州君公), the Man of Lin-ch'uan, that is, Fu-chow. His epithet is Wên-chêng (文正), and his literary designations are Lin-ch'uan and Ts'ao-lu (草廬). When he retired from office to his native place he lived in a wattled cottage with a thatched roof, and hence arose the familiar name Ts'ao-lu. In 1443 his tablet was placed in the Temple, but in 1530 it was removed; and in 1737 it was restored.

The contributions of Wu Ch'êng to the learning and literature of his country were very great. His wide range of reading, generous appreciation of whatever was good in books, and his candid spirit of enquiry have been acknowledged even by reluctant critics. Though a follower of Chu Hsi, he did not consider himself bound to accept all that philosopher's opinions. In the matter of dispute between him and Luh Chiu-yuan, which is very like the old difficulty as to whether " Virtutem doctrina paret naturane donet," Wu adopted a middle course. He held that teaching was necessary, but that it must presuppose a moral nature, pure and perfect. Wu was not afraid to breathe the free air of independent opinion, and not only did he dissent from many of the received judgments on the orthodox Classics, but he also strayed into the border-land of heresy. Of his *Shang*-shu-tsuan-yen (尙書纂言) Legge says—"Under the Yuen dynasty, about the beginning of the 14th century, Wu Chêng published his 'Digest of Remarks on the Shang Shoo.' The Work, so far as it goes, is well worthy of study. Chêng was a bold thinker and a daring critic. He handled the text with a freedom which I have not elsewhere seen."

Wu wrote similar " Digests of Remarks " on the Yih, the Ch'un-ch'iu, and the Books of Ceremonies; he edited and commented on the Tao-tê *Ching* and Chuang-tzŭ; and he revised and corrected several treatises of more recent origin. His works, however, have long been out of fashion, and they are little read except by such students as prefer learning to office. The taint of heresy still clings to him among superficial scholars and dim-eyed bigots. In his view Buddhism, Taoism, and Confucianism were three roads to virtue all diverging from that Ideal Truth which is one and eternal, but of the three the best and purest was Confucianism.*

---

* Tung-chien &c. (Supplement), Chs. 25, 26; Legge, Ch. Cl. III. Proleg. p. 36; Hsing-li-hui-yao, Ch. 13.

47. Ch'ên Hao (陳 澔). S. K'o-ta (可 大).

Of Ch'ên Hao's life very little is known. He was a native of Tu-ch'ang (都 昌), a town in the Prefecture of Nankang, and situated on the east side of the Po-yang Lake. His father, whose name was Ta-yu (大 猷), held office and rose to be Sub-Prefect of Huang-chou in Hupeh. Ta-yu was a man of ability and great learning, and he had made a special study of the Li-chi (禮 記), collecting materials for a commentary on that work.

Hao also became a man of extensive reading, and applied himself devotedly to the study of the ancient Classics. When the Sung dynasty was abolished he retired into obscurity and gave himself up to learning and teaching. For a large portion of his life he was afflicted with ill health, but he lived to be eighty years old, and died in 1341.

The literary designations of Ch'ên Hao, are Yun-chuang (雲 莊) and Ching-kuei (經 歸). These were given to him by his disciples of whom he had a large number. He is also known as Tung-huei-tsê (東 匯 澤) from the situation of his birth place. In 1724 he was admitted to the Temple of Confucius.

The fame of Ch'ên rests entirely on his one great work—the *Li-chi-chi-shuo*, which was finished about 1321. This treatise contains forty-nine *chuan* of text and a minute and very useful commentary. The author quotes largely from previous scholars specially those of the Sung dynasty. He shows great research and is terse and clear in his explanations. This treatise was added to the Imperial Library by the first Emperor of the Ming dynasty. It was afterwards, about the year 1440, made the text-book of the Li-chi for the official examinations, and it continues such to the present. In the Yung-lo period (1403 to 1425), however, Ch'ên's commentary and arrangement were already superseding those of the Han scholar Ch'êng Hsüan.*

* Li-chi-chi-shuo, (禮 記 集 說), Preface.

48. Hsü Ch'ien (許 謙) S. Yi-chï (益 之).

Hsü Ch'ien, who was born in 1270, was a native of Kin-hua-foo in Chekiang. At an early age he was left an orphan and fell to the care of an amiable and educated woman who taught him the Classic of Filial Piety and the Lun-yü by word of mouth. He was a quick, attentive boy and grew up to be a thorough lover of learning. In studying the four old Classics, viz :—the Yih, Shi, Shu, and Ch'un-ch'iu, he allotted separate tasks for day and night, and worked resolutely even when in ill health. In philosophy, and classical learning he had Chin Li-hsiang as his master and studied under that great scholar for several years. Chin introduced Hsü to the writings of Ho Chi and Wang Poh, and these four are often associated as the illustrious Chekiang men of the 13th century. It was through Chin also that Hsü became acquainted with the works of Chu Hsi and learned to admire and adopt their teachings. But his studies were not confined to the orthodox Classics and their commentaries. They extended to Astronomy, Law, Etymology, Natural philosophy and took in also Buddhism and Taoism. These last he investigated thoroughly in ordor to find the sources and causes of their errors and thus know how to refute them.

When Hsü had completed his education he retired to the Pa-hua (八 華) Shan, in the Prefecture of Kin-hua, and gave himself up to study and teaching. Here he became the chief of a large school, and had disciples of all kinds and from all quarters of the surrounding country. These he taught with careful assiduity and with remarkable success, training them to think for themselves and develope their natural abilities. He used the Four Books as his text-books and expounded these according to Chu Hsi's method and commentaries. But he refused to prepare students for the State examinations, because these, he alleged, cut off personal advantage from public duty.

For forty years Hsü led this philosopher's life, earning a noble fame without leaving the bounds of his lonely hamlet or in any way

seeking to be known among men.   Various efforts were made to bring
him into public life, but he utterly refused to take service even as
official Examiner under Barbarian Emperors.   He died in 1337, and
the historian records the event with minute solemnity.

During his life the disciples of Hsü Ch'ien generally spoke of him
as the Pai-yün-Hsien-shêng (白 雲 先 生), Mr. White-cloud, because
Hsü was wont to speak of himself as a White-cloud man.   Pai-yün
is consequently the common name for him in literature.   His posthumous epithet is Wên-yi (文 懿), Accomplished and Amiable, and
he was admitted to the Temple in 1734.

Hsü Ch'ien was the author of a celebrated work on the Shi-ching
entitled, Shi-chi-chuan-ming-wu-ch'ao (詩 集 傳 名 物 鈔) which Dr.
Legge describes as—" Examination of Names and Things, as given
in Choo He's She and commentary, from all sources."   It was intended to correct mistakes in the explanations which had been given
of the sounds of characters and of the names of objects mentioned in
the Shi.   He composed also treatises on the Four Books and the Shu-
ching.   To the latter he appended an examination of the history of
China, from the time of Fu-hsi down to the death of Ssŭ-ma Kuang,
in.1086.   His miscellaneous pieces are published in two volumes with
the title Pai-yun-chi (白 雲 集).   All his works are still current
among the literati of China and still hold a high rank.

A place has been assigned to Hsü Ch'ien in the Temple of Confucius partly because he revived the learning of Ho Chi, Wang Poh,
and Chin Li-hsiang, in the Province to which they all belonged, and
taught his numerous disciples to study and appreciate Chu Hsi.   But
a higher merit is that he abstained from office, refusing to accept place
or power in evil times.   The sceptre was wielded by barbarians and
there was no good government in the land.   It was the duty, accordingly, of a genuine Confucianist to embosom his principles and practise
them only in private life.   Hsü never felt the spur of fame nor knew
the tickling good of vulgar applause.   He wrote books only for the
sake of correcting error and spreading what he regarded as true
knowledge.   On account of his wide learning, his skill in the use of
language, and the nature of his doctrines, he was spoken of by the

scholars of his time, as an incarnation of Chu Hsi. Though he lived apart from the noisy strife of the world he did not lose his human sympathies, and when his countrymen were afflicted with famine and pestilence he was so distressed that he could not enjoy his food and became pale and thin.*

------◄►------

49. Fang Hsiao-ju (方孝孺). S. Hsi-chĭ (希 直). and Hsi-ku (希 古).

Fang Hsiao-ju, was born in the year 1357, at a village called Hou-ch'êng (緱 城), near the town of Ning-hai in Chekiang, and not far from the T'ien-t'ai Mountains. His father, K'o-chin (克 勤), was an official of great abilities and high character under the first emperor of the Ming dynasty, Ming T'ai Tsu. As a boy Hsiao-ju was noted for his bright, sparkling eyes and his unusual cleverness. From the excellence of his juvenile compositions and the ease with which they were written, he acquired among his fellow-villagers the soubriquet Hsiao-Han-tzŭ, that is, the little Han-yü. When sixteen years of age he went with his father to the latter's post at Ch'i-ning (濟 寧), in Shantung, and had much pleasure in visiting the places of classical interest in that Province. In 1375, his father was arrested and put in prison on a false charge and Hsiao-ju tried to be allowed to suffer for him. Next year he became a disciple of Sung Lien (宋 濂), a celebrated scholar and statesman of this period. But when his father was put to death he had the corpse carried to the family burying-place and followed it home. When the period of mourning was over he renewed his studies with Sung Lien who was now living in retirement at P'u-yang in the Lin-hua Prefecture, in Chekiang.

In 1382, Hsiao-ju was presented to T'ai Tsu, who was much pleased with his grave and dignified manner but thought it better not to put him in office at once. About ten years afterwards he became tutor to Prince Hsien, one of the Emperor's sons, and accompanied him to his Principality in Ssuchuan. Here he remained for several

* T'ung-chien &c., (Supplement), Yuen, Ch. 26; Legge, Ch. Cl. IV., Proleg. p. 179, et al.

years and won the esteem and affection of his pupil. He gave the name Sun-chĭ (遜 志), Yielding will, to his study, but the Prince changed this to Chêng-hsio (正 學), Orthodox learning, and the latter became Fang's literary designation.

When Hui Ti succeeded to the throne in 1399, he made Fang a Secretary of the Han-lin and Expounder of the Classics, and subsequently a Minister of State and a Doctor of the Han-lin. The Emperor consulted him about all difficulties not only in philosophy but also in government, and he drew up all the Imperial rescripts and Decrees. The reign of Hui Ti was a short and troubled one. He was the grandson of T'ai Tsu who had passed over all his own sons and named the son of the deceased Prince Imperial as his successor. This conduct created much jealousy and ill will between the young emperor and his uncles. The former acted cruelly and unjustly to the latter, stripping them of their rank or driving them to commit suicide, on slight or groundless suspicions. The Prince of Yen, one of the most ambitious and most accomplished of T'ai Tsu's sons, headed a rebellion and soon drove Hui Ti from his throne. It is not known what became of the unfortunate emperor, whether he burnt himself to death, or became a monk, or fled to Yunnan. The Prince of Yen ascended the throne in 1403, and adopted the style Yung-lo. He called Fang Hsiao-ju to resume his post as Chief adviser and drafter of Imperial Decrees. This, however, Fang refused to do, resolved not to serve a usurper, and he was thrown into prison. One of Yung-lo's ministers warned him not to put to death Fang, whose name and influence were great among all lovers of learning. Yang-lo summoned him into his presence and said—"I want to do as Chou-kung did for Ch'êng-Wang." "Is your Ch'êng Wang still living"? said Fang. "No, he has died by self-cremation." "Why not place his son on the Throne?" replied Fang. "The Empire requires a full-grown ruler." "Then why not set one of your Ch'êng-Wang's younger brothers on the Throne?" "That is a matter of our family," retorted the Emperor. He then picked up a pen and gave it to Fang, saying—"Without you the Decrees for the Empire cannot be drawn up." Fang weeping and chiding alternately, threw the pen on the ground. But being forced to take it up again he wrote in large characters—"The Yen rebel usurps the Throne." He ended by saying—"Put me to death if you will, but I cannot draft your Decrees." The Emperor became enraged and ordered him to be hacked to pieces in the market-place.

Fang heard his doom with composure and satisfaction, and in the interval before it was carried out he made a few lines—his swan-song before death. His younger brother was hewn to pieces at the same time, and all his friends and disciples who could be found were also brutally massacred. His wife and four children all committed suicide in order to avoid falling into the hands of the savage tyrant. In the night after the execution, some of Fang's disciples came by stealth and gathered up the pieces of his body. They buried them outside the South gate of Nankin, and a tombstone was placed at the grave which remains to this day.

The rage of Yung-lo was not appeased by the barbarous murder of Fang and the extermination of all his kindred. He ordered that all his writings should be burnt and forbade any one, under penalty of death, to hide them. Fang had composed treatises on the Yih and the Chow-li, and had written other works, and these were destroyed. He had published in 1397, a small collection of essays and miscellanies, and this was preserved by a faithful disciple. It was carefully edited and republished during the reign of Hsüan Tsung (1426-1435), with the title Hou-ch'êng-chi, from the name of Fang's native place. A new edition with a life of the author has been recently published as the Fang-chêng-hsio-chi (方 正 學 集). It contains a number of Letters, the Prefaces to his lost works, several Essays, some Memoirs and other miscellanies. The account which he gives of his father's official career is one of the most interesting in the collection, and some of the Fragments on political and philosophical subjects are also worth reading. Fang was a poet and a lover of poetry, and in conjunction with his master, Sung Lien, he edited the collection of lyrics made by Chang K'o-chiu (張 可 久), of the Yuan dynasty.

The literary soubriquets of Fang Hsiao-ju are Sun-chï (遜 志), and Chêng-hsio (正 學), derived, as has been stated, from names given

to his study, but the former is seldom used.   He is sometimes referred
to as the T'ien-t'ai Hsien-shêng, because his home was near the T'ien-
t'ai mountains.   In 1863, his tablet was placed in the Confucian
Temple, first of the Ming Ju. *

---

50. Ts'ao Tuan (曹 端). S. Chêng-fu (正 夫).

The native place of Ts'ao Tuan was Min-chï (澠 池), a town in
Ho-nan-foo, where he was born in the year 1376.   As a boy he was
marked for his filial piety and his diligence in study, and these virtues
remained with him throughout life.   He grew up to be a man of great
learning and of a gentle, amiable disposition.

In due time Ts'ao entered public life, and he held several offices
in succession.   For many years he was Director of Studies at Ho-
chow (霍 州), in Shansi, and here he earned his lasting fame.   He had
a large number of disciples to whom he communicated the learning of
the great Sung philosophers and the true meaning of the old canonical
books on Ceremonies and Music.   His death occurred in 1434, and
his loss was lamented wherever he was known.   The shops were
closed at Ho-chow and all the people felt saddened, the children cried
for him and the poor sorrowed as being left helpless and hopeless, and
his disciples mourned for him the full period of three years.

During life Ts'ao Tuan was called Yue-chuan-Hsien-shêng (月
川 先 生), and Yue-chuan became his literary designation.   He was
admitted to the Confucian Temple in the year 1860.   His published
works comprise explanatory commentaries on the Four Books, the
T'ai-chi-t'u, the T'ung-shu, Hsi-ming, and the Classic of Filial Piety.
His short pieces were collected and published in one volume with the
title Ts'ao-yue-chuan-chi.

---

* Fang-Chêng-hsio-chi; T'ung-chien, &c.; (Ming Suppl. 明 紀 綱 目), Ch. 384.;
  Wylie, Notes, &c. p. 205.

As a philosopher Ts'ao followed Chu Hsi and his predecessors of the Sung dynasty, and he was a diligent student and earnest expounder of their teachings. He was a determined enemy to Buddhism, Taoism, and all superstition and imposture including Fêng-shui. But he is known chiefly as the first Ming scholar in the departments of social observances and ancient music. On these subjects he lectured to his disciples and he revived the study of them in Shansi. By the example of his life, and the excellence of his teaching he wrought much good among the people of Ho-chou and other places.*

---

51. Hsie Hsüan (薛 瑄). S. Tê-wên (德 溫).

The home of the Hsie family was at Ho-chin (河 津), a town of Shansi, formerly within the Prefecture of P'ing-yang and now included in that of Kiang-chow. For several generations the family had produced men of genius and learning though the troubles of their times had kept them from seeing office. But Hsüan's father, named Chên (貞), a man of great abilities and high moral qualities, had accepted office early in the reign of Ming T'ai Tsu. Some years afterwards he was appointed Director of Studies at Yü-t'ien (玉 田), a town of Tsun-hua-foo in Chihli. It was in the College at this town that Hsüan was born in the year 1389 (though some place his birth in the year 1393). On the night of this event a man dressed in purple clothes and a tall hat appeared to his mother in a dream, and when she woke from sleep she was delivered of a son. But the sight of the infant horrified her, for his flesh was transparent like crystal and all his inwards were plainly visible. She wanted to destroy the baby, but the grand-father after hearing it cry interposed. "An infant with a transparent body (pure and clear), and strong powers of crying," he truly observed, "is no common child. He is destined to bring glory to his ancestors." Then the oracle was consulted, and, the answer proving favourable, Hsüan was "raised."   .

* Ming-shi, Ch., 282.

It is not surprising to learn that at seven years of age this child had the sedateness and gravity of a man, and that he had great powers of learning and remembering. His education was begun by his father who taught him first the Little Learning and afterwards the Four Books. When eleven years of age Hsüan, who had begun to write verses after the manner of youthful genius, was apprenticed to philosophy. Several eminent scholars were living in exile at Yü-t'ien and Hsie Chên invited them to the College and entrusted to them his son's education. Hsüan now applied himself to the study of the Classics, History, and the works of the great Sung philosophers. His progress was rapid for he had quick apprehension and unwearying industry. His teachers after a time ceased to regard him as a pupil and spoke of him as their "young friend."

In the early part of the Yung-lo period, Hsie Chên was transferred to Yung-yang in the Prefecture of K'ai-fêng. Here Hsüan became known to an official who was on duty in the district. This official was struck with the character and abilities of Hsüan and foretold his coming greatness. He wished to bring him to the notice of the Emperor for employment, but Hsüan refused to allow this, saying that he was not of suitable age and that his education was not finished. Afterwards becoming convinced that the writings of Chou Lien-ch'i and his followers were the artery in which divine truth flowed, he burnt his poetry, abandoned the course of study required for the State examinations, and resolved to devote himself to philosophy.

But a few years later, when his father was transferred to Yenling also in K'ai-fêng he yielded to his request and competed for the Chü-jen Degree. Having taken first place in this he next year, 1421, went up for the Chin-shi and obtained it also. The death of his father soon followed, and Hsüan observed the prescribed rules of mourning with the greatest strictness and with deep sorrow. When the period of retirement was over he applied for a literary appointment, and some time afterward he was made Superintendent of the Silver Mines of Hunan and Hupeh. While holding this office he did much to improve the people, and also continued his private studies. In 1435 he was made a Censor, and next year he was sent to Shan-

tung as Literary Chancellor, an appointment which gave him great
satisfaction. He introduced Chu Hsi's method of instruction, but
taught his disciples to place the practice of virtue first and literary
accomplishments second. His tenure of office was marked with great
success and he came to be known in literary circles as Hsie-fu-tzŭ
(薛 夫 子).

Through the action of a vile, but powerful creature of Ying Tsung,
named Wang Chên (王 振), Hsie was promoted to be a Sub-Director
of the Grand Court of Revision at the Capital, and soon after by the
same influence he was made Director. These appointments were
obtained by Wang merely because he wished to have a man from
P'ing-yang in the Court of Revision, and because he wanted to put
Hsie under an obligation. But the latter would not cringe to Wang
or show him any respect and even dared to defend a woman whom
one of his relatives was persecuting. Wang became enraged, ordered
Hsie to be arrested and put in prison, and was about to have him
executed. But seeing an old servant weeping in his kitchen and
learning that the cause of his grief was the report that Hsüan was to
be put to death, he thought it better not to proceed any further.
Accordingly Hsie was released and allowed to return to his native
place, where he remained for several years. Disciples came to him in
great numbers, and he taught them not only to know the old Classics,
but above all to make personal application of the truth which they
acquired.

In 1449 he was recalled to office and in the next year transferred
to the Grand Court of Revision at Nankin. One who did not bear
him any love said that he was the only good official in that city. In
1457 he was made Vice-President of the Board of Ceremonies at
Peking and also a Secretary in the Han-lin. The Emperor held him
in great esteem, but the government was largely in the hands of vile
favourites who loathed all virtue and nobility of character. Hsie
could not endure to serve under these and remain in office when his
counsels were set aside. So he obtained leave to resign, and went
back to end his days at home, poor as when first he sought employment. He rented a house in Ho-chin and gained a subsistence by

teaching. Disciples thronged to him until the house could not hold them all, and he taught them with untiring assiduity. His theme was still the same, to nourish the heart and restore the Heavenly nature—to find in philosophy practical rules of life and follow these with unfaltering earnestness. Having reached the age of seventy-five years he was one day sitting at his door composing some verses on the subject when he was suddenly seized with a severe illness. Knowing that the end was coming, he put on his robe and hat and sat down on a chair in the middle of the room. A thunder-storm arose which shook the house, a white vapour was seen to rise up through the atmosphere, and Hsie Hsüan was dead.

This was in the year 1464, and the Emperor gave him the posthumous rank of President of the Board of Ceremonies when the death was reported. Afterwards the epithet Wên-ch'ing (文清) Accomplished and pure, was given to him, the term *ch'ing* being that applied to him by his grand-father when he was newly born. His other designations are Ching-hsien (敬軒), Ho-fên (河汾), and sometimes Tung-ho (東河). Of these the first is Hsie's common name in literature, and the other two merely indicate the locality of his birth place. In 1572 he was admitted into the Temple of Confucius.

Hsie Hsüan did not write much and he destroyed a large portion of what he had written. The best known of his works is the Tu-shu-lu (讀書錄) or Notes of a Reader. This treatise as it now exists is a combination of two works which were published during the author's life time, with a new arrangement. It is a series of notes and reflections which he wrote down as they occurred to him while reading. His remarks are often good and are generally terse and pithy. It is much read and highly valued by native scholars, and Luh Lung-ch'i selects for special praise the views which it gives respecting the T'ai-chi. The author's reading extends over a large number of books and a great variety of subjects, embracing the canonical books, the Sung philosophers, early Confucianist, Taoist and Buddhist writers, and Natural History. The Tao-lun (道論) is a collection of thoughts and aphorisms uttered by Hsie and collected by some of his disciples. This also is a very interesting little book

and contains many striking reflections, some of which are scarcely
Confucian. In these treatises his favourite doctrine that all study
should be directed to the development and perfection of the inner self
is strongly inculcated. They are amongst the most suggestive and
thoughtful productions of all the Chinese philosophers. A collection
of Hsie's Letters, Biographical notices, Essays, and other short pieces
has been several times republished. One of the latest editions is that
by Chang Poh-hang which is entitled Hsie-ching-hsien-chi (薛 敬
軒 集).

The official career of Hsie was marked by some of the highest
human virtues. His fortitude was put to a severe test on several
occasions, and his love of justice and mercy was large and sincere.
Threats of imprisonment and death could not avail to mar his cheerful
spirits or turn him from the path of duty and honour. Incapable
of any meanness he lived pure and noble in the midst of vice, and corruption, and all debasement; faithful to his sovereign he was also
tenderly solicitons for the welfare of the people.

As a scholar and philosopher he was unrivalled among his contemporaries. The books which he read were very numerous, and, as
the Tu-shu-lu shows, he read with care and understanding. His
favourites were the works of the Sung philosophers and Chu Hsi
specially. The end of all learning with him was to regain the moral
nature which is man's pure and perfect birthright. So he laid great
stress on habitual self-reverence and self-control, on the necessity of
subduing the passions and thus leaving scope for the mind to devolope
itself. His views are often broader and more tolerant than those of
Confucianists generally, and he is not ashamed to own that there is
good in Taoism and Buddhism. From this latter he seems to have
borrowed some of his forms of expression and even one or two theories.
But he was a thorough adherent of orthodoxy, the great principles of
which he never wearied in studying and teaching. In the obituary
notice of Hsie written by a friend it is stated—" During the present
dynasty he stands alone in philosophy." *

* Hsie-ching-hsien-chi; T'ung-chien &c., (Supplement) Ming Chs., 6 &c.; Tu-shu-lu,
Vol. I, Introduction.

52. Ch'ên Hsien-chang (陳 獻 章) S. Kung-fu (公 甫).

The native place of Ch'ên Hsien-chang was a hamlet named Pai-sha (白 沙), near the town of Hsin-hui in the Prefecture of Canton, where he was born in the year 1428. In early life he lost his father, but he had a true-hearted, affectionate mother who trained him wisely and tenderly. From childhood he was grave and thought-ful, and fond of reading all kinds of books. He grew up to be a tall, fine-looking man though he had seven black spots on his right cheek.

In 1447 Ch'ên obtained his Chü-jen Degree, but he failed at the examination for the Chin-shi. When twenty-six years of age he attached himself as disciple to Wu Yü-p'i (吳 與 弼), a man of solid learning and stern integrity. Ch'ên remained with him, however, for only half a year and then betook himself to private study. Having built a house which he named Yang-ch'ün-t'ai (陽 春 臺) he shut himself up in it, and for several years neither went abroad nor received visitors.

Returning to the world after this period of voluntary seclusion he went to the Capital to study in the Imperial Academy. Here the Chief Examiner one day tested the students by giving them a poem by Yang Kuei-shan and telling them each to compose a poem on the same subject after the manner of Yang. Ch'ên's composition on this occasion was so good that the Examiner declared it to be superior to the original. This led to his becoming famous in the Capital and brought him to the knowledge of the Emperor. But he would not remain and went back to his native place where he was soon surrounded by numerous disciples. The Governor and the Provincial Treasurer of Kuangtung now recommended him for official employment, and he was consequently summoned back to the Capital. On arrival there he was ordered to attend the Board of Civil offices for examination but he refused and went away with the honorary title of a Graduate of the Han-lin. Of his after career nothing is recorded, but it is known that he died in the year 1500.

The posthumous epithet of Ch'ên is Wên-kung (文 恭), or the Reverent, which was conferred on him in 1584 at the time he was permitted to share in the honours of the Temple of Confucius. His literary appellation is Pai-sha from the name of his birth-place.

Of the philosophy of Ch'ên little is known as he refused to commit his theories to writing. But he is said to have taught that truth was to be reached by silent meditation and the absorption of the mind from all external influences. He was for many years a student of books but he came to think much reading a mistake. So he had recourse to quiet observation of his own mind and heart, and learned to know and control them thoroughly. Long training enabled him at length to keep his passions at heel, and he came to experience the happiness of virtuous thought developed into habit. But he slighted all book-knowledge and did not teach that virtue was for use in the daily business of life. Self-perfection by long mental exercise in complete isolation from the world was the end of his philosophy. Hence Hu Chü-jen is very wroth with him and calls him a Buddhist. Another scholar, however, declares him to be a follower of Chou Lien-ch'i and Ch'êng Ming-tao, and a contemporary spoke of him as a "living Mencius."

The filial piety of Ch'ên is famous, and there was a wonderful bond of affectionate sympathy between him and his mother. As in the case of Tsêng-tzŭ, when he was away from home and his mother longed for him, he at once felt his heart throb and went away to find her. He is also highly commended for his persistence in refusing to go into office while wicked men were in power and the principles which he held dear could not prevail. In the family circle and in public relations his life was preeminently good; and he had a great name and a wide spread popularity among his contemporaries.*

---

* Ming-shi Ch. 283; T'ung-chien &c (Suppl.) Ming Ch. 15.

53. Hu Chü-jen (胡 居 仁) S. Shu-hsin (叔 心).

Hu Chü-jen was born at Mei-k'i (梅 谿) now Min-ch'ing (閩 清) in the Prefecture of Foochow, but the home of his ancestors was Yü-kan (餘 于) in Jao-chow, a Prefecture of Kiangsi. His forefathers for several generations had been men of learning who did not care for office but preferred a life of quiet study and modest virtue. As a boy Hu was very careful about his words and actions, always correct in deportment and strictly honest, and full of high resolve. When he was twelve years of age his father removed from Mei-k'i to the village of Ta-yuan in the District of An-jen, a town near Yü-kan, and there the family continued to live for twenty years.

On settling at Ta-yuan, Hu became a close student, reading incessantly and preparing himself to compete for the Degrees which lead to office. But hearing of Wu Yü-p'i's fame he went on foot all the way to Ts'ung-jen and became a disciple of that philosopher. The effect of Wu's teaching was to make Hu cast aside his text-books and miscellaneous treatises and devote himself to the study of pure Confucianism.

In 1465 finding Ta-yuan too confined a place for a growing family he obtained his father's consent to a migration to Mei-k'i. A place was found in the neighbourhood of that town, the situation of which was good in every respect. There were a high plain, mountains, and streams which could supply crops, fuel, and fish, and afford healthful exercise. A geomancer selected the site for the house which was made of mud and thatched. Next year, however, his father died, and Hu performed his obsequies with every formality prescribed in the ancient rituals. He fasted until he could not rise without the help of a staff and looked like a breathing skeleton. Having to go to law about the site chosen for his father's grave, he dyed his mourning clothes in order that he might not have to change them before appearing in the magistrate's office.

Some time afterwards he travelled through several Provinces

visiting the famous mountains and rivers and making the acquaintance of illustrious scholars. While on this excursion he was invited by the Prince of Huai to stay with him and explain the meaning of the Yih Ching. He was also engaged as tutor or teacher by other persons, and was subsequently appointed Master of the White Deer College in the Lu mountains.

On his return to Mei-k'i young students came to him in such numbers that he had to build two houses for their accommodation. To these he expounded the old Classics and the philosophy of Chu Hsi. But he would not prepare any for the State examinations, and he impressed on all the paramount necessity of learning to control the feelings and purify the mind. He continued to study and teach for several years, but in the meantime his family had sunk to a state of utter poverty. This did not disturb the even dignity of his spirits, and he was content with his patched clothes and scanty fare. Little more is recorded of him but it seems that he died in the year 1485.

The watchword of Hu Chü-jen throughout all his life was Ching (敬), that is, Reverently circumspect. He called his study the Ching-chai (敬 齋), and his disciples transferred the name to himself. This is still his literary designation, and his posthumous epithet is Wên-ching, which was conferred on him in 1584, when his tablet was added to the Temple of Confucius.

The only treatise composed by Hu was the Chü-ye-lu (居 業 錄), which is regarded as a companion work to the Tu-shu-lu of Hsie Hsüan. The meaning of the title is Notes on Life Principles, and it is derived from a passage in Confucius' exposition of the third line in the Chien diagram (☰). The words in the Yih Ching are, "By regulating the outward expressions, and establishing sincerity within [the perfect man] becomes settled in principle." In 1488 as many of Hu's Essays, Poems and other miscellanies as could be collected were edited and published with the title Hu-ching-chai-chi (胡 敬 齋 集). These two works have since been several times reprinted, but it cannot be said that they are very popular. They contain, however, all Hu's philosophy and are interesting on that account. Though it was said of him that he had read all books and exhausted every subject, yet he taught his disciples to make reading subordinate to reflection. He insists on the supremacy of undisturbed thought, teaches that the heart should be nourished and the pure nature which is born with man be thus restored. But first and last the seeker after truth and virtue must have Reverence, and in this term he comprehends all that previous moralists had meant by fear, caution, sedulous attention, and similar expressions. He held that man's mind (or heart) and the moral law of the universe were originally one. In the Sages they are always so, and in those next below the Sages the mind and the law are in accord. The truths contained in the old Classics and developed in the works of the great Sung philosophers should be studied with reverent attention and when received into the mind be made the law of all conduct. A thorough scholar and a profound thinker, he had no patience either with the orthodox sciolists of his time or with Taoists and Buddhists. These indeed he "cudgeled with invectives more than cut with arguments," while showing that superficial resemblances between them and Confucianists overlay deep and radical differences. So near, however, are some of his doctrines to some of those in Buddhism that the charge which he brought against Ch'ên Hsien-chang of teaching that heresy has been preferred against himself. It was a vanishing boundary which parted his pet theories from Buddhism, and with some of his disciples the boundary quite disappeared.

In private life Hu Chü-jen showed all the stern and prickly virtues. So quiet, solemn, and decorous did he keep his family that his house was said to be like a temple,. He would not receive any visitors unless he was in full dress, and all his manner to them was cold, reserved, and rigorous in etiquette. Even with his wife he would not allow any familiarities and the two lived together as host and guest. In filial piety he went to ultra-canonical lengths, and he performed his duties towards brothers and distant relatives with strict conscientiousness. He kept a diary in which he wrote every evening the result of a self-examination with reference to the day's work, and he taught his disciples to keep similar diaries. In short he lived a Confucianist after the most straitest sect of that religion, honest but narrow-minded, learned but censorious, and virtuous, but formal and disagreeable.*

---

54. Ts'ai Ch'ing (蔡 清). S. Chie-fu (介 夫).

Ts'ai Ching was born at Chin-kiang (晉 江), in the Prefecture of Chin-chew, in the year 1453. He became a thoughtful, diligent youth and went to Foochow, in order to study the Yih Ching with Lin-P'i (林 玭), a native of that city celebrated for his learning. Having obtained a thorough acquaintance with the Yih, Ts'ai prepared for the official examinations, and in 1477, took first place among the Chü-jen of his district. In 1484, he became a Chin-shi and soon afterwards he received a subordinate appointment in the Board of Ceremonies. In this capacity he became known to Wang Shu (王 恕), a high and worthy statesman who made Ts'ai his intimate friend and confidential adviser. Ts'ai prepared two Memorials for Wang, in one of which he expounded the main principles of government and in the other recommended a number of good men for official employment.

Then his mother died and he had to go into retirement for the prescribed period. Immediately on his return to public life he begged for leave to go home and nourish his aged father. This was refused but he was transferred to the Imperial Academy at Nanking in order that he might be near his father. While here he one day felt a sudden throb at his heart and prayed earnestly to be allowed to return home. Leave was granted and he was enabled to attend his father during the illness which proved fatal to the latter at the end of a few weeks. For some time after the period of mourning was over, Ts'ai remained in retirement chiefly occupied in studying and giving private lessons. In 1506, he was again called to office and made Assistant Literary Chancellor for Kiangsi. In this position he distinguished himself by bold opposition to the unprincipled ways and ambitious schemes of the Prince of Ning. This conduct made the Prince his enemy, and Ts'ai saw that his wisest course was to retire from the

---

* Ming-shi, Ch. 282; Hu-ching-chai-chi; Chü-ye-lu; T'ung-chien, etc. (Supplement) Ming, Ch. 15.

public service. But he did not survive long, for his death occurred in 1508, while a new appointment was on its way to him.

From the title which Ts'ai gave to his study, arose his literary name Hsü-chai (虛 齋). The posthumous epithet conferred on him is Wên-chuang (文 莊), or *Chuang*, that is, sedate, and his introduction to the Confucian Temple occurred in 1724. '

Ts'ai Ch'ing's fame rests mainly on his labours in connection with the Yih Ching. Through all his life he was a diligent student of that hard book and he made himself a name among his contemporaries as being skilled in its mysteries. He wrote on it a treatise called the Yih-ching-mêng-yin (易 經 蒙 引), which is chiefly a selection of notes and commentaries with original observations. This work he left in Ms. and it was carefully transcribed by his son who presented it to the Emperor Shi Tsung, in 1529. The Emperor ordered it to be printed and put in circulation, and it has since remained a standard work on the Yih. Ts'ai wrote also the Ssŭ-shu-mêng-yin (四 書 蒙 引), which was published at the same time and in the same manner as the work on the Yih, but it has never held so high a place as the latter.

The leading theories of Ts'ai Ch'ing's teaching were similar to those of Ch'ên Hsien-chang and Hu Chü-jěn. In the early part of his career he made emotionless contemplation the ruling principle, but afterwards he taught the cultivation of Hsü (虛), or Emptiness. But he distinguished between this and the "emptiness" of Buddhism and Taoism. The latter was simple Vacuity—mere nothing, while his was the penetrable receptacle for all good according to the exposition of the Hsien (咸) Diagram in the Yih Ching. He had many disciples among whom were a few who afterwards rose to considerable eminence.

Ts'ai was a simple-minded generous man, equally contented with poverty and with philosophy. In official life he was careful and punctilious about all that concerned the honour and dignity of the Emperor. But he did not care for preferment and he had not his heart set on riches. *

---

* Ming-shǐ, Ch. 282.

55. Lo Chin-shun (羅 欽 順). S. Yun-shêng (允 升).

Lo Chin-shun was born in the year 1465, at Tʻai-ho (泰 和), in the Prefecture of Chi-an (吉 安), in Kiangsi. He early showed himself a lover of knowledge and a seeker after virtue. In his fourteenth year he wrote up over his door—" Persevere in efforts for excellence in yourself and toward others. " He became a Chin-shi in 1493, and thereupon received the title of Compiler in the Han-lin. As this did not oblige him to go into service he closed his door against all visitors and gave himself up to study. Becoming acquainted with a Buddhist monk at the Capital he had an opportunity of learning the principal doctrines of the Buddhist religion. They pleased him at first and he was specially charmed with the theory of ideal intellectual perfection, but he gradually came back to sound orthodoxy.

In 1502, he was appointed Tutor in the Imperial Academy at Nanking, and he betook himself with great earnestness to the study of the Canonical books and the works of Chow, Chʻêng, Chang, and Chu Hsi. The Academy had long been in a demoralized state and Lo set about making reforms by introducing discipline and periodical examinations to classify the students. In 1508, his term of office having expired, leave of absence was refused to him through the influence of Liu Chin (劉 瑾), an unprincipled creature of the Emperor, and because he would not pay court to this Liu he was dismissed from the public service. Soon afterwards, however, his enemy was put to death and Lo was recalled to office. He was made a Director in the Court of Sacrificial Worship and soon after Vice-President of the Nanking Board of Civil Offices. In each of these offices he tried to obtain the abolition of certain abuses which had lately sprung up but he was not very successful. In 1522, he was made President of the above Board, but the death of his father caused his retirement. When the period of mourning was over he was again appointed President, first of the Board of Ceremonies at Nanking and, on his refusing this, of the Board of Civil Offices at Peking. The administration of government was now, in 1527, chiefly in the hands of two very bad men, and as Lo would not serve with them he obtained leave to resign. Returning to his home in Kiangsi he spent the rest of his days in a quiet, happy manner, dividing his time among study, teaching, and gardening. He enjoyed the intercourse of literary friends and died in a ripe old age in the year 1547.

The name by which he is best known is Lo Chêng-ngan (整庵, adopted by himself. The epithet conferred on him posthumously is Wên-chuang (文莊), and he was allowed to share the Confucian worship in 1724, on the Petition of Chang Poh-hang,

Two works were published by Lo Chin-shun, the K'un-chï-chi (困知記), which appeared in 1528, and the Shï-wên-ts'un-k'ao (詩文存棄), which appeared in 1534. The former, a short but valuable treatise, discusses the supposed points of resemblance between Buddhism and Confucianism. The author argues not only against the ethics and psychology of the former, but also against the opinions of those Confucianists who tried to harmonize the two systems.

A selection from the Shi-wen has been lately published with several pieces not in the original work and entitled Lo-chêng-ngan-chi-ts'un-k'ao (羅 整 庵 集 存 稿). This contains some official documents and a few Essays and Letters, the last being the most interesting. Brisk but friendly controversies were carried on by Lo with two distinguished philosophers Wang Yang-ming (王 陽 明), and Tsan Kan-chuan (湛 甘 泉). Lo held that Ch'ên Hsien-chang was wrong in his expositions of Confucianism because he mixed them up with theories derived from Buddhism. Tsan on the other hand maintained that C'hên was perfectly orthodox and that the theories objected to were founded on passages in the Canonical books and the works of the Sung philosophers. The two old friends, "beyond seventy and in sight of eighty," discuss the subject in a genial pleasant manner with much skill and learning, but Tsan is apparently the winner.

Lo Chin-shun was an amiable, accomplished man with great decision of character. Strict wherever duty was concerned, he was at the same time kind and gentle to all and the influence of his example was felt wherever he lived. His way of living was plain and homely but he never forgot order and decorum. Honest and thorough in his own convictions, he was fair and courteous to those from whom he differed, and ready to bring to light the truth which lay hidden under error. His arguments against Buddhists and trimmers are not always strong or convincing, but native scholars judge of them in connection with the end for which he laboured.*

56. Wang Shou-jen (王 守 仁) S. Poh-an (伯 安).

The birth-place of Wang Shou-jen, was Yü-yao (餘 姚), a town in the Prefecture of Shao-hing and lying between that city and Ningpo. His birth, which occurred in 1472, was attended with un-usual circumstances, his mother having borne him in her womb for fourteen months. Shortly before the event, moreover, his grand-mother had a dream in which she saw an angel bring down an infant boy from a cloud. Hence when the son was born he received the baby-name Yun, that is Cloud. His father, Wang Hua (華), was an official of some distinction who rose to be President of the Board of Civil Offices. In early childhood Shou-jen was feeble and delicate, and he had attained the age of five years without being able to speak. One day about this period a strange being appeared who stroked little Cloud's head and advised his parents to change the name to Shou-jen. This was done and forthwith the child began to talk.

In his fifteenth year Wang set out on his travels, and led by chances or choice he made a long tour enjoying the beautiful scenery of his native land. When he returned to Shao-hing he fitted up a room in the Yang-ming (陽 明) Cave, in the Hui-ki (會 稽) Mountain, famed for its associations with Yü Wang who led the rivers in their proper courses and made order in the world. In this congenial dwel-ling place he took an extended course of reading in the literatures of Buddhism and Taoism. This did not interfere with his ordinary

---

* Ming-shi, Ch. 282; T'ung-chien, &c. (Ming.) Ch. 12; K'un-chï-chï; Lo-chêng-ngan-chi; Chêng-yi-t'ang-su-chi (正 誼 堂 積 集), Ch. 1.

studies and he was soon able to pass the Chû-jen Examination. But he had a youthful ambition for war, and though of a delicate constitution, he was fond of military exercises and became an expert in archery. Having obtained his Chin-shi, in 1499, he was called to office and soon afterwards made an Assistant Secretary in the Board of Punishments. Ill health obliged him to give up work for a time, and on his recovery he received a similar appointment in the Board of War. At this time Liu Chin (劉 僅) was high in the favour of the new Emperor Wu Tsung, and was abusing the power which he had gained by shameful means. In 1506, he arrested and imprisoned a Censor and twenty others who were obnoxious to him. Wang protested vigorously against this conduct and so enraged Liu who subjected him to the disgrace of corporal punishment and then banished him to a petty office in Kuei-chow. The place to which Wang was thus sent was a small Post Station in a wild part of Kuei-yang-foo, in the mountains inhabited by the Liao savages. He set himself to work for the improvement of these rude tribes, and taught them some of the ways of a better life. They were glad to receive his instructions and showed their gratitude by felling trees to make him a house. It was during the few years of this lonely exile that Wang began to work out his system of philosophy. Not having access to any books he proceeded to meditate on the teachings of the various systems with which he had become acquainted. But he could not find truth in any and came to the conclusion that it was to be reached by efforts directed to the mind itself—to be sought within and not from without.

In 1510 Liu Chin fell into disgrace and his enraged master ordered him to be hacked to pieces in the market place and all his ill-gotten treasures to be confiscated. Wang was now recalled to civilised life and received a succession of appointments. Serious rebellions arose throughout Kiangsi and in the parts of Fuhkeen, Kuangtung, and Hunan which border on that Province. Wang was sent to quell these insurrections, and beginning with Fuhkeen, in a few years he reduced the country to order. His military feats, though stained by the usual Chinese treachery towards enemies, were brilliant and successful. In 1519 he was able to report that all Kiangsi was free from rebellion and that Ch'ên Hao, the Ning Wang, was defeated and captured. Then he withdrew from public life to avoid the plots of jealous enemies, and devoted himself to the study and teaching of philosophy. In 1527 he was again called to serve in the field and sent against the wild tribes of Kuangsi who were ravaging that Province. Here again he was successful and within a year could announce that the Province was restored to tranquillity, the savages having been utterly routed and driven into the mountains. He had now attained the high position of President of the Board of War to which was added that of the Censorate, and he had been created an Earl (Poh), with succession to his heirs. But the glory of his achievments had brought him envy, and malicious accusations were brought against him. He asked for leave to resign and retire to his native hills as his health was quite broken down. Without waiting for the Emperor's reply he set off for Chekiang, but only survived to reach Nan-an, in Kiangsi, where he died in 1528.

Envy and malice followed Wang into the grave and his patent of nobility was canceled. But after a few years it was restored and the posthumous epithet Wên-ch'êng (文 成) added. In 1584, an Imperial Decree sanctioned his reception into the Temple of Confucius. From the name of the cave in which he lived for a time his friends called him Yang-ming (陽 明), and this has ever since been his usual designation.

Wang left a collection of Essays on various subjects, "but in after times when the original blocks were lost, extensive alterations and corruptions took place in later editions. In the latter part of the 17th Century 王 貽 樂 Wang E-lŏ, a fifth-generation descendant of the author, made a collection of his ancestor's writings, which he published under the title 王 陽 明 集 Wang-yêng-ming-tseih, in 16 books." This work had many readers and was soon out of print. In the reign of Chien-lung an enthusiastic admirer of Wang's philosophy by name T'ao Ch'un-t'ien (陶 春 田), had great difficulty in procuring a copy, but after much searching found what he calls "the priceless rare jewel" in an old-book shop in the Liu-li-ch'un in Peking. Ch'un-t'ien prepared notes for a new edition which he proposed to publish, but he died before the work was ready for the press. These notes, however, are incorporated in the edition which was published in 1826, under the care of several scholars. The first of the 16 books or *chuan* gives an elaborate biography of Yang-ming with notices of his posthumous fortunes, and the others contain his philosophical remains, notes of his teachings, Letters, Poems, official writings, and miscellaneous pieces. The style of his prose compositions is charming from its clearness and simplicity and his sentences have an easy graceful flow which is all their own. The explanations are generally distinct and precise, the arguments good, and an air of fairness and moderation prevails throughout. He did not shrink from any conclusions or fear any consequences even when maintaining opinions which seemed dangerous and schismatic.

The charge of teaching Buddhistic theories was incurred partly by the errors of his disciples who gave a one-sided development to his teachings. Partly it was the result of Yang-ming's generous efforts to rescue the name of Luh Chiu-yuan from unmerited obloquy and neglect. The followers of Chu Hsi branded Luh as a heretic and a feud had long existed between them and the followers of Luh. Yang-ming showed the disputants on both sides that they took imperfect views of their great masters' teachings, that they had dwelt too much on the points of difference, overlooking the essential agreement which existed between the two philosophers. For Chu, while maintaining the all-importance of learning, also insisted strongly on the paramount necessity of cultivating the mind and purifying the heart by internal processes; and Luh, though dwelling largely on the development of the native faculties from within, also laid stress on the study of the Ancient Classics. It was wrong and stupid, Yung-ming declared, for rival scholars to strive for mastery, one saying I am of Chu and another I am of Luh, for these two were disciples of one master and held the same general principles. Yang-ming was very courageous in his defence of Luh and succeeded, to use his own figure, in clearing the mud off his philosophical reputation. For this he has gained the lasting gratitude of all liberal and true-minded Confucianists.

Another subject which plays an important part in Yang-ming's philosophy is *liang-chĭ* (良 知). This is the faculty by which man gains his first and surest knowledge, without any aid from book or teacher or any instruction whatever. By it he knows "day and night," that is understands all subjects relating to brightness and darkness, life and death, ghosts and spirits. The expression liang-chĭ is taken from a passage in Mencius, and Dr Legge there translates it "intuitive knowledge." But with Yang-ming it has a large and varied use, and it sometimes answers to conscience and sometimes to consciousness, while at other times it is apparently instinct. It exists in all men throughout life but in different degrees of intensity and in the same person it not always equally active. To keep it pure and perfect as it is at birth and to develope its influence until it is followed unconsciously, should be man's constant endeavour. No amount of reading and learning can lead to this end which can be attained only by intense thought, calm meditation, and constant self-control. But there must be a basis and a rule and these are furnished by the ancient books and their orthodox commentators. For though Yang-ming discarded books and teachers for a time, yet he remained a strict Confucianist, and retained the canonical works as authoritative. But he explained such expressions as "resting in the highest excellence," "completing knowledge," and "investigating things," in the Great Learning as referring to the internal operations of the mind directed to itself. This of course savoured of heresy and Lo Ch'êng-ngan criticized Yang-ming's doctrines as inconsistent with the principles of Confucianism and as too much like Buddhism. He was afterwards accused of renouncing allegiance to the Sages and of trying to found a new school of philosophy. But he was strictly orthodox and considered that he was only taking the rational and proper interpretation of the words of Confucius and Mencius. To the objection that self-absorption and mere study as the means to attain spiritual perfection were tenets of Buddhism, he answered that they were also Confucianist, and pleaded that it was wrong to cast away those elements of orthodoxy which were common to it and heterodoxy. There were touches of goodness and hints of truth in Buddhism and Taoism derived from the one common source whence all had sprung. Yet he was not by any means partial to these systems or blind to their errors and defects against which he often warns his disciples. The charge of heresy and specially of a leaning to Buddhism, is indignantly repelled by the editors of his collected writings who refer to these confidently, and with justice, as thoroughly refuting the accusation. But they are not much read at present, for Yang-ming' criticized Chu Hsi's text and commentary of the Great Learning and wrote in favour of Luh Chiu-yuan, so the timid and indolent orthodox have still an apprehension about his soundness.

There are many points of more than superficial resemblance between the life and opinions of Wang Yang-ming and those of Descartes the study of which would prove interesting. Both were soldiers while cherishing an ardent love of philosophy, though the pagan fought in a nobler cause than the Christian. Both held that the mind possessed an innate faculty for knowing high truths and taught the great importance of self-dependence. But the Chinese philosopher had the courage of his opinions while Descartes feared the Pope and would not for all the world that from him should emanate a discourse " où il se trouvât le moindre mot qui fût désapprouvé d l' Eglisé. " He, however, also was accused of heresy and was buried without the becoming solemnities. *

---

* Wylie, Notes, &c. p. 188.; Wang-yang-ming-hsien-shêng-ch'uan-chi (王 陽 明 先 生 全 集), edition of 1826.

57. Lü Nan (呂 枏) S. Chung-mu (仲 木).

Of the life and character of Lü Nan, little seems to be recorded and little to be known. His native place was Kao-ling (高 陵), a town of Si-an-foo, in the Province of Shensi, and he was born in the year 1479. He did not become a Chin-shi until 1506, (or according to one authority 1508), and soon after he obtained this Degree he was made a Compiler in the Han-lin. The infamous Liu Chin wished to attach Lü to him as a friend but did not succeed. The latter in fact opposed the plots and devices of Liu, and ventured to present a Memorial to the Emperor Wu Tsung, who had given the active administration of the Empire into the hands of his favourite. Lü urged His Majesty to return to the Palace and resume the control of public business. By this Memorial he incurred the bitter enmity of Liu, and accordingly went out of office on the plea of ill health.

When Liu fell into disgrace and was put to death, Lü was summoned to take office again at the Capital. He now presented another Memorial to the Emperor in which he set forth the duty of paying attention to public education. After holding various appointments he was made a Vice-President of the Board of Ceremonies at Nanking, and he died in the year 1542. He had been greatly beloved and respected and his death was generally lamented; the people of Kao-ling closed their shops for three days, and his disciples wore the garb of mourning for the prescribed period.

The literary name of Lü Nan is Ching-ye (涇野), and his reception into the Temple of Confucius occurred in 1863. As a public servant he was firm and faithful, taking office when he felt it his duty to do so, and withdrawing when his counsels were unavailing. But his heart was set on learning and he was a devoted student of the ancient orthodox philosophy. He wrote useful commentaries on several of the Classics, and his house was frequented by a considerable number of disciples.*

---

* Ming Shi, Ch. 282.

58. Lü K'wun (呂 坤) S. Shu-chien (叔 簡).

The native place of Lü K'wun, was Ning-ling (寧 陵), a town of Kuei-tê-foo in Honan, where he was born in the year 1536. He obtained his Chin-shi Degree in 1574, and soon afterwards was made Magistrate of Hsiang-yuan in Shansi. His administration of this place excited admiration, and at the end of his term he was transferred to T'ai-t'ung in the same Province. From this he was promoted to a subordinate position in the Board of Revenue at the Capital. Then he became in succession Judge in Shansi, Treasurer in Shensi, and Governor of Shansi, with extraordinary powers. This last office he held for three years after which he was promoted to be a Censor and a Vice-President of the Board of Punishments. In 1597, he presented to the Emperor Shên Tsung a long and very remarkable Memorial on the unhappy condition of the country, its causes and the means of removing them. The four classes of persons, he states in this document, who have always been the originators of civil troubles are vagabonds, persons without moral principle, false teachers, and lovers of anarchy. He then contrasts the sad poverty and distress of the subjects with the luxury and extravagance of the Court, and describes eloquently the miseries of those who had to procure the massive trees required for Imperial buildings. He counsels His Majesty against listening to calumny and refusing access to faithful words. The Memorial contained further good advice and rebuke, but it was not heeded. Lü, accordingly, requested leave to resign and the Emperor granted his petition.

Several enemies of Lü K'wun now tried to work his ruin by interpolating treasonable passages in a work which he had published some years previously. But the clumsy imposture was discovered and the perpetrators of it were visited with severe punishment. Lü went home and lived in retirement all the rest of his life, engaged chiefly in studying and teaching. The only occasion on which he is recorded to have meddled in public affairs was when the Prince Fu was invested with 40,000 *ch'ing* (above 60,000 square acres) of territory in Honan.

He addressed the Emperor against the grant which was unprecedentedly large and greatly beyond what other Princes had obtained. He wrote also to the Ministers of State on the subject, and his efforts were successful, the Prince's endowment being diminished by one half. The Emperor could not be prevailed on to invite Lü back to office and he died at home in the year 1618.

His literary designation is Hsin-wu (新 吾), and he was admitted to the Temple of Confucius in 1826.

While holding office Lü K'wun published a treatise which he named Kuei-fan-t'u-shuo (閨 範 圖 說), meaning Notices of Model ladies of Imperial Harems with Portraits. In this, beginning with the famous Ma How, first concubine and afterwards Empress of Han Ming Ti, he gave historical accounts of all the eminently good women who had been Imperial wives or concubines. It was this treatise which was tampered with in order to bring ruin on its author. He wrote also a work on the principles of Confucian philosophy which has been highly praised. In 1598 an official named Chao Wên-ping (趙 文 炳), a disciple of Lü K'wun, made a collection of the political and official Essays of his master. Having arranged these he published them with the title Shi-chêng-lu, that is, Records of genuine Government. This is a book of great practical usefulness and very interesting for the information which it gives about the state of the empire at the period. Many of the Proclamations and other documents which Lü issued to the people in his various jurisdictions also form part of this treatise. They show him to have been a man of unusual mental activity, taking a practical interest in all the affairs of the people. He states the measures proper to be taken in the event of a famine, tells what should be done when a crime has been committed, warns all, but specially women, against extravagance in dress, and urges the formation of literary clubs for the improvement of education and the spread of culture. His language is plain and direct, and he enters into minute particulars about every subject of which he treats.

It is on account of his official career that Lü has received posthumous honours, and it would not be easy to out-do the language of eulogy in which this is described by Chao Wên-ping in his Preface to the Shi-chêng-lu. It is agreed that he was a man of strong will and decided opinions, of true courage and long perseverance. He always wrought for the material and intellectual welfare of the people, but he served an Emperor who could not appreciate his purity and devotion. In philosophy he is considered orthodox and a true expounder of Confucianism, though it is admitted the he introduced independent opinions. He had studied thoroughly the teachings of the Sung writers and adopted them to some extent. *

59. Liu Tsung-chow (劉 宗 周). S. Ch'i-tung (起 東).

Liu Tsung-chow was born in the year 1578, at Shan-yin Hsien (山 陰), in the Prefecture of Shao-hing. His father, who was a poor literary graduate, died before the birth of his son leaving his widow utterly destitute. She had to seek shelter and food for herself and infant in the home of her parents where Tsung-chow remained until he reached boyhood. Then learning that his grandfather Liu was in want and an invalid he went to nurse and serve him. So for several years he tended the old man and his wife cutting wood, carrying water, and preparing their gruel and medicine. He was a very frail, delicate boy and his mother was always anxious and distressed about the state of his health. Poverty, and sorrow added, brought on sickness which she bore with heroic patience until it ended in her death in 1601. Her son was at the time in Peking having just obtained his Chin-shi Degree. When the news reached him, he at once returned home and observed the rites of mourning with deep and lasting sorrow. Soon after this his grand-parents died and he kept the prescribed period of mourning for each of them.

His first appointment, on which he entered in 1611, was a small and unimportant one as a foreign correspondence clerk at the Capital. This he held only for a short time and resigned on account of the

---

* Ming-shi, Ch. 282; Shi-chêng-lu (實 正 錄); T'ung-chien, &c. (Suppl.) Ming Ch. 16.

growing power of wicked and adverse factions. In 1621, he was again summoned to office and made an Assistant Secretary in the Ceremonial Department of the Imperial Household. He now began his crusade against Court vices and political corruption by attacking an unprincipled and usurping Minister. He then urged that capital punishment should be inflicted on certain officials for past delinquencies, but the Emperor became annoyed and merely removed him to a higher post. On being afterwards transferred to another office he pleaded ill health and retired. In 1624 he was again summoned to Peking, but the enemy whom he had provoked before prevailed against him now, and he was soon stript of his official rank. On the accession of Chuang-Lie in 1628, Liu was made Governor of the Imperial Prefecture Shun-tien. Being compelled to accept this office he at once addressed a long Memorial to the Emperor. In this he calls His Majesty's attention to the dreadful condition of the empire, the result mainly of official rapacity. He describes how excessive and irregular taxation and the harsh insolence of the revenue collectors had made the peasants destitute and had broken their spirits. He then points out the tendency of the existing abuses and warns the Emperor of their consequences, advising him to employ only men of superior excellence and to have regard to the rural peasantry. His Majesty admired the loyal spirit of the Memorial but thought its suggestions too vague and speculative to be adopted. In 1629, when the Capital was in danger and the Emperor meditated flight, Liu implored him to remain as the only hope was in the preservation of the seat of government. He knelt a whole day at the palace door until he received the answer to his prayer. At this time he organised measures for the relief of the poor in Peking, and expostulated with the Emperor about his severe treatment of officials. Next year he again resigned and went home after drawing up a Prayer to Heaven for an enduring Decree. The Emperor's Prayer was to be a pure and noble life devoted to the welfare of his subjects.

After a few years Liu was summoned once more to the Capital but the profligate Court now "let alone" by Heaven couuld not endure his reproving presence and words which pricked to the heart.

Dismissed and recalled, his counsels were all set aside and his faithful rebukes only provoked the Emperor who at length deprived him of all rank as an official. Liu was not many months at home when the news came that Peking was in the hands of the rebels, and the ill-treated patriot at once shouldered his spear and set off to help a ruined cause. Failing to rouse any heroism in an official to whom he appealed, with the help of two friends he raised a volunteer force and offered his services unofficially to Prince Fu now reigning at Nanking. Even here, while the shadow of coming invasion was over the land, the honest counsels and faithful warnings of Liu made him bitter enemies. These sought day and night how they might kill him, and hired assassins to go to his residence at Tan-yang near Chinkiang and stab him. But these, witnessing the calm fearless manner of the man, dared not strike and went away without doing their deed. Then Liu, seeing that his services were useless, left the scene of ignoble strife and withdrew to his cottage.

Soon afterwards, in 1645, Nanking surrendered, Hangchow fell, and the Manchoos were lords of China. The news reached Liu as he sat at dinner, and bursting into tears he thrust the food away and went about to kill himself. To those who tried to turn him from his purpose he said that if only the Capital had been lost and the reigning Emperor deposed it might be a question whether to live or not. But not only had the sceptre passed and the dynasty perished, his own native land was lost to him and there was nothing for him but to die.

"Me si cœlicolæ voluissent ducere vitam,
Has mihi servassent sedes."

Having taken farewell of his ancestors' tombs he went out on the bay in a boat and tried to drown himself. The water was not deep and he was rescued by the sailors. Then he proceeded in a cool, deliberate manner to starve himself to death. For twelve days the only nourishment he took was a little tea occasionally, and all the time he received his disciples and discoursed to them as usual. Afterwards he became unable to swallow anything and in a few days died.

The literary designation of Liu is Nien-t'ai (念 臺), and he is sometimes called Chi-shan (蕺 山), from the old name of his birth-place. His admission to the Temple of Confucius took place in 1822. All his writings have been collected and published with the title Liu-tzŭ-ch'uan-shu (劉 子 全 書), forming more than 100 *chuan*. Chang Li-hsiang, who was his disciple for a time, made a selection from this work and published it with the title Liu-tzŭ-sui-yen (劉 子 粹 言), Pure words of Liu-tzŭ.

Liu Tsung-chow was a good scholar, an elegant writer, and a lover of learned society. Disgusted at the conduct of Wang Shou-jen's disciples in adopting Buddhistic theories, he founded a college in which the orthodox of his neighbourhood could meet for discussion. He taught his disciples that purity of mind was an essential antecedent to learning, that a feeling of reverence should always be supreme, that they should attend carefully to private meditation and secret, thorough self-examination, and that all thought of blessings and rewards should be rejected. He guarded them also against sliding into those errors in Buddhism which bore a superficial resemblance to truths of Confucianism. Yet he has been accused, and not without a show of reason, of having been influenced by Buddhistic teachings. This heretical tendency is seen chiefly in his Jen-pu (人 譜), or Man's Register, a short but very curious treatise. It describes first the moral constitution of man following the analogy of the T'ai-chi of Chou Lien-ch'i. It then unfolds the general character of the duties required of man as an individual and a member of society : and the last part enumerates the sins, secret and open, small and great which men are liable to commit, and adds rules for self-examination and correction.

As an official, Liu was honest and upright, bold in speech and ready in act. He sought to sweep away long-standing abuses and recall the rulers to the old ways of virtue, but it was too late. His counsels were, it is true, sometimes unpractical, for it was idle to hold up Yao and Shun as models and to object to Western fire-arms at a time when the pressing anxiety was to preserve existence. He was a good man with great abilities, but he was born out of time and belonged to the days of old-fashioned simplicity. When retiring from office to his native place he always travelled on foot, and at home ho had only cotton clothes and coarse fare, but he was happy with truth and contented with poverty. *

---

60. Huang Tao-chou (黃道周). S. Yu-p'ing (幼平).

Huang Tao-chou was born in the year 1585 at Chang-p'u (漳浦), a town of Fuhkeen in the Prefectural District of Chang-chou. His early life was full of toil and privation, and when he grew up to manhood he had to work all day in the fields in order to support his parents. It was not until the year 1623, when he was thirty-eight years old that he obtained his Chin-shi Degree. He was then made a Bachelor in the Han-lin and after a further examination was appointed a Compiler and Instructor in that institution. By his proud and dignified manner he soon became an object of aversion to the principled Minister Wei Chung-hsien, but his mother died and so he had to resign office. In 1629 he returned to public life and was made an Assistant Secretary in the Board of Education. Shortly before this an upright Minister named Ch'ien Lung-hsi had incurred the Imperial displeasure and he was now in prison under sentence of death. Huang addressed three Petitions in succession to the Throne pleading for Ch'ien, and His Majesty commuted the punishment of the latter, but dismissed Huang from office. In 1632, while still waiting for employment he was attacked by sickness and obtained leave to go home. Before setting out he presented a Memorial which was a practical discourse on the words of the Yih—"If it be an Emperor's destiny to establish a dynasty and keep up the family succession persons of low principles will not be in office." He shows that the troubles and disasters of the time arose from the selfish conduct of officials who deceived the Emperor and oppressed the people. The Emperor was displeased with the Memorial and still more with the explanation of an obscure passage in it which Huang gave at his command. The explanation was all directed against two powerful Ministers of bad character, but high in Imperial favour and so Huang was stript of his rank and dismissed from office.

* Ming-shi, Ch. 255.; T'ung-chien, &c. (Suppl.) Ming, Chs. 19, 20; Jen-pu.

In 1636, however, he was recalled to the Capital and restored to his old position. Next year when drought was added to the other disasters of the country he had the courage to expostulate with the Emperor on his inconsistency in praying to Heaven for rain while he kept two upright officials in prison. On being appointed to a higher office he drew up a paper giving his reasons for declining the appointment. He enumerated seven qualifications in each of which he had superiors among men well-known at the time. One of the names given was Chêng Man, or Wan (鄭 曼), and Huang said he was inferior to Chêng in literary and mental accomplishments. This was a bold thing to do for Chêng Man was at the time in prison on the terrible charge of having beaten his mother. The charge was a false one but the courtiers and officials generally affected to treat it as established. The Emperor was startled and when Huang proceeded to explain his words and plead for Man he gave him a severe rebuke. There were many evil-minded officials who saw in Huang's dauntless integrity an obstacle to their advancement and they were now glad to have the semblance of a reason for attacking him. They took the words "inferior to Man" from their context and treated them as a declaration by their author that he was beneath a man who had struck his mother. Some time afterwards the Emperor was again enraged at the faithful outspoken counsels of Huang and wished to put him to death, but he feared to do so on account of his high reputation. Then a charge of conspiracy was invented and Huang was degraded and sent to serve in a very low capacity under the Judge of Kiangsi. In the course of time the Governor of that Province recommended him to the Throne. For this offence he and Huang were cast into prison and beaten, the alleged crime being that they were in a league to create rebellion. In 1641 Huang was sent into perpetual exile in Kuangsi leaving his wife and only son in great poverty. Next year through the skilful and discreet mediation of some friends he was recalled and reinstated at the Capital. But after having an audience of the Emperor he obtained leave to resign and go home. Then Peking fell, the Emperor left without one faithful Minister or one loyal official committed suicide, and the Manchoos reigned. Huang now took service with the Prince reigning at Nanking, but his words and example were of no avail and he resigned. Then still wishing to help the Ming cause he joined himself to Prince T'ang, but though honoured with a high title he was treated with contempt. So having obtained leave he raised a large force of volunteers in Kiangsi and took the field in the vain hope of regaining the Empire. In an engagement fought at Wu-yuan, in the South of Anhui, he was defeated and taken prisoner. He was carried to Nanking and after a short detention there was led out for execution. As he was passing the tomb of the first Ming Emperor he begged to be put to death at that spot. His request was granted and he was beheaded near the Tung-hua Gate in the year 1646.

In the early part of his life Huang Tao-chou had chosen as a favourite place of study a natural rock-cavern in the T'ung mountain, and his disciples called him the Rock-Study Teacher—Shi-chai-hsien-shêng (石齋先生). Thus Shi-chai came to be his name in books, but it does not seem to be much used. In 1825 he was admitted to share in the worship offered in the Temple of Confucius. He was the author of three treatises of some celebrity but not much read—the Yih-hsiang-chêng (易象正), the San-yih-t'ung-chi (三易洞璣), and the T'ai-han-ching (太函經).

Huang was a public servant of unshaken loyalty and unswerving rectitude. Living at a time of utter degeneracy when nearly every trace of faith, honour, and humanity had disappeared, he kept his soul pure and stood aloof from all the vices of the age. No amount of injustice and ill-treatment could make him desert the cause of the Emperor, or cool his ardour. Even after his iniquitous exile when he was summoned to the Imperial presence he was moved to tears.

Huang was also a scholar of unusual attainments, not only well versed in all the literature of Confucianism but also skilled in astronomy and arithmetic. His favourite book of study was the Yih-ching, which he never wearied of reading and in which he found a clue to all history. His disciples were numerous, but they could not understand the abstruse philosophy of their master. He had a calm equable temper, unruffled by want, injustice, or ruin, and he continued his literary pursuits in the prison at Nanking until he was led out for execution. After his death a prediction of the year in which that event was to occur was found in his handwriting, and so it came to be believed that he could calculate future events.[*]

61. Sun Ch'i-fêng (孫 奇 逢). S. Ch'i-t'ai (啓 泰).

The native place of Sun Ch'i-fêng, who was born in the year 1584, was Yung-ch'êng (容 城) a town of Pao-ting-foo in Chihli. When thirteen years of age he passed the Hsiu-ts'ai Examination and next year became entitled to the Rice allowance granted by Government to deserving students. In 1600 he took the second or Chü-jen Degree but he does not seem to have tried for the Chin-shi. Soon afterwards his father and mother died in close succession and in their funeral rites he observed strictly all the requirements of ancient precept. His brothers and he built a hut near the graves and lived in mourning for six years. Filial piety like this was rare at the time and it was reported to the Emperor who decreed a memorial arch to the family. As he grew up Sun formed an intimate friendship with Lu Shan-chi, a man of learning and virtue, with whom he discussed the deep problems of philosophy. When the infamous Wei Chung-hsien seeking to suppress all virtue imprisoned three officials of known integrity who were natives of Pao-ting-foo, Lu and Sun combined in endeavouring to obtain their deliverance. The infatuated Emperor, however, listened to Wei who now brought the new charge of extortion against the three men. Sun did his utmost for them, collected a large sum of money, and rode day and night until he reached the Capital. But the money came too late for the innocent men had died under torture. All other friends of these three victims were paralysed with fear and Sun alone had the courage to speak out and clear their names. At the risk of his life also he removed their bodies and had them sent to their native place for burial.

Neither the bribes of the wicked nor the recommendations and invitations of the good could induce Sun to accept any official employment. The days were evil and only evil, and he would not cast his

---

[*] Ming Shi Ch. 255; T'ung-chien &c. (Suppl.) Ming Ch. 20.

pearls of high principle before the herd of swine which wallowed in all
wickedness and dishonour.   But he did not fail in duty when the time
came for him to be of service.   In 1636 Yung-ch'êng was attacked by
the rebel army of Li Tzŭ-ch'êng, and Sun maintained a vigorous
defence.   He collected his kindred and friends, armed them and appointed them to keep watch ; he repaired the ruined battlements and
all the while fought the enemy who returned again and again to the
attack.   The city held out bravely for a time but was at length taken,
and Sun escaped with his brothers to Yih-chow in the same Prefecture.
Here too he tried to stem the torrent of rebellion by raising a force and
stirring up the courage of the people, while amid the clashing of war
he observed the courtesies of peace and in the intervals of defensive
preparations he calmly pursued his studies.

From Yih-chou Sun went to the neighbourhood of Hui, a town
near the confines of Honan and Chihli.   This place was dear to him
for the memories which it held of Chao Fu and other great philosophers
of former times.   Here he settled with his wife and family and resolved
to make it his permanent residence.   The Manchoo Emperor Shun-
chih urged him repeatedly to accept office but he pleaded sickness and
refused all offers.   A friend presented to him a piece of land on the
Hsia-fêng Hill, and here he built a school or Hall.   His children and
grand children lived with him, supporting themselves and him by the
produce of a farm.   The fame of his learning drew many disciples to
his cottage and he spent the autumn of his life in tranquil happiness.
He continued to study and teach and enjoy the society of friends for
many years and died at the age of ninety-one in 1675.

Sun Ch'i-fêng is known by several names besides those given
above.   Thus his *hao* is Chung-yuan (鍾 元) : his literary designation
is Hsia-fêng (夏 峯), or sometimes Yung-ch'êng from the name of his
birth place : and his common soubriquet among the people of Wei was
Chêng-chün (徵 君), given to him because he was so often *summoned*
to take office and always declined.   He was the author of works on the
Four Books, the Yih, and the Shu, and of several other treatises which
are still read by scholars.   In 1828 he was admitted to the Temple as
the first of the " Scholars" belonging to the present dynasty.

In philosophy Sun tried to reconcile the opinions of Chu Hsi and Luh Chiu-yuan, but did not follow the latter or Wang Poh, as he considered that their teachings opened the way to heresy. Not caring for a vain reputation he did not seek to become the head of a school or sect, and taught his disciples to prefer the solid and useful in learning before what was merely ornamental. His learning was like a river from which many drew each according to his capacity but no one knew its depth. Sun was of a genial friendly disposition, liberal in his treatment of others, and so much beloved and respected by all who knew him. His affection for his parents remained with him through life, and when reading a book the sight of a note or remark in his father's hand-writing brought tears and he fasted that day. To his poor relatives he was kind and generous, cheerfully denying himself to help them. He lived to see peace prevail in the land once more, and virtue and learning lift their heads again. His children and grand children grew up at his knees, and many of his disciples rose to fame and honour, the greatest among them being T'ang Pin.*

---

62. Luh Shi-yi (陸 世 儀) S. Tao-wei (道 威).

The date of Luh Shi-yi's birth is not recorded nor is anything known about his parentage. He was a native of T'ai-tsang (太 倉) in the Province of Kiangsu, and lived during the first half of the seventeenth century. In youth he read much of Buddhism and Taoism, and studied the economy of the vital energies with the view of learning how to prolong life. He took delight in these pursuits for a time but when he came to reason on them he found them vain and unprofitable. It seemed to him that the suppression of all mental activity and of all the natural functions of the bodily senses for the sake of the vital spirits would make only a sorry man to whom long life would be of no use. So he abandoned Buddhism and alchemy and turned to Confucianism. Carrying his enthusiasm into the new pursuit he continued a course of thorough and severe study in philosophy for nearly

* Chao-tzŭ-yen-hsing-lu (趙 子 言 行 錄) Ch., 2.

thirty years. He now found that Reverence of Heaven is the door of
Virtue, and that to reverence one's own heart is to reverence Heaven.
A distinguished scholar named Ch'ien Chung-chie (錢 忠 介), but
better known as Chi-shan (蔌 山) from the name of a hill near his
native place in Chekiang, was about this time a public teacher at
T'ai-tsang. He became acquainted with Luh and foretold that he
would rise to the first place among the learned of the time. It was a
life-long regret to Luh that he did not carry out an intention he had
formed of becoming a disciple of Chi-shan.

For some time he was employed on the staff of a general as
secretary but he did not receive any substantive appointment, and the
offer of his services was declined by the Prince at Nanking. When
the Manchoos obtained possession of the empire he resolved to go into
seclusion. Accordingly he made an artificial lake with a small
island in the middle. On the island he built a small pavilion in which
he shut himself up for a time refusing to see any friends When the
winds and waves of war had subsided he left his hermitage and went
to Ningpo to pay the tribute of mourning at Chi-shan's tomb. Then
he returned home and, yielding to the requests of many students,
began his career as public instructor. The Ministers of Shun-chih
pressed him on several occasions to accept office but he persistently
refused. For some time he taught in the famous Tung-lin College
and afterwards at Ch'ang-chow-foo in Kiangsu, returning finally to
his native village. Of his subsequent history nothing is known but
his works show that it was not a blank. "Nec vixit male qui natus
moriensque fefellit."

The name which Luh Shi-yi gave his Lake-dwelling was Fu-
t'ing (桴亭), and this became his literary soubriquet. He was canonized in 1874 at the petition of the literati of T'ai-tsang presented by
the Governor of Kiangsu. The only treatise which he composed is
the Ssŭ-pien-lu (思 辨 錄) or Records of Reflections and Judgments.
The title is taken from the following passage in the Chung-yung—To
the attainment of Sincerity "there are requisite the extensive study
of what is good, accurate inquiry about it, careful reflection on it, the
clear discrimination of it, and the earnest practice of it." The work

was first published by his son with a Preface written at his request by Luh Lung-oh'i, a great admirer of the author. Recently an abridgement of it has been published under the editorship of Chang Poh-hang with the title *Luh-Fu-t'ing-ssŭ-pien-lu-chi-yao*. It begins with the Little Learning, that is, with reflections and suggestions on the education of children. It then goes on to the subject of settling the mind, and from that to the attainment of perfect knowledge, and soon through a variety of topics in practical philosophy.

Few books in Chinese literature are more delighful than the Ssŭ-pien-lu. Its style is pure, simple, and elegant, and its matter is generally excellent. The author had read widely and studied profoundly but his genius had " added feathers to the learned's wing And given grace a double majesty ". He knew Buddhism and Taoism well and so was able to " discriminate " between them and Confucianism. But he saw that there were elements of good in these despised systems and thought it was useful for boys to like them provided that orthodoxy supplanted them afterwards. He deals gently with the elder Confucianists when expressing dissent from their views and gives hearty approval to sentiments which seem to him right. His models were the great Sung philosophers, and he had a special admiration for Chu Hsi, of whose clear practical views, love of learning, and delight in nature he speaks in terms of genial appreciation.

Of the scholars who shed a lustre over the first reign of the existing dynasty Luh Fu-t'ing was one of the greatest and one of the least known. Some have not hesitated to declare him next to Chu Hsi, and as to this his latest editor merely says he " does not know." Though he was forgotten by the world during a large portion of his life he was all the time working to preserve and propagate the great principles of orthodox learning. Nor he did forget the more urgent needs of his country in the hour of her peril from rebellion. He used his pen to show that the rule of regular gradation in office should give way for the time to that of ability, and that efficient generals and other officers should be added to the army. Though he did not get office under the Ming rulers and would not take it under the new dynasty, yet the wisdom which he gained by long and patient study and which he freely imparted to others was of greater benefit to the people than a life of active service would have been. He taught men to seek for knowledge and practise virtue, but above and before all to establish and cherish the habit of reverence.*

---

63. Chang Li-hsiang (張 履 祥) S. K'ao-fu (考 夫) and Nien-chi (念 芝).

Chang Li-hsiang was born in 1611 at a small village called Yang-yuan (楊 園) or Willow Grove, situated about five miles in a North-westerly direction from T'ung-hsiang (桐 鄉), a District town of the Kia-hing Prefecture of Chekiang. Here his ancestors had been settled for some time and the family owned a small farm. The grand-father of Li-hsiang was a man of liberal education, and much esteemed in the neighbourhood specially on account of the interest which he took in the young. His father also was a lover of learning and distinguished for his filial piety, and his mother was a pattern of womanly virtues. Neither grand-father nor father took the higher Degrees or aimed at public employment.

The name Li-hsiang was given by the father to this, his second son, in the hope that he would become like Chin Li-hsiang, a great scholar and philosopher of the Sung period. The child's education was begun very early by his father teaching him the Classic of Filial Piety when he was four years of age. Two years afterwards he was sent to a school in T'ung-hsiang, the master of which was noted for his superior moral character and his general attainments. But his stay here was short, for his father died very suddenly in 1619, and left the family very poor. The grand-father took a small shop in the village town and the mother helped to maintain herself and children by spinning. She had a daughter and two sons, but the latter enjoyed all her care and devotion. For them she toiled and watched, denying herself the comforts of life that they might receive a good education. She urged them to diligence by the examples of Confucius and Mencius.

---

* Luh-Fu-t'ing-sau pien-lu-chi-yao (陸 桴 亭 思 辨 錄); San-yü-t'ang-wên-chi (三 魚 堂 文 集) Ch., 8.; Translations of Peking Gazettes, 1874 p. 66.

These, she said, were left fatherless children but because they had high resolves they attained to the rank of Sages. The grand-father continued to superintend the education of the boys and selected for them the best teachers of the neighbourhood. Thus for several years Li-hsiang studied under a succession of masters acquiring a wide knowledge of the ancient philosophical, historical and poetical literature. When he came of age he abandoned the designation Chi-jen (吉 人) or Blessed Man, which his relatives had given, and adopted instead the name K'ao-fu. He also married the niece of the amiable and accomplished master under whom he was studying at the time.

It was at this period that Chang first showed symptoms of standing aloof from the ways of the age. About 1628 habits of extravagance and display led to changing fashions in dress and he became noted for adherence to the tall hat and narrow sleeves of better times. He now lived at home happy in the loving services which he rendered his mother and grand-father, and in the pleasant society of intimate and congenial friends. But in 1630 the kind old grand-father died, and in the following year he lost his mother.

Soon afterwards Chang made the acquaintance of Yen Shĭ-fêng, a student with rare gifts both of heart and mind. They met at the school of a philosopher noted for a thorough acquaintance with the Yih-ching, and they read and studied together. A friendship thus grew up of the most cordial thorough kind, which lasted thirteen summers and winters and then the "Shadow fear'd of man" broke the fair companionship. Chang had hitherto been a desultory and miscellaneous reader and had been specially captivated by the teachings of Wang Yang-ming. About this time, however, he was induced to read the Great Learning and Chu Hsi's Chin-Ssŭ-lu. These works converted him, and he renounced heresy, abandoned Yang-ming, and became a devoted follower of the ancient Sages as interpreted by the brothers Ch'êng and Chu Hsi.

The rest of Chang's life was chiefly spent in teaching, writing, and farming. He did not obtain his Chü-jen Degree, nor did he take any open part in the troubles which now distracted the Empire. For a time, in 1644, he was at Chi-shan for the purpose of studying under

Liu Tsung-chou, to whose criticism he submitted some of his writings. Though he admired Liu at first he did not become a follower or accept all that philosopher's opinions. During a few years Chang taught a school at Hoochow but he spent nearly all his life in the immediate neighbourhood of T'ung-shan. The rebels burnt his cottage and the coffin of his grand-father which had been placed in a mat shed awaiting burial. This was his greatest distress and he was with difficulty dissuaded from committing suicide. When the rebel chief Li Tzŭ-ch'êng took Peking, and the Manchoos coming in afterwards gained possession of the Empire he fasted and mourned. But these and the other great events of the time did not effect any change in Chang's way of life. He refused to prepare students for the official examinations, and advised them in view of the serious troubles coming over the land to study only books of practical usefulness. Many disciples received instruction from him, and he continued to enjoy the happy though obscure life of a village philosopher until old age. In conjunction with his brother he built a house near T'ung-hsiang, and here he had lived for a short time when his death occurred in 1674. For some time before he had been wasting away with pain and sickness and at last was scarcely able to stand or sit upright. A very short time before he died an old friend called and wished to see him without formality. Ch'ang, however, quoted the dying words of Tsêng-tzŭ and received him with the observances due to a visitor. Death found him ready, waiting in his chair, solemn and composed.

From the name of his native Willow Grove Chang received the designation Yang-yuan Hsien-shêng by which he is best known. He was admitted to the Temple of Confucius in 1871 on the Petition of a high official. Until lately, however, his name and writings were little known, and even from his native place all memory of him had departed. But within the last few years a complete collection has been made of his Poems, Letters, Philosophical and other treatises, and notes of his lectures and discussions. The Compilation, which has been carefully executed, gives also a Minute Life of Chang with criticisms and summaries of his teachings. Among the Poems is one on the death of his beloved friend Yen, written in the manner of Sung Yü's lament for

Chü Yuan. He calls the spirit of his friend back to the chamber which his absence had made empty and to the world which needed his counsel and example. The Letters, which occupy thirteen *chuan*, are interesting chiefly for the detailed manner in which they state the writer's philosophical opinions. Among the larger treatises of Chang's composition are the Pei-wang (備 忘), Yuan-hsüo-chi (願 學 記), Yen-hsing-chien-wên-lu (言 行 見 聞 錄), Chin-ku-lu (近 古 錄) Pu-nung-shu (補 農 書) and Commentaries on some of the Classics. The Pu-nung-shu, or Supplementary Treatise on Husbandry, is very plain and practical. It gives minute directions about the various processes of farming, the keeping of cattle, rearing of silkworms, getting rid of snakes and other plagues. The Chin-ku-lu, first arranged for publication by Chang's disciples, illustrates the private, social, and public virtues by examples taken from modern history. It recounts instances of conduct which "came near to the ancients." This and the other treatises mentioned above were all prepared with the immediate end in view of supplying the wants of the author's family, disciples, and fellow-villagers.

In philosophy Chang Li-hsiang was a thorough adherent of Chu Hsi, adopting that scholar's readings and explanations of the Classics. From him he learned to admire Chow Lien-ch'i and the two Ch'êng and to see in them the true continuers and expositors of Confucian doctrine. Consequently he was opposed to Luh Chiu-yuan and his vindicator Wang Yang-ming. In the chain of transmission he links Hsie Hsüan and Hu Chü-jen with Luh Lung-ch'i. This last knew him and read some of his writings. All that Yang-yuan taught whether by lecture or book had a practical aim. He believed only in a philosophy which was of use to man in the affairs of every-day life. Man does not need, he taught, the wide space of the world, or an exalted position, or any high qualifications in order to lead a noble life and fulfill the requirements of duty. His own heart, the family circle, the little village are room enough; the occupation of a farmer and the most humble abilities will suffice as his equipment. Self-reverence can be practised in any place, and the moral law of humanity may be studied in any condition of life.

All Chang's writings are plain and simple without elegancies of style or any recondite meanings. He wanted to turn men away from the crooked paths which led to place and wealth, and to show them the more excellent way of a humble virtuous life. The only two occupations which he considered suitable for a good man were husbandry and learning, and these he thought were best united. As a farmer a man could be independent and lead a good life easily, while the official, mercantile, and mechanical employments were such that scarcely could a righteous man keep his integrity in any of them. He deprecated the unreasoning abuse which was dealt out to Buddhism and Taoism, but disliked the conduct of men like Liu Mèn-t'ai and Wang Yang-ming who denounced Buddhism and yet practically adopted several of its distinguishing theories.

In his own life Chang Li-hsiang exemplified all that he taught. With him filial piety was the root of all virtues and he possessed that in an eminent degree. It was not alone by the daily service before the tablets and the yearly worship at the tombs that he showed an affectionate remembrance of his parents and grand-father. For a long time he wore sackcloth under his ordinary dress, and still when the days of his father's and mother's deaths came round he kept them as solemn fasts. In all the relations of life he was true-hearted and self-forgetful, never forgetting a kindness and never alienating a friend. He had no sympathy with the restless, ambitious, and unprincipled seekers for wealth and power, and by the world generally he was quite unknown. His path has been that of the perfect man, which, the Chung-yung says, proceeds from obscurity to distinction. Though the tiny circle of village praise long since ceased it has been succeeded by the ampler circuit of enduring fame which includes him among the Confucian immortals.*

* Yang-yuan-hsien-shêng-ch'uan-chi (楊園先生全集).

64. T'ang Pin (湯 斌). S. K'ung-poh (孔 伯).

T'ang Pin was born in the year 1627 at Sui-chow (睢 州), a
District town of Kuei-tê-foo, in Honan. His father Tsu-ch'i (祖 契)
had held office under the last rulers of the Ming dynasty. He was a
man of good parts, affectionate, and careful of his son's education
though very poor. With his own hand he copied out books, marked
them off in chapters and sentences, and wrote down the meaning and
pronunciations of words. One day he had copied out twenty sections
and his arm became pained. Pin was only ten years of age at the
time, but he could never in after life take up these twenty sections
without shedding tears. When Li Tzŭ-ch'êng and his rebel army
besieged Sui-chow and took it the garden of the T'ang family was the
scene of a battle. Pin's mother, a loving tender-hearted woman
possessed with a spirit of pure devotion and self-sacrifice, was slain by
the rebels for her courageous loyalty. His father now fled from the
troubles of Honan and went to Chekiang where he remained until
1645 when he returned to his native place. In 1652 Pin became a
Chin-shi, then a Bachelor of the Han-lin, and afterwards a Graduate
in the Department of State History. While holding this rank he drew
up a paper in which he urged the Emperor to order a collection to be
made of all the local Histories and Biographies of the Ming period.
These works were then to serve as the material from which the annals
of that dynasty were to be compiled. He also brought forward the
precedents of the Sung and Yuan Histories to show that these annals
should contain records of those worthies who had from conscientious
scruples refused to give in their allegiance to the new dynasty. For
this proposition certain high officials thought the emperor should deal
severely with him as encouraging rebels, but His Majesty held a
different opinion. He promoted T'ang to be Taotai of T'ung-kuan, in
Shensi, and in 1659 transferred him to Ling-pei in Kiangsi, where he
distinguished himself by helping to crush a rebellion. Soon afterwards
he heard of his father's illness and at once obtained leave to go home.

The old man revived a little at the sight of his son who nursed and tended him with affectionate assiduity. It was only for a short time, however, and in 1664 he had to mourn the loss of his beloved parent.

When the required period of retirement was over T'ang did not care to return to public life, and having heard of Sun Ch'i-fêng as a great teacher in philosophy he went to the ·Hsia-fêng Mountains and became his disciple. He led the quiet life of a student and afterwards of a teacher also until 1678 when he was called to office by the Emperor Kanghsi. After an examination he was made a Sub-Expositor in the Han-lin and appointed to assist in the compilation of the Ming annals and to edit Shun-chï's Edicts. Afterwards he was made a "Sub-Chancellor of the Grand Secretariat," and helped to frame the Ta-ch'ing-hui-tien. The Province of Kiang-nan was now in a wretched condition and an able and upright Governor was needed in order to bring it to peace and order. The Emperor selected T'ang for this task and sent him to Soochow with many marks of his favour and confidence. T'ang's administration of this province was eminently successful in every respect. He drove out wizards and sorcerers, destroyed the temples and images of unlawful gods, purged the land of licentious books, and checked immorality of all kinds. In order to provide for the permanence of his reforms he obtained from the Emperor an Edict forbidding the people for ever to return to their evil ways. This Edict he caused to be engraved on a stone which he set upon a hill. But it was scarcely needed, for when the people saw that their dreadful gods did not harm the man who had thrown down their temples and cast away their images they went back no more to their foolish worship. T'ang also adjusted the taxes which had been the cause of much trouble, afforded speedy and efficient relief to the sufferers from flood and famine, and taught the people the advantages of furgality and temperance.

In 1686 Kanghsi called him to the Capital to be Tutor to the. Heir Apparent and made him a President of the Board of Ceremonies Next year by a little stupidity he incurred the Imperial displeasure, and his enemies at once came forward with accusations. The charges were referred to the Board of Censors which recommended that T'ang should be degraded from office, but the Emperor only took away his titles and retained him at his post. Shortly afterwards he was about to make him President of the Board of Works, but T'ang was attacked by sickness and begged leave to resign. He died in 1687 and the news of his death caused deep sorrow to the Emperor. When he heard of his illness he sent his own physician to him, and now he ordered his coffin to be carried to Honan by the Post-road, and restored his full title. He also decreed sacrificial honours to him at his tomb and in Halls dedicated to the worship of great statesmen.

The literary name of T'ang is Ch'ien-ngan (潛菴), and his posthumous epithet is Wên-chêng (文正). Further sacrificial honours have been decreed to him and in 1823 he was canonized. Besides his contributions to the historical and other works mentioned above T'ang wrote a treatise named Lo-hsüe-pien (洛學編) in which he developed the teachings of the great Sung philosophers. He composed also a number of Essays and Poems which he collected and printed, at the Emperor's request, with the title Shi-wên-chi (詩文集). His official papers, Letters, and other Miscellanies were collected and edited by some of his disciples, and published as the T'ang-tzŭ-yi-shu (湯子遺書). Some of the Essays and Memorials in this collection are very interesting, specially those which relate to T'ang's measures at Soochow against immorality and religious imposture. The Lives of his father and mother are beautiful as well for the piety and affection which they reveal as for their simple and graceful narratives. The work contains some of his Letters to Sun Ch'i-fêng and the Preface which he wrote for Sun's Miscellanies. It includes also the Essays and Poems of the Shi-wên-chi, or at least a number of them.

T'ang Pin spent the greater part of his life in office, and he was throughout a zealous and faithful servant. He gained the affection and esteem of the Emperors Shun-chi and Kanghsi, and he carried out their wishes in winning over the people to contentment with the new dynasty and healing the wounds made by war and rebellion. Being himself a good scholar and an orthodox philosopher he exerted himself to revive learning and restore Confucianism to its proper position.[*]

---

[*] T'ang-tzŭ-yi-shu; T'ang-chien-ngan-chi (湯潛菴集), edited by Chang Poh-hang.

65. Luh Lung-ch'i (陸 隴 其).   S. Chia-shu (稼 書).

Luh Lung-ch'i was born of poor parents in the year 1630 at P'ing-hu (平 湖), a town in the Kia-hing, Prefecture of Chekiang. As a boy he was not clever or remarkable in any way except that he was fond of reading all kinds of books, and truthful and honest. His education was acquired by steady perseverance maintained for many years in the midst of hardships, and he had to earn his living as a private tutor. The key note of his life was struck when he told his first employer that he was not anxious to have a large salary.

It was not until 1670 that Luh was able to obtain his Chin-shi, and after that he had to wait five years before receiving an appointment. He was then made District Magistrate of Chia-ting (Ka-ding) in Kiangsu, a place of great importance and hard to be governed. Here he endeared himself to the people by his unwearied labours for their good. He was of inflexible virtue and without reproach in all his ways, and he set the people an example in sobriety of life and diligence in business. His heart was set on having his District free from crime, but he had not much experience of the world, and was too indulgent in the matter of tax-collecting for he loved the people as his children. The Governor of Kiangsu, not satisfied with Luh's conduct, proposed that he should be transferred to a post more suited to his character and abilities. The Peking Government, however, degraded him and ordered him to remain in charge of Chia-ting. But just at this time a serious murder occurred within his jurisdiction and his management of the case called forth severe censure. The Emperor now dismissed him from office to the great sorrow of the people over whom he had been presiding. Luh would not sue for pardon or allow any one to intercede for him, though a deputation did actually go to the Governor to pray that Luh might be retained. When he was going away the citizens thronged the streets and weeping tried to stop his sedan. After he was gone every household set up his effigy and gave him the worship due to a parent.

In 1678 Luh was, on the recommendation of a high official, again summoned to the Capital, but before the day of Examination came his father died and he had to go into retirement. His next appointment was that of Magistrate at Ling-shou in Chibli, a post which the Emperor selected as suited to Luh's high moral character and small administrative abilities. Next year the Governor General was able to report that already Luh had effected great improvements, and that it was his duty to recommend him to the Throne. Ling-shou was a poor district and its inhabitants were rude and lawless. Luh encouraged agriculture, diffused learning and established the laws and customs of orginized society. His hands were never soiled by a bribe nor his conscience wounded by an unkind or unjust action.

In 1690 he was called to Peking and promoted to be Censor for the Circuit of Ssu-chuan. One of his first acts after reaching the capital was to petition the Emperor to remit the taxes due by the inhabitants of Yuan-shan who had suffered very severely from continuous bad seasons. The prayer was answered by the remission of the taxes for a year and-a-half. Shortly afterwards he besought His Majesty to forbid the Governor of Hunan to remain in office while observing mourning for a parent. If the Governor were allowed, he said, to do this his conduct would become a precedent and thus work great mischief. This request also was granted and without delay.

Next year the military operations of Kanghsi required large sums of money beyond what the ordinary revenue afforded. The expedient of selling offices, promotions, and official pardons was now resorted to though not without opposition. Luh Lung-ch'i was among the officers appoint to deliberate and report on the matter. He proposed that all purchasers of office should be considered on trial for three years and that, if at the end of that period they were not recommended by their superiors, they should be dismissed. This was shown to be impracticable, and as Luh persisted and was opposed to the sale of office under any other conditions he was accused of wanton and perverse attempts to injure the national finances. His accusers recommended that he should be degraded from office, but the Emperor more just and humane, proposed to give him a new though inferior appointment.

Luh would not continue to serve, and having resigned on the plea of ill health he went to his native place. Here he lived in poverty and sickness for a few months, and died in the winter of 1692.

Luh was admitted to the Temple of Confucius in 1724 and in 1736 the epithet C'hing-hsien (清 獻), Pure and Intelligent, was conferred on him by the Emperor Chien-lung. · The Ceremonial Code of the dynasty did not allow of posthumous honours being given to officials of the Fifth Rank, but the Emperor got over this difficulty by conferring on Luh the rank of a Sub-Chancellor of the Grand Secretariat and Vice-President of the Board of Ceremonies. His literary name is P'ing-hu (平 湖) or sometimes Tang-hu (當 湖), the latter being the old name of P'ing-hu, Luh's birth-place.

The personal character of Luh Lung-ch'i is uniformly described as very excellent. He was without genius and without ambition, but he was settled in principle and faithful in conduct. Also, first and last and above all he was a student and teacher of the great works of former Sages. He was a Confucianist of the strictest orthodoxy and a thorough follower of the two Ch'êng and Chu Hsi. The services which he rendered to the cause of learning were great though he was not a profound or original thinker. He assisted in the publication of several books for the use of young students, among them being the Hsiao-ssŭ-shu or Four Books for Boys, a valuable little treatise. His labours on the Classics extended over many years and their results are given in a number of books. The Sung-yang-chiang-i (松 陽 講 義) is an elaborate commentary or rather a series of popular lectures on the Four Books. It is the substance of his discourses to the students at Ling-show arranged and edited by himself. In another treatise on the Four Books he gives notes and comments derived from a great variety of scholars with occasional reflections by himself. Besides these he wrote several other works on the Classics, compiled an official account of Ling-show, and composed several other treatises. His Letters and Remains were published with the title San-yü-t'ang-chi (三 魚 堂 集) to which an addition as Wai-chi was afterwards added. This is not a book of any peculiar value, but some of the Letters and Essays are interesting for their criticisms on Wang Yang-ming. Luh never misses an opportunity of attacking Wang whom he treats as a Buddhist in disguise, and whose theories he regards as utterly pernicious. This book is of value also for the many short notices and observations it has on the works and authors of the Ming and other periods. Luh was of a very practical and methodical turn of mind and he was wont to write down reflections which occurred to him as he read, and to copy out passages which he regarded as important. Some of his extracts from Chu Hsi's writings have been printed as a separate book under the editorship of Chang Poh-hang who seems to have had for Luh a veneration like that which the latter had for Chu Hsi.*

* Kuo-ch'ao-hsien-chêng-shi-liao (國朝先正事畧) ch. 9 ; San-yü-t'ang-chi ; Chêng-yi-t'ang-su-chi, Ch. 4; Tu-chu-sui-pi (讀朱隨筆). Preface.

The Ch'ung-sheng-t'zu (崇 聖 祠)
or Temple to Ancestors glorified as Sages.

The Ch'ung-shêng-t'zŭ is a chamber properly at the back of the large Hall in the Temple of Confucius, but in many of his temples throughout the Provinces it is outside the main building and adjoining its eastern wall.

In the year 1008 Sung Chên Tsung ennobled Confucius' father Shu-liang-ho with the title Ch'i-kuo-kung (齊 國 公), Duke of Ch'i, and at the same time erected a temple to his honour at Ch'ü-fou (曲 阜) in Shantung. The Emperor Wên Ti of the Yuan dynasty in 1330 conferred on Shu-liang-ho the higher title Ch'i-shêng-wang, Sage-producing Prince, and erected a temple to him at each Government College throughout the Empire. Under the Ming dynasty, in 1437, the fathers of the Four Associates and afterwards the fathers of the great founders of the Sung philosophy were admitted to share in the worship offered to Confucius, father. The name of the Hall was also changed to Ch'i-shêng-wang-tien. In 1724 other progenitors of Confucius to the fifth generation were made Princes and Sages and placed beside his father in this Hall which had its name again changed, being now called the Ch'ung-shêng-t'zŭ. This title indicates that the building is devoted to the worship of ancestors, that is, in the first place of Confucius' ancestors, and that these men owe their saintships to the merit of their descendant.

The Hall is dedicated to their worship and their tablets are placed in a row at the upper end. They are called Chêng-ssŭ-wu-wei (正 祀 五 位), the Five places of principal worship. They are, beginning with the middle.

1. Chao-shêng-wang Mu-chin-fu-kung (肇聖王木金父公).

Chao-shêng denotes the Sage who founded the family, that is, the most remote ancestor to whom Confucius' merits have been allowed to extend. Mu-chin was the son of K'ung chia (孔 嘉) a high officer in the State of Sung. A minister of the same State named Hua-tu (華督) fell in love with Mu-chin's wife and in order to obtain possession of her killed her husband in the year B.C. 709. Nothing beyond this is known of his history. His titles and those of the three immediately following were conferred by the Emperor Yung-chêng in the year 1724.

On the left hand of Mu-chin is

2. Yü-shêng-wang Ch'i-fu-kung (裕聖王祈父公).

The name of this man, who was a son of the above, is also variously given as Kao-i (皋 夷) and Yi-i (睪夷), but the Yi is generally said to be a mistake for Kao, though some consider Yi-i to be the correct form.

On the right hand of Mu-chin is

3. I-shêng-wang Fang-shu-kung (詒聖王防叔公).

This man, son of Ch'i, was the first of the K'ung family to settle in the State of Lu, whither he fled to avoid the powerful enmity of Hu-tu's descendants. In his adopted country he soon received official employment, and he was for a time Chief Magistrate of Fang (防), a town near the site of the modern Pi-Hsien (費 縣), in the Yen-chow Prefecture of Shantung. His proper name has not been handed down, and he is known only as Fang-shu from his connection with the above town.

On the left hand of No. 2 is

4. Ch'ang-shêng-wang Poh-hsia-kung (昌聖王伯夏公).

Poh-hsia was a son of the preceding, and nothing more is known about him except that he was the father of Shu-liang-ho.

On the right hand of No. 3 is

5. Ch'i-shêng-wang Shu-liang-kung (啓聖王 叔梁公).

Shu-liang-ho was for some time Chief Magistrate of Tsou (郰) another town situated within what is now the Prefecture of Yen-chow. He is represented in tradition as a man of gigantic size and of extra-ordinary strength, noted for his military prowess. His wife, however, bore him only daughters and nine of them, while a concubine gave him a son who was a deformed cripple. After this one does not wonder to learn that he became "austere" and married again. When above seventy years old he asked a neighbour named Yen (顏) for one of his daughters in marriage, and Yen, who had three, gave him the young-est, the Cordelia of the family. Sse-ma Ch'ien says that Shu-liang-ho and Yen's daughter, whose name was Chêng-tsai, only met in the country, but he is not to be believed. Perhaps he meant, as one suggests, that they were unequally yoked as January with May, or the two characters may be misprints. The young wife prayed and so became the mother of Confucius, but the old father died when his son was only three years of age.*

——◆◆◆——

At the upper end of the East wall and apart from the others is a tablet inscribed Hsien-hsien-K'ung-shi-Mêng-p'i (先賢孔氏孟皮).

Mêng-p'i, known also as Poh-ni (伯尼), was the son of Shu-liang-ho by a concubine and so nearly half-brother to Confucius. He was deformed in the feet and consequently could not take office. Nothing is known about his life except that he had a daughter whom Confucius gave away in marriage to a good man named Nan-jung. Mêng-p'i was admitted to this Hall in 1857, and in some temples his tablet is smaller than the others, a hard-hearted way of recalling his bodily defects.

---

* Legge Ch. Cl. I, Proleg. Ch. 5 sec. 1.; Chia-yü Chuan 9, ch. 39; Hsiang-tang-t'u-k'ao (鄕黨圖考), Chs. 1 & 2.; Shi-chi, Ch. 6, p. 77.

The Four Associates succeed. These are placed and arranged in positions corresponding to those of their sons in the principal Hall.

———————

1. Hsien-hsien-Yen-shi (先賢顏氏).

Yen Wu-yao (顏無繇) or Yen-yao. S. Chi-lu. (季路) or Lu. When Confucius began to teach in his native place Yen Wu-yao, who was only six years his junior, became a disciple. When his son Hui died he asked the Master to sell his carriage and give him the proceeds to buy an outer coffin for Hui's corpse. Confucius refused, and little more is known about the life of Wu-yu. Posthumous honours and titles were conferred on him at different times, and in 1530 he and the three who immediately follow were made the Four Associates in this Hall.

———————

2. Hsien-hsien-Tsêng-shi (先賢曾氏).

Tsêng Tien (曾點) S. Hsi (皙) or Tzŭ-hsi.

Tsêng Tien, or as he is more commonly designated, Tsêng Hsi, was also a disciple of Confucius who apparently held him in some esteem. But he was not a man of any great merit or abilities, and was said by Mencius to be one of those who Confucius said were reckless (" ambitious " in Legge's translation), that is talking wildly about the ancients and not following them in conduct. When the Master on one occasion asked certain among his disciples what were their aims in life, Tien who was among them at first did not care to answer. Being pressed he said, " In *this*, the last month of spring, with the dress of the season all complete, along with five or six young men who have assumed the cap, and six or seven boys, I would wash in the E, enjoy the breeze among the rain-altars, and return home singing." The Master gave his " approval to Tien." Titles of honour were conferred on him also during the T'ang, Sung, and Ming dynasties.

3. Hsien-hsien K'ung-shi (先 賢 孔 氏).

K'ung Li (孔 鯉).   S. Poh-yü (伯 魚).

Li was the only son of Confucius and the father of Tzŭ-Ssŭ. He
was born in B.C. 532 and the name Li was given to him in honour of
Duke Chao of Lu who sent the Sage a present of some carp (Li 鯉)
on the occasion of his son's birth. Of his life we have only a few
incidental notices, and it does not seem to have been in any way distinguished. His father observed "a distant reserve" towards him, and the
only teaching he is recorded to have given Poh-yü was a warning
against neglecting the Odes and Ceremonies. The warning caused his
son to study these treatises. When Confucius' wife died, though she
had been divorced from her husband Poh-yü mourned for her piously
until his stern father ordered him to desist. He died before his father
perhaps in the year 482, but there are conflicting accounts of the
length of his life. He was first canonized in A.D. 1267 and the usual
honoray titles were conferred on him at different periods.

4. Hsien-hsien Mêng-sun-shi (先 賢 孟 孫 氏).

Mêng-sun Chi (孟 孫 激).   S. Kung-yi (公 宜).

Nothing is known of this man beyond the fact that he was the
husband of Mencius' mother, and that he died while his son was an
infant. It is not quite certain even what was actually his surname.
Titles similar to those of the three preceding were conferred on him,
and in 1436 he was first admitted to the Confucian Temple.*

* Legge Ch. Cl. I. Proleg. Ch. V., 1. p. 179, 112, II. p. 375 &c; Chia-yü. Ch. 39.

FORMER CONFUCIANISTS.

1. Hsien-ju Chou-shi (先 儒 周 氏).

Chou Fu-ch'êng (周 輔 成).

The date of Chou Fu-ch'êng's birth is not known nor is anything recorded about his early life. He became a Chin-shi in A.D. 1015 and soon afterwards received an official appointment. The rest of his life was chiefly spent in the public service and the last position he held was that of Magistrate of Kuei-ling (桂 嶺) a town situated within the present Prefecture of P'ing-lo in Kuang-si. His reputation as an efficient administrator was very great and he was highly esteemed by all who knew him. He was twice married and it was his second wife, named Chêng (鄭), who was the mother of Lien-ch'i. Fu-ch'êng died in the year 1031, and was posthumously promoted to be a Censor. His tablet was placed in this Hall in 1595.

2. Hsien-ju Chang-shi (先 儒 張 氏).

Chang Ti (張 迪).

Chang Ti, the father of Tsai, was the son of a scholar who rose to high position in the State. The dates of his birth and death are not known and little is told of his life. He held office during the reign of Sung Jen-tsung, A.D. 1023 to 1063, and died while in charge of Fou-chow (涪 州) in what is now the the Prefecture of Chung-king in Ssuch'uan. He was buried near the town of Mei (郿) in Shensi, and his tablet was placed in this Hall in 1724.

3. Hsien-ju Ch'êng-shi (先 儒 程 氏).

Ch'êng Hsiang (程 珦). S. Poh-wên (伯 溫).

The native place of Ch'êng Hsiang, the father of Ming-tao and I-chuan was Lo-yang in Honan-foo, and he was born in the year 1006. His father and grand-father had been men of merit and distinction in the public service and through this he received his first appointment, a subordinate office at Huang-p'i (黃陂) near Han-yang. After some time he was promoted to be Magistrate of Hsing-kuo hsien in Kiangsi. This was a place of bad repute for the disorderly character of its inhabitants and their love of litigation. By gentle means Ch'êng in a short time reformed the people and his prisons became empty. The law-suits about land which plotting knaves had raised and complicated he settled with off-hand decision. It was here that he met Chou Lien-ch'i whose great abilities he was the first to discern and make known. So highly did the people of Hsing-kuo esteem Ch'êng and his services, that when he was removed they had a temple built in the town for his worship.

The next place to which he was appointed was Kung-chow, in Kuangsi. The chief of a wild tribe near this place had lately been executed and a report now arose that the chief's ghost had ordered the people to build him a temple. The people were about to do so when Ch'êng quashed the affair by causing the tablet of the intended divinity to be thrown into the river. From Kung-chow he was transferred to P'ei Hsien in Kiangsu, where he saved the peasants from famine during a flood by having beans planted over a large extent of country still under water. When the " new measures" of Wang An-shi were set on foot Ch'êng, who was at the time Prefect of Han-chow, in Ssŭchuan, though almost single-handed, opposed them with energy as bad for the country. By this he incurred the displeasure of the Imperial Commissioner appointed to enquire into the working of the measures, resigned office, and went home. Here he died at the age of eighty-four in the year 1090.

Though Ch'êng had written his own epitaph and enjoined on his sons not to ask for a funeral eulogy two of his old friends reported his death to the Emperor and praised his purity as an official and his self-restraint. He was buried at the public expense and received posthumous titles. In 1530 his tablet was placed in the Hall of Confucius' Ancestors.

The gentle and stern virtues were happily combined in Ch'êng Hsiang's character. He was affable and kind-hearted but at the same time strict and firm. His house was full of little ones, sons, grand-sons, and nephews, and he was always anxious to have the young people and the servants happy and comfortable. If any one did any-thing naughty, however, he was certain to be punished. Ch'êng out of his small salary helped all his poor relatives who with his own family shared his care and affection. He had an abhorrence for all heresy and would not even run to see a blazing Buddha. His aim in life was to do what was right and this he taught his two illustrious sons, introducing them also to the teacher whom he loved and esteemed, and who, he knew would guide them in the path of true philosophy.

4. Hsien-ju Chu-shi (先 儒 朱 氏).
Chu Sung (朱 松). S. Ch'iao-nien (喬 年).

The birth-place of Chu Sung was near Wu-yuan in Anhui, and he was born in the year 1097. As a child he was remarkable for unusual cleverness and in youth he became a wide and miscellaneous reader. But becoming a disciple of Lo Tsing-yen and Yang-shi he turned his attention to philosophy and became a devoted student of the ancient Classics. Having obtained his Chin-shi in 1118 he received a small appointment at Chêng-ho (政 和) a town of Kien-ning-foo in Fuhkeen. Here his father died and Sung had to go into mourning. He was too poor to have his father's remains carried back to Anhui and so they were buried at Chêng-ho.

On his return to public life he was sent to Yu-ch'i (尤 溪) also in Fuhkeen and here his son Hsi was born. From this subordinate office Chu Sung rose through a series of appointments to be a Secretary in the Board of Civil Office, and in all gave satisfaction. But when Ch'in K'uei came into power and urged peace with the Kin invaders Chu opposed him vigorously, and by so doing incurred the enmity of Ch'in. Malicious charges were brought against him and he considered it to be his wisest course to retire from public life. Accordingly in 1140 he resigned and went home to Kien-chou where he died in 1143. A posthumous title was conferred on him, and in 1530 he was admitted to this Hall.

The literary designation of Chu Sung is Wei-chai (韋齋), which is derived from the name he gave his study. *Wei* is a leather belt and is here used in the sense of gentle restraint. Chu was himself disposed to be desultory in reading and impetuous in thinking, and he took this word as the name of his study to remind him that he must proceed gently and exercise self-restraint. He was man of great learning and of a quiet modest disposition, born to poverty, and living and dying poor. To his son he gave all he had to give, a good example and the foundation of an education, and on his death-bed he provided for his future training in wisdom.

* * *

5. Hsien-ju Ts'ai-shi (先 儒 蔡 氏).

Ts'ai Yuan-ting (蔡 元 定). S. Chi-t'ung (季 通).

Ts'ai Yuan-ting was born in the year 1135 near Kien-yang in Kien-ning a Prefectural District of Fuhkeen. In boyhood he was distinguished for his love of reading, his power of learning quickly, and his very retentive memory. His father, a scholar of some repute, gave him the writings of the two Ch'êng, Shao and Chang, telling him that in these flowed the true doctrines of Confucius and Mencius. Yuan-ting studied these works carefully and throughly, taking them with him to the Hsi-shan or Western Hills, where he lived for a time as a hermit. Hearing of Chu Hsi's fame he went to that philosopher resolved to become his disciple. But Chu finding that he was man of solid learning and profound genuis refused to call him disciple and made him a friend and fellow-student. The two philosophers lived together and thoroughly enjoyed each other's society often prolonging their conversation on the deep meanings of the sacred books until long after midnight. They worked together at the correction and explanation of the texts of the Four Books and other Classics and at the compilation of the great National History. Yuan-ting sketched the outline and drew up the draft of the work which Chu afterwards elaborated into the Chi-mêng.

Though repeatedly recommended for office he refused to accept any appointment and when Chu Hsi went away he returned to the Hsi-shan. Persecution arose against him and he was falsely accused of teaching false doctrines. The charge was actually levelled at Chu but Yuan-ting was also involved. He was banished to Tao-chao in Hunan, and thither he proceeded on foot attended only by his affectionate son Ch'ên. Chu Hsi who was again at home, along with a large party of friends gave him a farewell entertainment, and when the friends wept he kept his cheer. We clasp hands, he said to Chu, and part with a smile, and do not cry like children. At Tao-chow disciples came from far and near to hear him read and expound the old canonical writings. Nor did he forget those whom he had left in Fuhkeen, but wrote counselling them to be true to themselves and not be frightened by what had befallen him.

One day in the year 1198 he said to Ch'ên, Decline all visitors. I want to have peace and quietness while restoring to Providence (my maker) its old property. He knew the end was near at hand and after two or three days he died. Posthumous honour was conferred on him and he received the epithet Wên-chie (文節), Accomplished and of rigid principle. His usual name in literature is Hsi-shan (西山), from the name of the mountain, the still cold peaks of which he chose to be his place for undisturbed study. His tablet also was placed in this Hall in the year 1530.

Ts'ai Hsi-shan was one of China's greatest scholars and profoundest thinkers. Not only did he know thoroughly with the understanding and the heart the literature of Confucian philosophy but he was also well acquainted with history, astronomy, arithmetic, and other subjects. He left manuscripts of several works in a more or less unfinished condition, the most celebrated being that of the Hung-fan-chie which his son Ch'ên afterwards completed and published. Chu Hsi says of Yuan-ting—Accurate in knowledge, unique in abilities, inflexible of will and inexhaustible in argument, his like can never be seen.[*]

---

* Chou-Lien-ch'i-chi Ch. 10; Shang-yu-lu, Ch. 11; Chu-tzŭ-nien-pu, Ch. 1; Shang-yu-lu, Ch. 18; Hsing-li-ta-ch'uan, Ch. 24.

It is understood that the subject of the following brief notice has lately been admitted to the Temples of Confucius, but up to the time of printing this the official announcement of the fact has not been published.

Chang Pai-hsing (張 伯 行). S. Hsiao-hsien (孝 先).

The native place of Chaug Pai-hsing was I-fêng (儀 封), a District town of K'ai-fêng-foo in Honan, where he was born in the year 1651. Of his early life little seems to be recorded, but he tells us that while still young he lost both his parents, a statement which is at variance with the official biography of Chang. In 1685 he obtained the Chin-shi Degree, and was thereupon appointed a clerk in the Grand Secretariat, but soon afterwards he was transferred to the Imperial Patent Office. The death of his father obliged him to retire from office for a time, and he returned to his native place. Here when the period of mourning was over in 1699, he made himself useful by organising a band of workers and repairing an embankment to the north of I-fêng. This brought him to the notice of the Governor General of the Huang Ho on whose recommendation Chang was appointed to duty in connection with that troublesome river. All through his life he had a liking for hydraulic engineering and evidently took great pains in studying the subject.

In 1703 Chang was appointed Taotai of C'hi-ning in Shantung and held that post for three years when he was promoted to be Judge in Kiangsu. The Emperor Kanghsi visited this Province in 1707, and was much pleased with the good reputation which the Judge had achieved. "I have ascertained," he said to his Courtiers, "that Chang Pai-hsing administers his office with great purity, such as it is very difficult to obtain; he is thorough and sincere, and not afraid of his enemies." Accordingly the Emperor promoted him at once to the Governorship of Fuhkeen, and in this office Chang not only won golden opinions among the people, but also made himself an immortal fame. One of his first official acts at Foochow was to obtain the remission of the Land Tax for three Districts in Formosa which had been afflicted with a continued drought. In the same year food was very dear in Fuhkeen and he obtained from the Imperial Treasury 50,000 Taels which he used in the purchase of rice from other provinces, selling it to the people at the ordinary price. Next year, 1708, he prayed the Emperor to make permanent the increase of ten to the number of Chü-jen Degrees allowed to the Province. The petition was granted and the number of Degrees was fixed at 84, to the delight of the literary class which was increasing with very rapid growth. In the meantime Chang built a college for the use of advanced students, and collected in it many rare and valuable treatises. Here also he superintended the studies of those aspiring to literary honours, and occasionally lectured to them on the old learning. Moreover he organised a Committee for reprinting a number of useful treatises which were out of print or hard to be obtained; he revised these works, corrected errors, and contributed to nearly all Prefaces or Introductions. It this time a nefarious custom prevailed in parts of Fuhkeen of selling young girls into perpetual slavery, and Chang set himself vigorously to abolish the custom. Many other goods works also were wrought by him among the people of this Province and the memory of them still remains.

In 1709 Chang was transferred to Kiangsu, and here his troubles commenced. The Governor General, whose name was Koli 噶 禮 was a Manchoo. He was an accomplished, clever man, but devoid of all principle; he sold official protection, the subordinate posts in his Provinces, and the Chü-jen Degrees. The trouble which arose in connection with this last crime made it necessary for Chang to accuse Koli to the Emperor. But Koli made up seven charges against the Governor and submitted them to his Majesty also. Commissions were sent to Kiangsu to investigate the matters, and the men who composed them, coming under the influence of the Governor General, decided the that he was innocent and the Governor guilty. But Chang submitted a long memorial to the Emperor in which he took up the seven charges in succession and refuted them. The Emperor set aside the verdicts and recommendations of the Commissions, degraded the Governor General, and restored Chang to the post from which he had been temporarily removed for the purposes of investigation.

In 1714 Chang did a good service to the people of his jurisdiction, specially those concerned in shipping. This consisted in obtaining from the Emperor a Decree requiring that every war, merchant, and fishing Junk should have its number and the names of its Province and town displayed on its sides aft, and that every master of a vessel should always carry with him his Certificate of Registration.

About this time Chang came into collision with the Provincial Finance Commissioner whom he accused of harbouring a pirate. Again commissions were sent to make inquiry and again Chang's enemies declared him guilty. They even pronounced him worthy of death, but the Emperor knew his faithful and tried servant to be in the right, and brought him to the capital. At first he was appointed to do duty in the Imperial College of Inscriptions, but he was soon entrusted with more difficult work. He had risen to be a Vice President of the Board of Revenue when Kanghsi died and Yung-chêng, in 1723, came to reign in his place. The new Emperor, obeying the promptings of filial piety, showed honour and kindness to the faithful counsellers and upright servants of his father. Among these was Chang Pai-hsing whom Yung-chêng promoted to be President of the Board of Ceremonies. But Chang was now an old man, and the years of his dog-and-horse-service were nearly ended. His heart still owned the noble debt of gratitude, however, and he would not vacate his post. At the beginning of 1725 illness came upon him, and he soon knew that the end was at hand. His last thoughts were for the good of his country, and shortly before dying he drew up a memorial for the Emperor. In this he prayed His Majesty to go on as he had begun—to keep good ministers—to encourage pure officials by liberal salaries and repress the avaricious by setting forth the laws—to foster the kind and gentle and send away the rude and violent—and the memorial ended with an earnest prayer for *His* Majesty's eternal welfare. It was in the second month of this year that Chang died, and the Emperor decreed to him a public funeral and posthumous honours. The epithet he selected was one which the deceased had well deserved, Ch'ing-Ko (清 恪). The former of these words means pure, that is, unsullied by the acceptance of a bribe or the influence of a mean motive, and the latter denotes earnest attention to the duties of one's office or position.

Chang Pai-hsing was not a man of brilliant genius or great tact, and he had by no means a yielding disposition. Self-sufficient and self-possessed he recked little of the good or ill opinion of others, and did not fear the power and influence of his superiors. To himself he was strict and rigorous, abstaining from many of the ordinary comforts and luxuries of life, and devoting much of his income to the relief of the distressed. To serve his ruler and his country faithfully was the one study of his life, and his idea of service was not limited by any narrow bounds of official rule or custom. It embraced everything by which the welfare of the people in the present and for the future could be promoted. It was in this spirit that he applied himself to learn the nature and circumstances of the lakes, canals, and rivers in Middle and North China in order to help in the prevention of out-breaks and overflows. Under the title *Chü-ch'i-i-té* (居濟一得) he published a collection of essays which he had written at various times on these sub-jects, on the general principles of hydraulics as laid down by the ancient sages. His thoughtful kindness extended to all classes and conditions. It raised the despised female child from the rank of a chattel to that of a human being; it softened the severity of men and gods towards the homeless vagrant; it helped the poor student by smoothing some-what the path of learning and enlarging the hope of the great reward; it sought to give purer morals and simpler manners to the people, and to extirpate all heresy in philosophy and religion. His memorial to the Throne respecting Roman Catholic missionaries and their converts may still be read with interest. The chief objections he urges against

Christianity are that it teaches children to forsake their parents and follow persons called "spiritual Father," that it divides between Heaven and Heaven's ruler making these two, that it forbids the worship of sages and ancestors, and that so it shows contumacy to Heaven, contempt towards the sages, and opposes the traditions and customs of the country. He recommends that the foreign missionaries, except those employed for astronomical purposes at the capital, be ordered to leave the empire within a fixed period, that the native converts be required to return to orthodoxy, and that the chapels be converted into free public schools.

In philosophy Chang Pai-hsing was an earnest and thorough follower of Confucianism as taught by the school of which Chu Hsi is the representative. It was in the teachings of Chu and his masters that Chang found the true exposition and development of the truths held by Confucius and Mencius. The plain, moderate, practical character of the philosophy of these men also pleased Chang who would have no learning or wisdom that was not attainable by man and which did not aim directly at man's improvement. Hence he opposed with vigour and earnestness the philosophy of Ch'ên Pai-sha and Wang Yang-ming as vague and unprofitable. On the other hand he was ready to spend time, study, and money in order to extend what he regarded as the only true and useful learning. His contributions to literature and philosophy are considerable and are all published in the Chêng-i-t'ang collection. The *Lien-Lo-Kuan-Min-Shu* 濂 洛 關 閩 書, which appeared in 1709, contains extracts from the writings of Chou-tsŭ (Lien), the two Ch'êng (Lo), Chang-tsŭ (Kuan), and Chu Hsi (Min), and the extracts are accompanied by notes and comments from the pen of Chang. The *Tao-nan-yuan-wei* (道 南 源 委), which was based on a M.S. Work of Chu Hêng (朱 衡) a great scholar and statesman of the Ming dynasty, is a book of considerable value. It gives detailed notices of the Confucianists who carried on Yang Kuei-shan's work of spreading Ming-tao's teachings in the South, that is, chiefly, in Chekiang and Fuhkeen during the Sung, Yuan, and Ming dynasties. The *Hsiao-kuei-lei-pien* (學 規 類 編) is a large collection of extracts from the recorded sayings and the writings of eminent philosophers, intended for the use of students in the public schools. The *Yang-chêng-lei-pien* (養 正 類 編) is a short treatise on the conduct of life also compiled for the use of the young. Chang's Letters, State papers and other official documents, Essays, and Memoirs are contained in the *Chêng-i-t'ang-wên-chi* and Chêng-i-t'ang-suh-chi. Even a hasty reading of these two collections will show that this man's life was full of active services for the good of his fellows, and that he well deserves to share the feasts in the Temples of Confucius. In these modern times few have deserved so well of the Sage in teaching his principles and in carrying them out in all the ways of personal, domestic, social, and political life.*

* For Chang Pai-hsing's life and work see the *Chêng-i-t'ang-ch'uan-shu-tsung-mu* (正 誼 堂 全 書 總 目), and the *Chêng-i-t'ang-wên-chi* 文 集 and Suh-chi (續 集).